The Perfect Name
for the Perfect Baby

ALSO BY JOAN WILEN AND LYDIA WILEN

*Chicken Soup & Other Folk Remedies**
*More Chicken Soup & Other Folk Remedies**
Live and Be Well
*Name Me, I'm Yours!**

*PUBLISHED BY FAWCETT COLUMBINE

The Perfect Name for the Perfect Baby

Joan Wilen
and Lydia Wilen

Fawcett Columbine
New York

A Fawcett Columbine Book
Published by Ballantine Books

Library of Congress Catalog Card Number: 92-90401

ISBN: 0-449-90654-X

Cover design by Georgia Morrissey
Cover illustration by Vicki Wehrman

Manufactured in the United States of America
First Edition: April 1993
10 9 8 7 6 5

Contents

Acknowledgments

Big thanks to Joëlle Delbourgo for making this publishing house a home for our book.

To our editor, Elizabeth Rosalie Zack, who pushed us mercilessly and refused to settle for second best, our gratitude and our respect. (This is probably the only page on which we won't have to do more work!)

To Elise Marton, our copy editor and Oops!-preventer, we truly value the masterful job you've done.

Our great appreciation to the writers whose research is in the public domain.

And to all the women and men who choose to be parents, many blessings!

A Wilen Welcome

Aside from life itself, one of the first and most influential gifts parents give their newborn babe is a name. Think about it: You're making a major decision for another person, one that's quite a responsibility. We're not looking to scare you here, but we *are* looking to prepare you. That's the whole reason for this book.

The Perfect Name for the Perfect Baby is a practical, informative, and informal guide to aid parents in the traditional and pleasurable task of naming their child. As you will see soon enough, this book is not intended as a scholarly work on onomatology—the study of names. In fact, that's as scholarly as it gets!

Instead, we have lists to inspire you (saints' names, biblical names, names of angels), lists to take you down memory lane (names in songs), lists of winners (tennis players and marathon runners), lists that will take you back to your roots (foreign names), lists that will remind you of your favorite people and things (names from literature, soap opera characters, flowers, gemstones, and celebrities), and much more. Somewhere among them all is *sure* to be the right name for your own child.

So, with our book as your collaborator, enjoy the search and trust in your decision; the name that you finally select will be *perfect*!

Ready to get started? Take a pen or pencil and get prepared to record your list of possibilities on the pages at the end of the book. (You may also want something to munch on. Baby-naming has been known to work up *quite* an appetite.) Now make yourself comfortable, and—let the names begin!

"People have within themselves a level of prophecy, and they experience it at least once in their lives — when they name a child."

HASSIDIC RABBI

The Perfect Name
for the Perfect Baby

Considerations to Keep in Mind when Selecting the All-Important Name(s)

START BY THINKING ABOUT YOUR OWN FIRST NAME

Would you give yourself the same name you already have? Before you answer that, take the time to go down memory lane. As a child, were you ever teased because of your name? Did you always change your name when you played "pretend" games? Did you go through stages when you asked your family and friends to call you by another name? If your answer is yes to any of these, figure out why. Once you've analyzed your "whys," it would be wise to take them into consideration when naming your own child.

THEN THINK ABOUT YOUR LAST NAME

If it's short and simple — Smith, Chan, Gold — then you might want to pair the last name with a long, intriguing first name — Aurora, Granville, Evander.

3

On the other hand, if the last name is long — Whitticomb, Yamaguchi, Costellano — you might want to think in terms of a short and easy-to-remember first name — Dawn, Glenn, John.

If your last name is obviously ethnic, be sure to read about ETHNIC NAMES on page 7.

A MIDDLE NAME

We are definitely in favor of giving today's child a middle name. At a time when everything is computerized, a middle name can be a real plus for identification purposes. There may be a lot of Molly Smiths out there, but how many Molly *Wilson* Smiths are there?

And keep in mind that during certain stages of your child's growing up, he or she might not be too crazy about his or her first name. This way the child has a choice; he or she can use that middle name you so thoughtfully chose for him or her years before.

It's important that your child not be an "NMI" (no middle initial). We've heard about people in the military who have filled out forms stating that they have no middle name; from that point on, the computers actually list "NMI" as their middle name on military records.

Almost every United States president, from John Quincy Adams to William Jefferson Blythe Clinton, has had a middle name. And four-fifths of the people in *Who's Who* have middle names. So by all means, give your child a middle name . . . or, at the least, a middle initial. Which brings us to another important consideration. . . .

INITIALS

Ah, superstition! It is said that people whose initials spell out a word will be wealthy. If you believe the superstition, then rig it so that your child's name will spell out a word. But be kind.

Make sure the word is one with which your child will want to be associated.

It's great when initials spell out words like TEN, FUN, or WOW. But be sure to steer clear of initials with questionable associations like BAD, PIG, or DUD. Did the parents of our lovely young editor, Elizabeth Zack, consider initials when naming their baby girl? Yes! That's one reason Elizabeth has a middle name, so that she would not be saddled with the nickname EZ.

You might also want to consider initials that are an acronym for a nickname. For instance: Theodore Evan Dodd. The initials are TED, the nickname for Theodore.

Our eighteenth president was baptized Hiram Ulysses Grant. As the story goes, the young student anticipated with dread the teasing he would get from his West Point classmates when they realized his initials spelled out HUG. Fortunately, the congressman who nominated him to West Point thoughtfully changed Hiram Ulysses Grant to Ulysses Simpson Grant (Simpson being the maiden name of Ulysses' mother). That took care of one problem for Ulysses, but created another: his nickname became "Useless"!

NICKNAMES

A Hungarian proverb says, "A child that is loved has many names." And most nicknames *are* a sign of affection. Studies have shown that people with nicknames tend to be better adjusted. Plus, nicknames seem to promote a certain intimacy and indicate a readiness for friendship on the part of the owner.

It might be wise, then, to select a name for your child that lends itself to one or more nicknames — Elizabeth (Liz, Lizzie, Beth, Bess, Bets, Bette); or William (Willie, Will, Billy, Bill).

Then there are those non-name-related nicknames — The Boss, The Queen of Mean, and so on. These names are earned, and they either say something about your child's personality or physical appearance or an event associated with him/her. They arise from the creativity — and, unfortunately, occasional cruelty — of his or her peers. It's a shame, but these names are beyond a parent's control.

INFORMAL VS. FORMAL NAMES

Throughout the last quarter of this century in America, there continues to be a trend toward informality in name-calling. Just as very few employees now address their boss as "Mr. or Ms. So-and-so," so does this informal trend extend itself to baby-naming. Names once considered nicknames are showing up on birth certificates all throughout the country.

While there's nothing wrong with naming your baby Vicki instead of Victoria, or Danny instead of Daniel, we think that a formal name serves the baby better when (s)he is an adult and can choose to be known by either the formal or the informal version of the name.

ALL KIDDING ASIDE

A funny name can be hysterical, and it's guaranteed to make people laugh. But will its owner — your child — be happy to be the brunt of a joke?

We've spoken to — or heard about — Ilene Forward, Rusty Hammer, Herbert Sherbert, Flip Side, Otto Graph, Rita Sedita, Rose Bush, Candy Barr and Clark Barr, Marsha Mellow, Solomon Gemorrah, and the Boston stockbroker's daughters Cash, Gamble, and Chance. We've been told there's the Dwopp family with a son named Wayne (a song cue if ever there was one): "Wayne Dwopp keeps falling on his head. . . ."

Are these names funny? Yes. Is it fair to give one to a child? We've met people with names that provoke laughter who love their names for that very reason. But we've also met people who regard their names as bad jokes, and they've never forgiven their parents for it.

So let your conscience (and not your sense of humor) be your guide.

ETHNIC NAMES

It's wonderful to remember your roots when it comes to naming a child, but there are a couple of other things to remember: Mixing two different nationalities — Vito McDonald, Zeus Feinberg, Mustafa Swenson — can sound comical; also, if you have an extremely ethnic last name and want to keep with tradition by giving your child a matching ethnic first name, take into account how hard the name may be to spell.

On his first day of kindergarten in America, a little boy from Israel told the teacher his name: "Yitzhak Menachem Eisenstadt." The teacher asked, "How do you spell that?" Yitzhak replied, "My mother helps me."

Funny, sure, but more than to amuse you, we tell the story to spark an awareness of possible problems that can accompany complex names that have not been Americanized.

There's a bit more we have to say about spelling, so read on.

SPELLING

Our first inclination was to say, keep the spelling conventional so that your child doesn't have to go through life correcting everybody. But our attitude changed once television personality Sharron Lovejoy shared her story with us.

It all happened during World War II. Captain Lovejoy, a pilot in the Air Force, told his pregnant wife, "If we have a girl, name her Sharron and spell it with two r's. That way, if I don't make it home from the war, my little girl will think of her daddy every time she has to tell someone how to spell her name correctly." Unfortunately, Sharron's dad did not make it home from the war. And yes, she thinks of him each time she has to correct the spelling of her name.

A TOUGH ACT TO FOLLOW

It might be traditional to give a boy his father's name, tacking on a "Junior" or "II" or "III," but we think you can do better than that. *Give your son his own name!*

It's downright confusing having two guys with the same name around. To avoid such confusion, the inevitable happens. The father becomes "Big Whomever" and the son becomes "Little Whomever," or, worse yet, the boy is called Junior or some cutesy nickname.

Also, one child's having the father's name may make other siblings a wee bit jealous. After all, it stands to reason that Dad might feel closer to his namesake. And maybe he even *expects* more from that namesake.

So we are not in favor of Juniors, IIs, IIIs, etc. (Come to think of it, you're probably not either. If you were, you wouldn't be reading a baby-name book!)

TRENDS

Jennifer! Jason! Jessica! Amanda! Need we say more? (Maybe not, but we haven't let that stop us before!)

It's no fun to be in a classroom with six other children who have the same first name as you. Do your child a favor: Steer clear of all those trendy names.

RHYTHM

You may be surprised to know that there's a general rule that comes into play here: Names that follow each other should not have the same number of syllables, such as Barbra Streisand (2 and 2), Glenn Close (1 and 1), and Warren Beatty (2 and 2). See how it held all of them back? (That only goes to show that there are many exceptions to the rule.)

In general, though, it *does* sound better to vary the number of syllables in each name. Start with the given — your last name. Count the number of syllables in it. Select a first name that has fewer or more syllables than the last name. Then select a middle name with a different number of syllables than either the middle or last names.

Our parents instinctively did right by us: Lydia (3) Hope (1) Wilen (2), and Joan (1) Wilen (2). (They do lose points, however, for not giving Joan a middle name.)

If you have a very short last name, you can make up for it with a long first name or a long middle name. A good example is Alexander (4) Graham (2) Bell (1). Doesn't it have a nice *ring* to it?

RELIGION AND TRADITION

It's a wonderful idea to let religion and tradition influence you in baby-naming.

The Catholic religion, for instance, requires its followers to have the name of a saint as a first or middle name. (For a listing of saints' names and feast days, turn to pages 34 through 80.)

Frequently Jewish children are named for someone special who has passed on. Thus the child becomes a living memorial to that deceased relative or friend.

In parts of Africa, a naming-day ceremony takes place about a week after the birth of a baby. The oldest member of the tribe whispers the name to the very newest member; once the baby has heard his or her own name for the first time, the name is then announced to the rest of the celebrants.

Today, many African-Americans are both changing their own names and giving their children African or Moslem names in recognition of their heritage before slavery.

One of the Chinese naming traditions is changing names. About a month after the baby is born, s(he) is given a "milk" name. For a girl it usually represents something of beauty; for a boy, the name is usually plain so that he will go unnoticed by the Devil. After the milk name, there may be a going-to-school name, then a marriage name, also an occupational name, and a casual name used just between friends.

It's a tradition of Hispanic-Americans to give a child the names of several male and female saints.

In a typical Russian family, children are given formal names known as "passport names." When each child is sixteen, s(he) is given the father's first name as his or her middle name, at which time s(he) adds on the appropriate feminine (-evna or -ovna) or masculine (-evich or -ovich) ending.

Greek tradition holds that the firstborn child be named after the paternal grandparent of the same sex.

By speaking to your particular religious leader you can learn about special religious and traditional guidelines associated with naming a child.

IS IT A BOY, OR IS IT A GIRL?

Robin, Terry, Carson, Jan, Corey, Lindsay, and Jamie make up the troop. But are they Boy Scouts or Girl Scouts? Judging solely by the names, it's anyone's guess.

If you're thinking about a unisex name for your child, talk to youngsters who have them. When we did, we found that while the girls *liked* having unisex names, the boys would have preferred names that didn't leave anyone guessing.

THE "MEANING" OF IT ALL

The meanings of names go way back to the beginning of recorded history, and it all depends on which historical record you go by. In other words, one name, because of different derivations, can have different meanings. For example, in Old High German "Alice" means "of noble birth" while in Greek it means "the truth." Our A-to-Z listing of names in the back of the book includes each name's most popular meanings. But if you attach special importance to the original meanings of names and have narrowed your choice down to several names, you may want to do additional research at the library. Start with the Subject catalogue, under "Names, Personal."

For more on the meanings of names, see the Introduction to the Main Name List (page 182).

SOUND IT OUT

When you find a name you like, link it with a middle name and with your last name. Say it out loud again and again. Does it sound good? Our cousin thought she came up with the perfect combination of first and middle names: Amanda and Lynn. Then she said them out loud, "Amanda Lynn," and realized it was a swell name for a musical instrument, but not for her beautiful little girl. "Amanda Leigh" sounded a lot better.

Check and make sure that your name choices have different last syllables. The same ending syllables for first and middle names sound funny when said together (Arthur Luther, Norma Sondra, Norman Simon), and the same holds true for first and last names said together (Madeline Bailin, Robert Talbert).

Keep in mind that when the first name ends with the same sound with which the last name begins (Phillip Pratt, Jane North, Michael Lear), it's hard to tell where the first name ends and the last one begins.

TEST MARKET THE NAME

In a notebook or on index cards, write down each name you're interested in like this:

> Full name — Benjamin Jay Chandler
> Initials — BJC
> First and last names — Benjamin Chandler
> Nicknames — Ben, Benny, Benjie, BJ, BC

Once the name works for you on paper, repeat the name out loud to others and ask them to tell you the picture that the name brings to mind. (That is, if you're not concerned about keeping your name choice a secret.) It's a good way to get insight on the reaction your own child will eventually get from his or her name.

CREATING THAT SPECIAL NAME

Here's your chance to be the mother or father of invention! And why not? Since your baby is a unique, special someone, create a name to reflect that uniqueness. Here are some ways to do just that:

Combining Syllables or Names

Use syllables from two names to create a new name. But don't do what our neighbor was going to do. She wanted to name her child after her father, Ferdinand, and her mother, Eliza. The child would then have been called Ferdiliza! But seriously . . .

Albert and Victoria = Altoria
Andrew and Claudine = Andine
Prince Charles and Princess Diana = Charlana

Or combine any two names that flow together: Lauralynn, Rosellen, Leeanna. (This doesn't seem to work well for boys — except maybe for those in Texas, like Billybob.)

Acronyms

Find a phrase, a line of poetry, or a grouping of words that's meaningful to you, and use the first letter of each word to form an acronym that can be used as a name. We know a couple named Charles and Lillian who named their baby Cally. It's an acronym for Charles And Lillian Love You.

One couple named their baby girl Camise. It's an acronym for Conceived At Maple Inn, South Evanston.

The Yagers — Ann Victoria and Earl Russell — had a little

boy. They used their initials to create a name for the baby and it worked out great. In fact, each time that their son, Avery, who is now a young adult, has to spell out his name for someone, he says, "A as in Ann, V as in Victoria, E as in Earl, R as in Russell, and Y as in Yager."

A young man introduced himself as Boothe. When we asked about the name, he explained that it stands for *B*orn *O*ut *O*f *T*wo *H*earts *E*mbracing.

Ain't love grand? Well, so are acronyms!

Anagrams

Take a word you love and juggle the letters around to form a pleasing name for your little angel. Hey, there's an idea:

Angel = Elgan, Engal, Galen, Glane, Glena, Lange, Nagel

Or select an anagram based on a word that has special significance for you and your partner. For instance, if you got married in April, or if the baby was conceived or born in April, then you may want to use an anagram of the name of the month:

April = Alpir, Piral, Prila, Pirla,
Parli, Prali, Plair, Lipra

Ananyms

When you spell a word or a name backward to form another word or name, that's an ananym. Try it with a word or name you love, or one with significance, and see if the result is pleasing. Here are some examples:

Adam = Mada
Asset = Tessa
Lyric = Ciryl
Six A.M. = Maxis
Nomad = Damon
Iron = Nori

How about your own name spelled backward? Would it make a good name for baby?

Name Dropping

Take a word or name that has some special meaning to you, and drop letters from it to form a new name:

Computerized = Cotie, Merie, Perie, Terie
Sagittarius = Sari, Sita, Gia, Tari, Taris

ALL IN THE FAMILY

Consider a family name for a first (or middle) name. Hume Cronyn and Jessica Tandy did so when they named their daughter Tandy. Please bear in mind, however, that some family names may be a little sophisticated for a tiny tot. Ask yourself if there's a shortened version (a nickname) of that name that would be appropriate until the child is old enough to carry the weight of an "important" name.

While you're at it, when you come up with a name that's fine for a baby, make sure it will suit an adult as well.

A SPECIAL NOTE FOR PARENTS: Despite all we've mentioned in the previous pages, there are countless numbers of people with names that defy every consideration. Among those people are the rich and the famous, the happy and the healthy. For instance, Arnold Schwarzenegger. "Arnold" is generally thought of as a nerdy, wimpish name. Schwarzenegger is hard to pronounce, difficult to remember, and impossible to spell. For all we know, his middle name starts with an S, making his initials . . . . Well, as of this writing, Arnold Schwarzenegger, the former Mr. Universe, married into the Kennedy family, heads the President's Fitness Program, and is one of the world's top movie stars. Did he become a bodybuilder to compensate for his name? Would he be such a big box-office success today if his name were as simple and common as Jim Larson? It's something to think about . . . but not for *too* long! You have more important things to do, like find the perfect name for your own baby.

Those Little Angels!
Angelic Names for Your Child

The Hebrew term *mal'akh,* which originally meant "the shadow side of God," was translated by the Greek to *angelos* and came to mean "messenger." Thus angels are often thought of as messengers of light, reflecting God's radiance. Wouldn't those words also be the perfect description of a baby—a reflection of God's radiance? That's reason enough to consider giving your baby the name of an angel!

Initially we thought that compiling a list of angel names would be easy. All we'd have to do is look through the Old and New Testaments and gather together all the names. But while angels appear in just about every book of the Bible, and in many cases their appearances are crucial to the situations, they often don't get any billing at all. With the exception of Michael and Gabriel, the Bible reveals very little information on the personalities, natures, or names of angels.

However, the Bible tells us, "Seek and ye shall find." We did, and in so doing, came up with a stellar collection of angel names.

Before you read on, however, there are a few things you

should know. We've omitted the angel names that are extremely long and unusual, difficult to spell, or hard to pronounce. We've also left in names that can be pronounced a variety of ways. We figure that if you love the name, you should be the one who says how it's pronounced. We know three women named Andrea. Each pronounces the name differently: *An'-dree-a, Ahn'-dree-a,* and *Ahn-dray'-a.* Remember, when it comes to names, there's no right or wrong pronunciation; *there's only your choice.*

Based on interpretations of scriptural passages in several foundational texts, including the *Summa Theologica* by Thomas Aquinas, there are three orders of angels, with three choirs in each, that surround the Divine Core. (The Divine Core is also called the Throne of Glory, or His Presence, or the Divine Source of Light and Love, and yes, it's God.) The First order of angels is seraphim, cherubim, and thrones; the Second order is dominions, virtues, and powers; and the Third order is principalities, archangels, and angels. (Please note, however, that no two sources seem to agree on the order of importance.)

While we were able to collect names of angels, we couldn't always find out which choir they belong to, or which culture or religion they're from. In most cases, we don't even know whether they're male or female! We're counting on your good judgment to determine whether a name is more suitable for a girl or for a boy.

Enough said. Here's the list of angel names. They're *heavenly* and certainly worth considering.

ANGELS

Arael — Angel of Birds.

Arel — Angel of Fire. According to *The Sword of Moses* by Moses Gaster, Arel is an angel who's summoned when ritual magic is practiced.

Dabria — According to *Revelation of Esdras IV,* Dabria is one of five angels who transcribed the books that the Hebrew prophet Ezra dictated. Also see ETHAN and SAREA or SARGA.

Dara — Angel of Rains and Rivers (according to Persian mythology).

Dina — Guardian Angel of Wisdom and of the Law, as is written in the Torah. Dina is also the angel said to have taught a total of seventy languages to new souls at the time of Creation.

Elijah — When he lived on earth, this Hebrew prophet was known as "the grandest and the most romantic character that Israel ever produced." Many legends about Elijah exist. One is that he ascended to Heaven in a chariot of fire; another is that he was transformed into the angel Sandalphon; and still another is that he was an angel from the start. All *we* know is that Elijah is a strong and interesting name. Cher thought so too, and gave her son that name.

Ethan — One of five angels who transcribed the books the Hebrew prophet Ezra dictated. Also see DABRIA and SAREA or SARGA.

Farris — Angel who governs the second hour of the night.

Gabriel — One of what we call the two "superstar" angels among the Jewish, Christian, and Islamic religions. (Michael is the other.) Thought to sit on the left-hand side of God, Gabriel presides over Paradise, and — as if that weren't enough! — he is the Angel of Joy, Judgment, Mercy, the Holy Spirit, Annunciation, Resurrection, Truth, Vengeance, Death, Revelation, Mercy, Prayer, Mysteries, Dreams, and more.

Geron — The angel who's called upon in magic-based prayer.

Hamal — Angel of Water. Hamal is invoked in Arabic ritual prayers.

Hariel — Angel of Tame Animals. This cherub is also the ruler of science and the arts.

Irin — Along with his twin Qaddis, he is among the most exalted of angels serving God.

Javan — Guardian angel whose territory is Greece.

Joel — According to *The History of the Life of Adam and Eve* by Frederick G. Conybeare, Joel is the archangel who gave Adam and Eve one-seventh of our earthly paradise. Joel is also recognized for his suggestion that Adam name all things.

Kadi — An angel who presides over Friday. He is summoned from the West and serves in the Third Heaven, according to Francis Barrett's *The Magus II*.

Laila, Lailah, or Layla — According to Exodus, "an angel appointed to guard the spirits at their birth."

Manuel — Angel whose dominion is the Zodiac sign Cancer.

Michael — One of the two "superstar" angels among the Jewish, Christian, and Islamic religions. (Gabriel is the other.) Michael is the Chief of Archangels, Prince of the Presence, Ruler of the Fourth Heaven, Angelic Prince of Israel, Purifier of People and Places Plagued with Disharmony and Evil, and Angel of Repentance, Righteousness, Sanctification, Mercy, and more. According to Maldwyn H. Hughes in *The Greek Apocalypse of Baruch,* Michael "holds the keys of the kingdom of Heaven." As recently as 1950, Pope Pius XII named Michael the Patron of Policemen. This angelic name has been on the list of the most popular boys' names in the Northeast since 1948, and number one in popularity for boys since 1980. Since the early seventies, when actress Michael Learned starred in the TV series *The Waltons,* it's no longer rare to meet a girl named Michael.

Miri — An angel from "Sagesse," a poem by Hilda Doolittle in her book *Tribute to the Angels.*

Neria — The name means "lamp of God" and is thought to be the same as *Neriel* who, in The Sixth and Seventh Books of Moses, is one of the angels governing the mansions of the moon.

Nitika — Angel of precious stones.

Oriel — Angel of Destiny and one of the rulers of the tenth daylight hour.

Paniel or Pariel — These angel names, according to *Hebrew Amulets* by T. Schrire, are enscribed on charms to ward off evil.

Raphael — One of the seven holy angels who attend the throne of God. Raphael is Ruling Prince of the Second Heaven, Guardian of the Tree of Life in the Garden of Eden, Governor of the South, Guardian of the West, and Overseer of the Evening Winds. Raphael, whose name means "God has healed," is, appropriately, the Angel of Healing. He is also the Angel of Science, Knowledge, Repentance, Prayer, Joy, Light, Love, and more.

Sarea or Sarga — One of five angels who transcribed the books the Hebrew prophet Ezra dictated. Also see DABRIA and ETHAN.

Sofiel — Angel of Fruit and Vegetables.

Suria — An angel-warden of the First Hall of the First Heaven. According to *The Zohar* by Harry Sperling and Maurice Simon, Suria is the "high angelic being who takes up all the holy words that are uttered at a table and sets the form of them before the Holy One."

Tabris — Angel of Free Will, according to occult lore.

Talia — One of ten angels who escort the sun on its daily course, according to an ancient Gnostic sect of Mesopotamia.

Tariel — Angel of Summer.

Uriel — The name means "fire of God," and, as evinced by his credits, there's a lot of firepower here. Uriel is said to be the "spirit who stood at the gate of the lost Eden with the fiery sword" and the angel who brought alchemy down to earth, and is supposedly the inspiration of writers and teachers. He's also the Angel of Prophecy and the Angel of September, and is described in Milton's *Paradise Lost* as the "sharpest sighted spirit of all in Heaven."

Yael, Yale, or Yehel — An angel who attends the throne of God and is summoned at the conclusion of the Sabbath for magic rituals.

Yahriel — Angel of the Moon.

Zachriel — The angel with dominion over memory.

Zaniel — An angel who presides over Monday. He is summoned from the West and has dominion over the Zodiac sign Libra.

Zazel — The angel summoned for love invocations when King Solomon practiced magic arts. According to *The Magus* by Francis Barrett, Zazel is the spirit of Saturn and has the cabalistic number 45.

And if these aren't enough angel names for you, read on!

ANGELS WHO GOVERN THE WINDS

Uriel — South Wind
Michael — East Wind
Raphael — West Wind
Gabriel — North Wind
Nariel — Noonday Winds

ANGELS ASSIGNED TO THE DAYS OF THE WEEK

Michael — Sunday: Angel of Earth
Gabriel — Monday: Angel of Life

Zamael — Tuesday: Angel of Joy
Raphael — Wednesday: Angel of Sun
Sachiel — Thursday: Angel of Water
Anael — Friday: Angel of Air
Cassiel — Saturday: The Earthly Mother

ANGELS WHO GOVERN THE MONTHS OF THE YEAR

Gabriel — January
Barchiel — February
Malchidiel — March
Asmodel — April
Ambriel or Amriel — May
Muriel — June
Murdad — July
Hamaliel — August
Uriel — September
Aban — October
Azar — November
Anael or Dai — December

THE ANGELS OF THE HOURS OF THE DAY AND NIGHT

Hours Day.	Angels and Planets Ruling SUNDAY.	Angels and Planets Ruling MONDAY.	Angels and Planets Ruling TUESDAY.	Angels and Planets Ruling WEDNESDAY.	Angels and Planets Ruling THURSDAY.	Angels and Planets Ruling FRIDAY.	Angels and Planets Ruling SATURDAY.
	Day.	*Day.*	*Day.*	*Day.*	*Day.*	*Day.*	*Day.*
1	☉ Michael	☽ Gabriel	♂ Samael	☿ Raphael	♃ Sachiel	♀ Anael	♄ Cassiel
2	♀ Anael	♄ Cassiel	☉ Michael	☽ Gabriel	♂ Samael	☿ Raphael	♃ Sachiel
3	☿ Raphael	♃ Sachiel	♀ Anael	♄ Cassiel	☉ Michael	☽ Gabriel	♂ Samael
4	☽ Gabriel	♂ Samael	☿ Raphael	♃ Sachiel	♀ Anael	♄ Cassiel	☉ Michael
5	♄ Cassiel	☉ Michael	☽ Gabriel	♂ Samael	☿ Raphael	♃ Sachiel	♀ Anael
6	♃ Sachiel	♀ Anael	♄ Cassiel	☉ Michael	☽ Gabriel	♂ Samael	☿ Raphael
7	♂ Samael	☿ Raphael	♃ Sachiel	♀ Anael	♄ Cassiel	☉ Michael	☽ Gabriel
8	☉ Michael	☽ Gabriel	♂ Samael	☿ Raphael	♃ Sachiel	♀ Anael	♄ Cassiel
9	♀ Anael	♄ Cassiel	☉ Michael	☽ Gabriel	♂ Samael	☿ Raphael	♃ Sachiel
10	☿ Raphael	♃ Sachiel	♀ Anael	♄ Cassiel	☉ Michael	☽ Gabriel	♂ Samael
11	☽ Gabriel	♂ Samael	☿ Raphael	♃ Sachael	♀ Anael	♄ Cassiel	☉ Michael
12	♄ Cassiel	☉ Michael	☽ Gabriel	♂ Samael	☿ Raphael	♃ Sachiel	♀ Anael
Hours Night	*Night.*	*Night.*	*Night.*	*Night.*	*Night.*	*Night.*	*Night.*
1	♃ Sachael	♀ Anael	♄ Cassiel	☉ Michael	☽ Gabriel	♂ Samael	☿ Raphael
2	♂ Samiel	☿ Raphael	♃ Sachiel	♀ Anael	♄ Cassiel	☉ Michael	☽ Gabriel
3	☉ Michael	☽ Gabriel	♂ Samael	☿ Raphael	♃ Sachiel	♀ Anael	♄ Cassiel
4	♀ Anael	♄ Cassiel	☉ Michael	☽ Gabriel	♂ Samael	☿ Raphael	♃ Sachiel
5	☿ Raphael	♃ Sachiel	♀ Anael	♄ Cassiel	☉ Michael	☽ Gabriel	♂ Samael
6	☽ Gabriel	♂ Samael	☿ Raphael	♃ Sachiel	♀ Anael	♄ Cassiel	☉ Michael
7	♄ Cassiel	☉ Michael	☽ Gabriel	♂ Samael	☿ Raphael	♃ Sachiel	♀ Anael
8	♃ Sachiel	♀ Anael	♄ Cassiel	☉ Michael	☽ Gabriel	♂ Samael	☿ Raphael
9	♂ Samael	☿ Raphael	♃ Sachiel	♀ Anael	♄ Cassiel	☉ Michael	☽ Gabriel
10	☉ Michael	☽ Gabriel	♂ Samael	☿ Raphael	♃ Sachiel	♀ Anael	♄ Cassiel
11	♀ Anael	♄ Cassiel	☉ Michael	☽ Gabriel	♂ Samael	☿ Raphael	♃ Sachiel
12	☿ Raphael	♃ Sachiel	♀ Anael	♄ Cassiel	☉ Michael	☽ Gabriel	♂ Samael

A table showing the hours of the day and night during which certain angels rule, along with the related zodiacal signs. From Barrett, *The Magus*.

Names from the Bible

The Bible is known as the Good Book. And it *is* a good book in which to find beautiful names.

"God formed man of the dust of the ground" (Gen. 2:7, 19). That refers to God naming the first man Adam, which means "of the earth." Adam named the cattle, birds, and wild animals, then *finally* got around to naming the first woman: "And the man called his wife's name Eve [meaning 'life']; because she was the mother of all living" (Gen. 3:20).

The tradition of choosing biblical names for newborns in America started way back, when the Puritans attempted to establish the Kingdom of God in the New World — in other words, at the time of America's colonization. In keeping with that divine tradition, we've compiled a list of names selected from both the Old and New Testaments. (Please note that our list does not differentiate between the two, simply because both books do belong to everyone . . . and with so many crossovers, it's too complicated to say who belongs where.)

Our research indicates that many children in the Bible had names that were apropos of their destiny in life, while others were named for their time of birth, circumstance at the time of birth, or place of birth. Children were also given names from nature, names that expressed how much like a treasure a baby is, and names that reflected the pain of childbirth.

Since there are *over* three thousand Biblical names, we've naturally chosen only a small number to list here, veering away from the names that reflect pain and steering more toward the precious names that sound good. We've also included names you already know, just to make sure you're aware they're from the Bible.

Many names represent more than one person in the Bible, so we've confined our brief profile to the most prominent namesake. The meaning of each name is given in parentheses.

One more thing: We found some wonderful men's names that we thought, in this day and age, would work better as women's names, and so we've *deliberately* included them in the *women's* list. (We're telling you this ahead of time because we don't want you to think we misplaced some names!)

Now, "Seek and ye shall find."

WOMEN OF THE BIBLE

Abigail (father's source of joy) — Beautiful wife of Nabal; later, wife of King David.

Ada, Adah (ornament, beauty) — Wife of Lamech.

Adria — Place name: a town near the River Po.

Ahava (pronounced Uh-hah'-va; water) — Place name: a river, on the banks of which Ezra collected the second expedition which returned with him from Babylon to Jerusalem.

Anna (grace) — A prophetess in Jerusalem of the tribe of Asher.

Apollonia (belonging to Apollo) — Place name: a city of Macedonia through which Paul and Silas passed.

Ariel (lioness of God) — In the Book of Isaiah, it is used as another name for Jerusalem.

Atarah (pronounced Uh-ta'-ra; crown) — Wife of Jerahmeel; mother of Onam.

Bathsheba (daughter of the oath) — Beautiful wife of Uriah; later, wife of King David; mother of Solomon, Shimea, Shobab, and Nathan.

Bernice (bringing victory) — Daughter of Herod Agrippa I.

Beth — A general word for a house or habitation; specifically, a house of worship, usually used as the first word of a compound name, i.e. Temple Beth-Sholem.

Bethany — Place name: an obscure village near Bethabara where John baptized Jesus.

Beulah (pronounced Bew'-lah or Byou'-lah; married) — The name Israel will have when "the land shall be married."

Candace, Candice (prince of servants) — A dynasty of Ethiopian queens.

Carmel (fruitful place or park) — Place name: Mount Carmel is a mountain ridge that extends about fifteen miles across northwestern Israel to the Mediterranean.

Cassia, Kazia, Kezia (plant or shrub that produces cinnamon) — One of Job's three beautiful daughters, born to him after the restoration of his prosperity.

Chloe (green herb) — A woman mentioned in 1 Corinthians.

Claudia (lame) — A Christian woman mentioned in 2 Timothy as saluting Timotheus.

Damaris (heifer) — An Athenian woman whom St. Paul converted.

Deborah (bee) — One biblical Deborah was Rebecca's nurse; another, a Hebrew prophetess who helped the Israelites conquer the Canaanites.

Delila, Delilah (delicate) — Mistress and betrayer of Samson.

Diana (the divine) — The representative of the Greek Artemis, the tutelary goddess of the Ephesians.

Dinah (judgment) — Beautiful daughter of Jacob and Leah.

Eden (pleasure) — The residence of the first couple, Adam and Eve, before they were cast out.

Edna (pleasure, delight) — Mother of Abraham.

Elisheba, Elisabeth, Elizabeth (God is her oath) — Old Testament: Wife of Aaron. New Testament: Wife of Zacharius; mother of John the Baptist; cousin of the Virgin Mary.

Esther (star) — Wife of Ahasuerus who saved the Jews from Haman's plotting.

Eunice (good victory) — Mother of Paul's disciple, Timothy.

Eve (life) — The name given in Scripture to the first woman.

Hali (necklace) — Place name: a town on the boundary of Asher.

Hannah (grace) — Wife of Elkanah; mother of the prophet Samuel.

Hava (life) — The Hebrew name for Eve.

Jael (pronounced Yah-ale´; to ascend) — A courageous Kenite woman who slew Sisera with a tent stake.

Janna (flourishing) — Son of Joseph; father of Melchi.

Japhia (pronounced Ja-fee´-yah or Ya-fee´-yah; splendid) — King of Lachish at the time of Canaan's conquest by the Israelites.

Jarah (honey) — A descendant of Saul; son of Micah; great-grandson of Mephibosheth.

Jemima (dove) — One the three beautiful daughters born to Job after the restoration of his prosperity.

Joanna (grace or gift of God) — Wife of Chuza.

Judith (praised) — Wife of Esau; slayer of Holofernes during the siege of Bethulia.

Julia (feminine of Julius: soft haired) — Wife of Philologus who was saluted by St. Paul.

Leah (wearied) — Daughter of Laban; first wife of Jacob; mother of Reuben, Simeon, Levi, Judah, Issachar, Zebulun, and Dinah.

Lois (agreeable) — Mother of Eunice; grandmother of the Apostle Timothy.

Lydia (voluptuous beauty) — Place name: an ancient country in Asia Minor. Seller of purple-dyed cloth; the first European convert of St. Paul.

Magdalene (high tower) — With the first name of Mary, a disciple and friend of Jesus, who inspired her to go from sinner to saint.

Marsena (worthy) — One of the seven princes — "wise men which knew the times" — of Persia.

Martha (lady) — Sister of Mary and Lazarus; friend of Jesus.

Mary (rebellion, bitter, tear) — There are several women named Mary in the Bible. The most noteworthy is the Mary who was the Virgin Mother of Jesus.

Michal (who is like God?) — Daughter of Saul; wife of King David.

Miriam (rebellion) — Prophetess; daughter of Amram; sister of Moses and Aaron.

Moriah (chosen by Jehovah) — Place name: the mountain where Abraham was to sacrifice his son Isaac to God.

Myra — Place name: an important town in ancient Lycia.

Naomi (my delight, sweetness) — Wife of Elemelech; mother of Boaz; mother-in-law of Ruth. After the death of her husband and sons, she wished to be known as Mara (bitterness).

Ophrah (fawn) — Place name: a town probably in Manasseh, five miles east of Bethel.

Orpah (pronounced Or'-pah; gazelle) — Wife of Naomi's son Chilion.

Peninnah (pronounced Pa-neen'-ah; coral, pearl) — Wife of Elkanah.

Phoebe (radiant) — One of the most important Christian women, she strove to have deaconesses admitted to the apostolic Church.

Priscilla (ancient) — Energetic wife of Aquila who is used as an example of all that the married woman can do to serve the Church.

Rachel (female sheep) — Beautiful wife of Jacob; mother of Joseph and Benjamin.

Rainbow — The token of the covenant that God made with Noah when Noah emerged from the ark. It assured that flood waters would no longer destroy all that lived. And so the rainbow became a symbol of hope and an emblem of God's faithfulness and mercy.

Rebecca, Rebekah (trapper) — Beautiful daughter of Bethuel; sister of Laban; wife of Isaac; mother of Jacob and Esau.

Rhoda (rosy) — A maid who announced Simon Peter's arrival at Mary's house after his miraculous release from prison.

Ruth (female friend) — Wife of Mahlon; later, wife of Boaz. After her second husband's death, Ruth devoted herself to her mother-in-law Naomi, telling her, "Whither thou goest, I will go. . . ."

Salome (peace) — Daughter of Herodias and stepdaughter of Herod Antipas. Before she would please her stepfather's guests with her famous dance, she asked for the head of John the Baptist on a silver platter.

Samaria (watch mountain) — Place name: a city thirty miles north of Jerusalem, one rich in Old Testament history.

Sara, Sarah (princess); Sarai (my princess) — Mother of Isaac, she changed her name from Sarah to Sarai when her husband changed his name from Abram to Abraham.

Sharon (flat plain) — Place name: a plain in western Palestine noted for its fertility, especially the growing of roses.

Shobi (pronounced Show'-bee; glorious) — Son of Nahash and one of the first to meet David at Mahanaim.

Susanna (lily) — The heroine of the story of the judgment of Daniel.

Tabitha (gazelle) — Known as Dorcas by St. Luke, she is noted most for her good works.

Tamar (palm tree) — Daughter of King David and Maachah; mother of twins Pharez and Zarah.

Tirza, Tirzah (pronounced Teer′-zah; delight) — Place name: the capital of Samaria. The youngest of Zelophehad's five daughters.

Veronica (true image) — The woman who wiped Jesus' brow when he was carrying the cross to Calvary.

Zipporah (pronounced Zeh-poor′-ah; bird) — Daughter of Jethro; wife of Moses; mother of Gershom and Eliezer.

Zoe (life) — Egyptian translation of the name Eve.

MEN OF THE BIBLE

Aaron (to sing, to teach, messenger, mountain) — Brother of Moses and Miriam; son of Amram and Jochebed; first High Priest of the Israelites.

Abel (breath, vapor) — The son of Adam and Eve who was slain by his brother, Cain.

Abner (father of light) — Saul's first cousin and commander-in-chief of Saul's army; slain by Joab.

Abraham (father of many) — Forefather of the Jews; husband of Sarah; father of Isaac and Ishmael. Originally named Abram (God is exalted), he was renamed Abraham by God after he journeyed to Canaan.

Adam (of the earth) — According to the Book of Genesis, the first man created by God.

Adlai (refuge of God) — Father of Shaphat; overseer of David's herds.

Alexander (helper of men, brave) — The son of Philip and Olympias, Alexander III, as the king of Macedon, was given the epithet "the Great."

Alva, Alvah (injustice or height) — Member of Esau's family.

Amal (work, labor) — A member of Asher, one of the twelve tribes of Israel.

Amon (builder) — One of Ahab's governors.

Amos (to be burdened) — A shepherd and dresser of sycamore trees who was called by God's Spirit to be a prophet.

Amram (an exalted people) — Husband of Jochebed; father of Aaron, Miriam, and Moses.

Andrew (manly) — Disciple of John the Baptist; brother of Simon Paul; one of Jesus' apostles.

Ara (the altar) — Son of Jether and descendant of the tribe of Asher.

Aram or Arni (high, heights) — Place name: the country lying northeast of Palestine. Noah's grandson.

Ariel (lion of God) — Under Ezra, one of the chief men who led the caravan back from Babylon to Jerusalem.

Asa (physician, healer) — Son of Abijam; grandson of David. A king of Judah who reigned for forty-one years.

Asher in the Old Testament, Aser in the New Testament (blessed) — Eighth son of Jacob by Zilpah, Leah's handmaid. One of the twelve tribes of Israel.

Barnabas, Barnabus (son of exhortation) — Disciple of Paul; one of the first Christian missionaries.

Bartholomew (hill) — In the Gospel of Mark, he is listed as one of Jesus' twelve apostles.

Baruch (blessed) — Secretary and friend of Jeremiah.

Ben (son) — This Levite was one of the porters appointed by David to tend the Ark of the Covenant.

Benjamin (son of my right hand — denoting the favorite) — Youngest of Jacob's twelve sons. Originally named Benoni (son of my sorrow) for the pain his dying mother, Rachel, suffered during his birth, he was renamed Benjamin by his father.

Caesar (to cut, the hairy one) — The Roman emperor; the sovereign of Judea.

Caleb (faithful like a dog, brave) — One of Moses' spies sent to Canaan.

Cyrus (sun) — The founder of the Persian empire. Legend has it that his courage and genius led to numerous conquests.

Dan (judge) — The fifth son of Jacob and the first of Bilhah, Rachel's maid. Leader of one of the twelve tribes of Israel.

Daniel (judgment of God) — A great prophet whom God saved from the lions.

Darius (upholder of good) — The name of several kings of Media and Persia. One Persian king with this name was responsible for throwing Daniel to the lions.

David (beloved) — Slayer of the giant warrior, Goliath; great and wise king of Israel; father of Solomon, who was his successor.

Demetrius (lover of the earth) — The silversmith of Ephesus.

Elam (eternity) — Place name: a country south of Assyria and east of Persia. Son of Shem.

Elazar, Eleazar (God has helped) — The son of Aaron, he succeeded his father as high priest.

Eli (ascension) — Israel's high priest and last judge.

Elihu (pronounced El'-eh-hue; he is my God) — David's brother; chief of the tribe of Judah.

Elijah or the Greek form, Elias (the Lord is my God) — Prophet who went to Heaven in a chariot of fire, traveling there in a whirlwind. He is said to be "the grandest and most romantic character that Israel ever produced."

Emanuel, Emmanuel, Immanuel (God is with us) — A name given to Jesus Christ by the Apostle Matthew, because Jesus was God united with man and was God living among men.

Enoch (dedicated) — The eldest son of Cain, the son of Adam and Eve, who slew his brother, Abel.

Enos (mortal man) — Great-grandson of Adam and Eve; son of Seth.

Ephraim (double fruitfulness) — Son of Joseph and Asenath. Also a place name: a portion of Canaan named after Ephraim.

Esau (pronounced Ee'-saw; hairy) — Son of Isaac and Rebecca who sold his birthright to twin brother Jacob.

Ethan, Etan (strong, substantial, enduring) — One of the four sons of Mahol, whose wisdom was excelled by Solomon.

Ezekiel (the strength of God) — Son of a priest named Buzi, he was one of the greatest prophets and a member of a community of Jewish exiles who settled on the banks of the Chebar in Babylonia.

Ezra, Esdras (help, salvation) — A prophet and a great leader who was responsible for religious reforms among the Palestine Jews.

Felix (happy) — Husband of Drusilla; brother of Pallas. A Roman procurator of Judea appointed by the emperor Claudius.

Gabriel (God's strength) — One of the four angels who stood around the throne of God. Michael, Raphael, and Uriel are the other three. Also, the angel who announced to Zacharias the birth of John the Baptist, and to Mary the birth of Christ.

Garrison (to place erect) — A column erected in an enemy's country as a token of conquest; a fortified post.

Gideon (he that cuts down, mighty warrior) — One of the Judges of Israel; warrior-hero who defeated the Midianites.

Haran (mountaineer) — Third son of Terah; youngest brother of Abram.

Herod (herolike) — Herod the Great was the King of Judea.

Hillel (praise) — One of the Judges of Israel; father of Abdon.

Hiram (noble) — King of Tyre who helped Solomon build his temple and David his palace.

Hosea (salvation) — First of the minor prophets; son of Beeri.

Ira (the watchful of a city) — One of the heroes of David's guard.

Isaac, Isaak (laughter) — Son of Abraham and Sarah; half-brother of Ishmael; husband of Rebecca; father of Esau and Jacob.

Isaiah (salvation of the Lord) — Son of Amoz; one of the greatest prophets who also fought civil corruption in Judah.

Israel (prince that prevails with God, wrestling with God) — The name given to Jacob after he wrestled with one of God's angels. It became the national name of the twelve tribes collectively (see next entry).

Jacob (supplanter, to take the place of) — Son of Isaac and Rebecca; brother of Esau; husband of Leah and Rachel. The twelve tribes of Israel evolved from Jacob's twelve sons: Asher, Benjamin, Dan, Gad, Issachar, Joseph, Judah, Levi, Naphtali, Reuben, Simeon, and Zebulun.

James (Greek form of Jacob: supplanter, to take the place of) — There are two apostles named James in the New Testament: James the Greater, and James the Less. The latter, however, was not *less* important than the former, but was given that name because he came *after*. It was simply a way of distinguishing between the two.

Japhet, Japheth (pronounced Jay'-fit or Jay'-fith; enlargement) — Son of Noah.

Jared, Jered (to descend) — Place name: the original name of the River Jordan. Son of Mahalaleel; father of Enoch.

Jason (the healer) — Entertainer of Paul and Silas.

Jeremiah, Jeremy (exalted of the Lord) — A major prophet.

Jesse (wealthy) — Son of Obed; father of David.

Jethro (his excellence) — Father of Zipporah, who married Moses; Midianite priest or prince. He is also called Reuel, which is thought to be his proper name; Jethro is his official title.

Joel (to whom the Lord is God) — Eldest son of Samuel the prophet; father of Heman the singer.

John (God is gracious) — There are eighty-four saints named John. The most notable may be John the Apostle, brother of the

Apostle Peter, who is mentioned in five books of the Bible and who wrote his own book, the Gospel of John.

Jonah, Jonas (the dove) — Prophet who was thrown into the sea, swallowed by a whale, and yet survived.

Jonathan (God has given) — Son of Saul; friend of David; famous warrior.

Joram, Yoram (the Lord is exalted) — Son of Ahab, king of Israel.

Jordan (the descender) — Place name: the one river in Palestine, with a course of over two hundred miles.

Jose, Joses (exalted) — Son of Eliazer in the genealogy of Christ.

Joseph (increase) — In the Old Testament, he was the son of Jacob and Rachel, and was known for his prophetic dreams. In the New Testament, Joseph, the man of Nazareth, was the husband of Mary, the mother of Christ.

Joshua and its various forms: Hoshea, Oshea, Jehoshua, Jeshua, and Jesus (savior) — The successor of Moses who led the Israelites to the Promised Land.

Josiah (whom Jehovah heals) — The son of Amon and Jedidah, he succeeded his father as king of Judah when he was only eight years old.

Judah (praised, celebrated) — Fourth son of Jacob and Leah; founder of one of the twelve tribes of Israel.

Julius (soft-haired) — The Roman centurion to whose charge St. Paul was delivered as a prisoner.

Kenan, Cainan (possession) — Son of Enos. He begat a son at age seventy and died 840 years later at age 910.

Lazarus (Greek form of the Hebrew Elazar: whom God helps) — The brother of Mary and Martha whom Jesus raised from the dead.

Lemuel (dedicated to God) — Thought to be the king or chief of an Arab tribe that dwelt on the borders of Palestine.

Levi (joined) — Son of Jacob and Leah; father of Gershon, Kohath, and Merari.

Linus (net) — After the apostles, the first bishop of Rome.

Lucas, Luke (an abbreviated form of Lucanus: giving light) — A companion of the Apostle Paul; one of the four evangelists; the "beloved physician" credited with the Gospel of Luke.

Malachi, Malachy (pronounced Mal'-a-ky' or Mal-ah'-ky; messenger of the Lord) — The last of the Hebrew prophets.

Marc, Mark (of Mars; warlike) — One of the four evangelists; credited with the Gospel bearing his name.

Matthew (a contraction of Mattathias: the Lord's gift) — Named Levi at birth, this apostle wrote the Gospel of Matthew.

Matthias (gift of God) — The apostle elected to fill the place of the traitor Judas.

Michael (who is like God?) — One of the four angels who stood around the throne of God. Gabriel, Raphael, and Uriel are the other three.

Mordecai (pronounced Mor'-deh-kigh; little man, worshiper of Mars) — Uncle of Esther; with her aid, he saved the Jews from Haman's plotting.

Moses (drawn — i.e., from the water) — Son of Amram; brother of Aaron and Miriam; husband of Zipporah. This legislator led the Israelites out of Egyptian bondage to the Promised Land.

Nathan, Nathaniel (gift of God) — A prophet who reproved King David for causing Uriah's death.

Nehemiah (the Lord's comfort) — A Jewish leader who was empowered by Artaxerxes to rebuild Jerusalem.

Noah (rest, comfort) — The son of Lamech, he escaped the Great Deluge by building an ark. Father of Ham, Japheth, and Shem.

Omar (eloquent, talkative) — Son of Eliphaz, the firstborn of Esau.

Oren (pine tree) — One of the sons of Jerahmeel; the firstborn of Hezron.

Paul (small, little) — Named Saul at birth by his Jewish parents, this tentmaker became the best known and most revered of the apostles.

Peter (rock, stone) — One of the twelve apostles, he was born Simon bar Jonah and nicknamed the Arabic version — Peter — by Jesus.

Phares, Pharez, Perez (burst forth) — Twin brother of Zarah or Zerah; son of Judah.

Philip (lover of horses) — One of the twelve apostles.

Raphael (God's healer) — One of the four angels who stood around the throne of God. Gabriel, Michael, and Uriel are the other three.

Reuben (behold a son) — Jacob's firstborn child with Leah; founder of one of the tribes of Israel.

Rufus (red) — Son of Simon the Cyrenian; he was saluted by the Apostle Paul as "elect in the Lord."

Samson (like the sun) — The son of Manoah who, it was said, was endowed with supernatural power and undaunted bravery; he was betrayed by Delilah.

Samuel (asked of the Lord) — Hebrew judge and prophet; son of Elkanah.

Saul (desired) — Of the tribe of Benjamin; son of Kish; the first king of Israel.

Seth (compensation) — Son of Adam; father of Enos.

Shiloh (pronounced Shy′-lo; place of rest) — Place name: the city of Ephraim, one of the earliest and most sacred of the Hebrew sanctuaries.

Silas (contracted form of Silvanis: woody) — One of the leaders of the Church at Jerusalem.

Simeon (heard) — The second of Jacob's sons by Leah.

Simon (contracted form of Simeon: heard) — A Canaanite; one of the twelve apostles (see Peter).

Solomon (peaceful) — Lastborn son of David; the king of Israel who reigned for forty years and was noted for his extreme wisdom.

Stephen (crowned) — The first Christian martyr, he was chief of the seven appointed to assist the apostles.

Thaddeus (wise) — Another name for Jude the Apostle.

Thomas (twin) — One of the apostles. According to Eusebius, his real name was Judas.

Timothy (God-fearing) — Child of a mixed marriage whose father's name is unknown; his mother is Eunice and his grandmother Lois.

Tobias (Greek form of Tobiah: goodness of God) — Father of Johanan; an Ammonite who opposed King Nehemiah.

Uri (fiery) — Father of Bezaleel; one of the architects of the Tabernacle.

Uriah — Devoted husband of Bathsheba; sent to death in battle by David, who wanted Uriah's wife for himself.

Zachariah, Zechariah (remembered by God) — The fourteenth king of Israel, who reigned for only six months; son of Jeroboam II.

Zacharias (Greek form of Zachariah) — Husband of Elizabeth; father of John the Baptist.

Zalmon (shady) — Place name: Mount Zalmon, near Shechem. An Ahohite; one of David's guard.

Zared (brook) — Place name: a brook or valley running into the Dead Sea near its southeast corner.

Names of Saints

A saint is a person who has lived a life of exceptional holiness, filled with good deeds and often the working of miracles. The Roman Catholic Church formally recognizes saints through the process of canonization and believes saints possess the ability to intercede for humans on earth.

At a baptism, the Christian custom is to give the baby the name of a saint from the Roman Martyrology, or Calendar of Saints. That saint then becomes the guardian and inspiration for his or her young namesake. Down the road a bit, at confirmation, the child may select the name of another saint as a protector and role model.

Many Christians observe their saint's "feast day" as their "name day" — in other words, by celebrating the same way you celebrate a birthday. In most cases, the saint's feast day is the day the saint died. Instead of it being a time of mourning, it is regarded as the saint's "heavenly birthday" and a time for celebration.

There is a feast day for every day of the year. In fact, since there are thousands of saints, most days belong to more than one saint. Also, there are many saints with the same name. For instance, there is St. Elizabeth of Hungary, whose feast day is

November 17; St. Elizabeth of Portugal, whose feast day is July 4; and St. Elizabeth Ann Seton, whose feast day is January 4. For this book we've selected one saint for each day of the year and, when appropriate, have noted what (s)he is the patron saint of, or why (s)he has been honored by the Church.

There aren't many saints from America, and, of those that are, most were canonized long ago. That means that many of their names are foreign and very old-world, like Wulfric, Theodosius, and Maximus. The Church allows us to take the liberty of turning these names into modern-day derivatives. Wulfric might become Wilfred; Theodosius might become Theo or Theodore; and Maximus might become Maxwell, Maxie, or Max. (The main A-to-Z name list, found at the back of the book, can help you with derivatives.)

Also, bear in mind that you can use the feminine version of a male saint's name. For example, the feminine version of St. Brendan could be Brenda; the feminine version of St. Charles could be Charlene, Charlotte, Cheryl, Carla, Carol, Caroline, even Arlene or Arlette. While the male version of a female saint's name can be used, chances are, though, that the female name is *already* a derivative of a male name. For example, St. Louise could be Louis, Lewis, even Aloysius — and probably was!

To learn even more about the choice of saintly names available to you, check the reference section of your local library; *Butler's Lives of the Saints* is indispensable.

Meanwhile, to help preserve this truly beautiful and meaningful custom, let's let the saints go marching in!

NOTE: What follows first is an alphabetical listing of the saints we've profiled, so that you can quickly see what names appeal to you and/or find out if your favorite saint appears here. They are all cross-referenced by date, so that if a particular saint appeals to you, you can then look him/her up in the list that follows, which profiles each saint according to his or her feast day.

NAMES OF THE SAINTS WE'VE PROFILED AND THEIR FEAST DAYS

Aaron — 7/3
Abraham — 10/27
Abraham Kidunaia — 3/16
Abraham of Smolensk — 8/21
Adalbert of Egmond — 6/25
Adamnan — 9/23
Adela — 12/24
Adelaide — 12/16
Adele (See: Adela) — 12/24
Adrian of Canterbury — 1/9
Adrian of Nicomedia — 9/8
Aedan (See: Aidan of Lindisfarne) — 8/31
Aedh (See: Macartan) — 3/26
Agape — 4/3
Agatha — 2/5
Agnes — 1/21
Aidan of Ferns — 1/31
Aidan of Lindisfarne — 8/31
Albert the Great — 11/15
Alexander Akimetes — 2/23
Alexander of Lyons — 4/22
Alexis — 7/17
Aleydis (See: Alice) — 6/15
Alice — 6/15
Aloysius Gonzaga — 6/21
Alphonsus Mary Liguori — 8/2
Alphonsus Rodriguez — 10/30
Amator — 5/1
Amatre (See: Amator) — 5/1
Amatus — 9/13
Ambrose — 12/7
Ambrose Barlow — 9/10
Amé (See: Amatus) — 9/13
Anastasia — 12/25; 4/15
Anastasia Patricia — 3/10
Anatolia — 12/23

Andrew — 11/30
Andrew of Fiesole — 8/22
Andrew Hubert Fournet — 5/13
Andrew Kim Taegon — 9/20
Angadrisma — 10/14
Angela Merici — 5/31
Angelina of Marsciano, Blessed — 7/21
Angelo — 5/5
Anne (Also see: Susanna) — 7/23; 7/26
Anselm — 4/21
Anthelm — 6/26
Anthony of Padua — 6/13
Antonia of Florence — 2/28
Antony the Abbot — 1/17
Antony Mary Zaccaria — 7/5
Anysia — 12/30
Apollo — 1/25
Arsenius the Great — 7/19
Athanasius — 5/2
Audrey — 6/23
Augustine of Canterbury (See: Austin) — 5/27
Augustine of Hippo (See: Austin) — 8/28
Aurea — 3/11
Aurelius — 7/27
Austin of Canterbury — 5/27
Austin of Hippo — 8/28
Bairre (See: Barry) — 9/25
Barbara — 12/4
Barnabas — 6/11
Barry — 9/25
Bartholomew — 8/24
Basil the Great — 1/2
Basilissa (Also see: Basilla) — 4/15; 5/20
Basilla — 5/20
Beatrice of Ornacieu — 2/13
Benedict — 7/11
Benedict Biscop — 1/12
Benen — 11/9
Benet (See: Benedict Biscop) — 1/12
Benignus (See: Benen) — 11/9
Benjamin — 3/31

Bernadette — 4/16
Bernard — 1/23
Bernard of Clairvaux — 8/20
Bertilla Boscardin — 10/20
Bertinus — 9/5
Bertrand — 6/30
Bibiana (See: Viviana) — 12/2
Blaan (See: Blane) — 8/11
Blaise — 2/3
Blane — 8/11
Boris — 7/24
Brendan — 5/16
Brigid — 2/1
Bruno — 10/6
Caedmon — 2/11
Cajetan (See: Gaetano) — 8/7
Camillus De Lellis — 7/14
Canice (See: Kenneth) — 10/11
Casimir — 3/4
Cassian of Imola — 8/13
Castor — 9/2
Catherine of Alexandria — 11/25
Catherine of Genoa — 9/15
Catherine of Sweden — 3/24
Ceadda (See: Chad) — 3/2
Cecilia — 11/22
Cecily (See: Cecilia) — 11/22
Chad — 3/2
Chaermon — 12/22
Charity — 8/1
Charles Borromeo — 11/4
Chionia — 4/3
Christina of Aquila — 1/18
Chrysanthus — 10/25
Ciaran (See: Kieran) — 3/5
Clare of Assisi — 8/12
Clement I — 11/23
Colette — 3/6
Colm (See: Colum) — 6/9
Colman of Lindisfarne — 2/18
Colum — 6/9

Columba — 6/9
Conrad of Piacenza — 2/19
Cormac — 9/14
Cosmas — 9/26
Cyprian — 9/16
Cyran — 12/5
Cyril of Alexandria — 6/27
Cyril of Jerusalem — 3/18
Damasus I — 12/11
Damian — 9/26
Daniel — 10/10
Daria — 10/25
David — 3/1
David I of Scotland — 5/24
Deirdre (See: Ita) — 1/15
Demetrius — 10/8
Denis — 10/9
Dewi (See: David) — 3/1
Dominic — 8/8
Dominic of the Causeway — 5/12
Dominic of Silos — 12/20
Dominic Savio — 3/9
Donald — 7/15
Donatus — 10/22
Dorotheus of Tyre — 6/5
Dunstan — 5/19
Dymphna (See: Dympna) — 5/15
Dympna — 5/15
Eadbert (See: Edbert) — 5/6
Edan (See: Aidan of Ferns) — 1/31
Edbert — 5/6
Edmund the Martyr — 11/20
Edward the Confessor — 10/13
Elizabeth — 11/5
Elizabeth Ann Bayley Seton — 1/4
Elizabeth of Hungary — 11/19
Elizabeth of Portugal — 7/4
Elmo — 6/2
Eric IX of Sweden — 5/18
Ernest — 11/7
Etheldreda (See: Audrey) — 6/23

Eucherius — 2/20
Eulalia of Mérida — 12/10
Eve — 9/6
Fabian — 1/20
Faith — 8/1
Felicity — 3/7
Felix of Nantes — 7/7
Fergus — 11/27
Fidelis of Signaringen — 4/24
Fina (See: Seraphina) — 3/12
Finbar (See: Barry) — 9/25
Flavian — 2/24
Flora — 11/24
Flora of Beaulieu — 10/5
Florence — 12/1
Florian — 5/4
Frances Xavier Cabrini — 11/13
Francis of Assisi — 10/4
Francis Caracciolo — 6/4
Francis De Sales — 1/24
Francis of Paola — 4/2
Francis Xavier — 12/3
Frederick of Utrecht — 7/18
Fulbert — 4/10
Gabriel — 9/29
Gabriel Possenti — 2/27
Gaetano — 8/7
Gatian — 12/18
Gelasius I — 11/21
Gemma Galgani — 4/11
Genevieve — 1/3; 5/8
George the Great — 4/23
Gerald — 4/5
Gerard of Brogne — 10/3
Gerard Majella — 10/16
Gerlac — 1/5
Germain — 5/28
Germanus (See: Germain) — 5/28
Gertrude of Helfta — 11/16
Gilbert of Sempringham — 2/16
Gildas the Wise — 1/29

Giles — 9/1
Gleb (See: Boris) — 7/24
Godfrey — 11/8
Godric — 5/21
Gregory Barbarigo — 6/18
Gregory the Great — 9/3
Gregory Nazianzen — 5/9
Guido (See: Guy of Cortona) — 6/16
Guy of Anderlecht — 9/12
Guy of Cortona — 6/16
Hannah (See: Anne) — 7/26
Harvey — 6/17
Helena — 8/18
Henry of Cocket — 1/16
Herbert — 3/20
Hervé (See: Harvey) — 6/17
Hilary of Poitiers — 1/13
Hilda — 11/17
Hope — 8/1
Hugh of Rouen — 4/9
Hyacinth — 8/15
Hyacintha Mariscotti — 1/30
Ida (See: Ita) — 1/15
Ida of Herzfeld — 9/4
Irenaeus of Lyons — 6/28
Irene — 4/3
Irmina — 12/24
Isaac the Great — 9/9
Isabella (See: Elizabeth of Portugal) — 7/4
Isidore of Seville — 4/4
Ita — 1/15
Ivo of Chartres — 5/23
James — 4/30
James the Greater — 7/25
James the Less — 5/3
Jane Frances Fremiot DeChantal — 12/12
Januarius — 9/19
Jason — 7/12
Jerome — 9/30
Jerome Emiliani — 2/8
Joachim — 7/26

Joan of Arc — 5/30
Joan Delanoue, Blessed — 8/17
Joan De Lestonnac — 2/2
John the Baptist — 6/24
John Baptist De La Salle — 4/7
John of the Cross — 12/14
John of Egypt — 3/27
John the Evangelist — 12/27
John of God — 3/8
Jordan of Saxony — 2/15
Josaphat — 11/12
Joseph — 3/19
Joseph of Cupertino — 9/18
Jude — 10/28
Julia Billiart — 4/8
Julian — 2/24
Julian the Hospitaller — 2/12
Juliana Falconieri — 6/19
Julitta of Caesara — 7/30
Julius — 7/3
Julius I — 4/12
Justin De Jacobis — 7/31
Justin Martyr — 6/1
Justus — 8/6
Kateri Te Kakwitha, Blessed — 4/17
Kenneth — 10/11
Kevin — 6/3
Kieran — 3/5
Laisren (See: Laserian) — 4/18
Lambert of Lyons — 4/14
Landericus (See: Landry) — 6/10
Landry — 6/10
Laserian (See: Laisren) — 4/18
Laurence O'Toole — 11/4
Laurence of Rome — 8/10
Leger — 10/2
Leo I the Great — 11/10
Leo IX — 4/19
Leodegarius (See: Leger) — 10/2
Leonard Casonova — 11/26
Leonard Murialdo — 3/30

Leonard of Noblac — 11/6
Lilian — 12/8
Lillian (See: Lilian) — 12/8
Lily (See: Lilian) — 12/8
Louis of Anjou — 8/19
Louis Mary of Montfort — 4/28
Louise de Marillac — 3/15
Lucian — 10/26
Lucian of Beauvais — 1/8
Lucius — 2/24
Lucy of Syracuse — 12/13
Lughaidh (See: Molua) — 8/4
Luke — 10/18
Macarius the Wonder-Worker — 4/1
Macartan — 3/26
Madeleine Sophie Barat — 5/25
Maedoc (See: Aidan of Ferns) — 1/31
Marcellus — 11/1
Marcian — 4/20
Margaret — 7/20
Margaret Clitherow — 3/25
Margaret of Cortona — 2/22
Maria Goretti — 7/6
Marian (Also see: Marcian) — 4/20; 4/30
Marina (See: Margaret) — 7/20
Marius — 1/27
Mark — 4/25; 10/24
Martha — 7/29
Martin (See: Mark) — 10/24
Martin I — 4/13
Martin De Porres — 11/3
Martin of Tours — 11/11
Mary — 1/1
Mary Magdalen Postel — 7/16
Matilda — 3/14
Matthias — 5/14
Maura of Troyes — 9/21
Maximilian Mary Kolbe — 8/14
May (See: Marius) — 1/27
Meda (See: Ita) — 1/15
Medard — 6/8

Melania the Younger — 12/31
Mercedes — 9/24
Michael — 9/29
Mildred of Thanet — 7/13
Modan — 2/4
Molaisse (See: Laserian) — 4/18
Molua — 8/4
Monica — 8/27
Montanus — 2/24
Narcissus — 10/29
Natalia — 7/27
Nestor — 2/26
Nicholas — 12/6
Nicholas Von Flue — 3/22
Nino — 12/15
Non (See: Nonnita) — 3/3
Nonna (Also see: Nonnita) — 3/3; 8/5
Nonnita — 3/3
Norbert — 6/6
Odo of Cluny — 11/18
Oliver Plunket — 7/1
Olympias — 12/17
Otto — 7/2
Owen — 8/23
Paschal Baylon — 5/17
Pastor — 8/6
Patricia — 8/25
Patrick — 3/17
Paul — 6/29
Paul of the Cross — 10/19
Paul Miki — 2/6
Perpetua — 3/7
Peter Canisius — 12/21
Peter Damian — 2/21
Peter Fourier — 12/9
Peter Julian Eymard — 8/3
Philip Evans — 7/22
Philip Neri — 5/26
Quentin — 10/31
Quintinus (See: Quentin) — 10/31
Radbod — 11/29

Raphael — 9/29
Raphaela Mary Porras — 1/6
Raymond of Peñafort — 1/7
Raymund — 5/29
Regina — 9/7
Reine (See: Regina) — 9/7
Richard Gwyn — 10/17
Richard of Lucca — 2/7
Rita of Cascia — 5/22
Robert Francis — 9/17
Robert of Newminster — 6/7
Roderic — 3/13
Romanus — 8/9; 10/23
Rosaria — 10/7
Rose of Lima — 8/30
Rudericus (See: Roderic) — 3/13
Rufina — 7/10
Rufinus — 6/14
Rupert of Salzburg — 3/29
Sabina — 8/29
Samson — 7/28
Sava — 1/14
Scholastica — 2/10
Secunda (See: Rufina) — 7/10
Senericus (See: Serenus) — 5/7
Seraphina — 3/12
Serapion — 3/21
Serenus — 5/7
Silverius — 6/20
Silvin — 2/17
Simeon Metaphrastes — 11/28
Solangia — 5/10
Stephen the Deacon — 12/26
Stephen of Hungary — 8/16
Stephen of Perm — 4/26
Sunniva — 7/8
Susanna — 7/23
Tarasius — 2/25
Teilo — 2/9
Teresa of Avila — 10/15
Teresa of the Child — 10/1

Teresa of Jesus — 8/26
Ternan — 6/12
Theodora of Alexandria — 9/11
Theodore — 12/28
Theodosius the Cenobiarch — 1/11
Thomas Aquinas — 1/28
Thomas Becket — 12/29
Thomas More — 6/22
Thomas of Villanova — 9/22
Thrasius (See: Tarasius) — 2/25
Timothy — 1/26
Tobias — 11/2
Tutilo — 3/28
Urban V — 12/19
Ursula — 10/21
Valerius — 6/14
Valentine — 2/14
Veronica Giuliana — 7/9
Victor Maurus — 5/8
Victoria — 12/23
Victorian — 3/23
Victorinus (See: Montanus) — 2/24
Vincent De Paul — 9/27
Vincent Pallotti — 1/22
Viviana — 12/2
Walter of L'Esterp — 5/11
Wenceslaus — 9/28
Wilfrid — 10/12
William of Bourges — 1/10
William of Eskill — 4/6
Wolstan (See: Wulfstan) — 1/19
Wulfstan — 1/19
Wulstan (See: Wulfstan) — 1/19
Zachary — 11/5
Zita — 4/27

PROFILES OF THE SAINTS, ORGANIZED BY FEAST DAYS

January

1 **Mary**, the Blessed Virgin, has many feast days. The Solemnity of Mary, Mother of God — which is celebrated on the first day of the year — is one of them.

2 **Basil the Great**, one of the Four Doctors of the Greek Orthodox Church, is the patriarch of Eastern monks and the patron of Russia.

3 **Genevieve** is credited with saving Paris from the ravages of Atilla the Hun through her prayers and fasting. She is patron of Paris and its disasters, including drought and torrential rains.

4 **Elizabeth Ann Bayley Seton** founded the Sisters of Charity, the first religious society in America. Elizabeth was the first American-born saint and was canonized in 1975 by Pope Paul VI.

5 **Gerlac**, to atone for the sins of his youth, spent seven years in Rome nursing the sick and doing penance. He then returned to his native Holland, gave all his possessions to the poor, and lived as a hermit in the hollow of a tree.

6 **Raphaela Mary Porras** overcame great opposition to start the congregation of the Handmaids of the Sacred Heart, which was devoted to educating children. She was canonized in 1977 by Pope Paul VI.

7 **Raymond of Peñafort** was famous for his preaching and was the confessor of Pope Gregory IX. He opposed heresy and is the patron of lawyers.

8 **Lucian of Beauvais**, a missionary in Gaul, was said to be the companion of St. Dionysius of Paris.

9 **Adrian of Canterbury**, a great scholar and abbot, is revered for his miracles, which helped students in need.

10 **William of Bourges** was named archbishop of Bourges by order of Pope Innocent III. He lived an extremely austere life, was known for helping the poor and the penitent, and defended the rights of the Church — even against the king.

11 **Theodosius the Cenobiarch** built a monastery for hermits and

hospices for the sick, the aged, and the mentally disturbed. He was buried in a cell called the Cave of the Magi; the wise men who came to find Christ after his birth were said to have lodged in it.

12 Benedict or **Benet Biscop**, abbot, built many monasteries and is the patron of the English Benedictines.

13 Hilary of Poitiers, bishop and Doctor of the Church, was one of the most esteemed theologians of his time and a staunch defender of Christ's divinity. He is the patron against snake-bites.

14 Sava, a trainer of young monks, was respected for his gentleness and leniency. He was also credited with teaching his people effective ways to farm the land, and about using windows — instead of doors — to let in air and light. He is the patron of the Serbian people.

15 Ita, also known as **Deirdre, Ida**, and **Meda**, is a virgin credited with creating an Irish lullaby for the Infant Jesus. In Ireland, she is second in popularity to St. Brigid.

16 Henry of Cocket was a Dane who had a religious calling very early in life. He became a hermit on the island of Cocket, off England's coast of Northumberland. He had only one meal a day — bread and water — which he ate after sunset.

17 Antony the Abbot, the founder of Christian monasticism, is the patron of those with skin diseases, of domestic animals, of basketmakers, and of gravediggers.

18 Christina of Aquila, baptized Matthia, became an Augustinian hermit at Aquila. She was known for her devotion to the poor and for her gifts of prophesy, ecstasy, and miracles.

19 Wulfstan or **Wolstan**, bishop, washed the feet of twelve poor men daily and was highly regarded for his humility. He was also an ardent advocate of clerical celibacy.

20 Fabian, a martyr for his faith, supposedly was elected pope because a dove landed on his head during the election.

21 Agnes, at age thirteen, refused to compromise her purity and so was tortured and murdered. It is said that when her clothes were torn off, her hair spontaneously grew long to cloak her body, and that a man who assaulted her went blind, until she asked that his sight be restored. One of the most famous Roman martyrs, she is, appropriately, the patron of virginal innocence.

22 Vincent Pallotti founded the Society of Catholic Apostolate, performed exorcisms, and is considered the forerunner of Catholic Action.

23 **Bernard**, archbishop of Vienne, was known for his insistence on strict ecclesiastical discipline.

24 **Francis de Sales**, bishop and Doctor of the Church, was known as "the Gentle Christ of Geneva." He is the patron of writers, editors, and the Catholic press.

25 **Apollo**, abbot, founded a community of monks at Hermopolis when he was close to eighty. The most astonishing miracle accorded to him is the continual multiplication of bread during a time of famine.

26 **Timothy**, bishop, was a missionary companion of Paul the Apostle and was called "the Almsgiver" because of his care for the poor. He is the patron against stomach disorders.

27 **Marius** or **May** was a monk who was cured of a serious illness at the tomb of St. Denis in Paris. Every year he spent the forty days of Lent alone in a forest. During one such period, he had a vision of the barbarians invading Italy and the subsequent destruction of his monastery. Unfortunately, both visions came true.

28 **Thomas Aquinas**, priest and Doctor of the Church, was one of the Church's most prolific writers and theologians. He is the patron of all universities, scholars, philosophers, theologians, and booksellers.

29 **Gildas the Wise**, abbot, is a celebrated teacher and thought of as the first English historian.

30 **Hyacintha Mariscotti**, named Clarice at birth, was forced by her family to enter a Franciscan convent. For more than ten years she was rebellious. Then, after surviving her second serious illness, she changed her ways and adopted the strictest of religious life-styles. She helped found two congregations that ministered to the sick, the aged, and the poor.

31 **Aida**, **Edan**, or **Maedoc of Ferns**, was a Bishop of Ireland known to be extremely kind, especially to animals. He is said to have performed many miracles.

February

1 **Brigid (Bride) of Ireland** is the second patron of Ireland and "the Mary of the Gael." She is the patron of poets, dairy workers, blacksmiths, and healers.

2 **Joan de Lestonnac** got married, had four children, and was widowed. As soon as the children were on their own, Joan entered the religious life and founded a community of nuns dedicated to educating young girls. She was canonized in 1949.

3 **Blaise** or **Blase**, bishop, healed sick and wounded animals. He is the patron of wild animals, wool combers, and those who suffer from throat problems. He is also invoked to help heal sick cattle.

4 **Modan** was an extremely austere monk who, against his will, became the abbot of his Scottish monastery. He then lived as a hermit.

5 **Agatha** was tortured and killed because she promised her virginity to God. She is the patron of nurses, wet nurses, and fire fighters.

6 **Paul Miki** was a Japanese Jesuit preacher who was martyred. His canonization, along with that of his martyred companions, led him to become one of the protomartyrs of the Far East.

7 **Richard of Lucca** was respectfully given the name "Richard the King" by the people of his town. His real name is unknown. Three of his children — Willibald, Winebald, and Walburga — also became saints.

8 **Jerome Emiliani** is the founder of the Somaschi, which saw to the education of youth in colleges, academies, and seminaries. He is the patron of both orphans and abandoned children.

9 **Teilo**, known as Eliud in his native Wales, was a successful preacher who founded several monasteries.

10 **Scholastica**, the twin sister of St. Benedict, is the patron of Benedictine nuns and is called upon for help against storms. Upon her death, her brother had a vision in which he saw her soul ascending to heaven.

11 **Caedmon**, a laborer or herdsman at an English monastery, is said to have had a vision that taught him how to compose verses in praise of God. He became the first Anglo-Saxon writer of religious poetry and is called "the Father of English Sacred Poetry." His sole surviving hymn is said to have been composed during a dream.

12 **Julian the Hospitaller** is the patron of innkeepers, travelers, and boatmen.

13 **Beatrice of Ornacieu** lived an austere life and was gifted with

visions of Christ. She was so moved by the sight of him that it was thought she would injure her vision by her abundant shedding of tears.

14 **Valentine**, a physician and priest from Rome, is a martyr and the patron of lovers and greetings. The medieval belief that birds begin to pair together on this date is thought to have inspired the sending of Valentine cards.

15 **Jordan of Saxony**, whose real name was Gordanus or Giordanus, was a powerful preacher who directed his charismatic energies toward young students. He has been called "the first university chaplain." His writings about St. Dominic are the prime source of information about the founder of the Dominicans.

16 **Gilbert of Sempringham**, along with seven young women and the approval of Pope Eugene III, established the Gilbertine Order, the only religious order to originate in England during the medieval period. It eventually grew to twenty-six monasteries.

17 **Silvin** canceled his marriage plans to embark on a religious life of devotion to the needy. He used his wealth to build churches and to ransom slaves from the barbarians. He died a Benedictine monk.

18 **Colman of Lindisfarne**, bishop, was a staunch defender of Celtic, but not Roman, ecclesiastical practices. When King Oswy ruled in favor of the Roman way, Colman gave up his bishopric and moved from Lindisfarne to the Isle of Inishbofin to found a monastery in which he could practice Celtic rites.

19 **Conrad of Piacenza** was a Franciscan hermit who lived a life of extraordinary piety. He is invoked to heal hernias.

20 **Eucherius**, bishop, took an unpopular stand in France against using Church revenues for war expenses. He spent much of his life in prayer and contemplation.

21 **Peter Damian**, bishop, cardinal, and Doctor of the Church, worked zealously for the internal reform of the Church and fought against practices such as simony. He wrote some of the most beautiful poetry in medieval times.

22 **Margaret of Cortona** had an illegitimate son, but when her lover was killed, she saw it as a sign of God's disfavor and thereafter strove to resist "temptation." She then spent most of her life helping the sick and the poor.

23 **Alexander Akimetes**, a native of Asia Minor, was a convert to Christianity who retired to Syria to practice asceticism.

24 **Montanus** and his companions **Lucius, Flavian, Julian,** and **Victorinus** were all slain for upholding their faith. They share this feast day.

25 **Tarasius** or **Thrasius**, bishop and secretary to ten-year-old Emperor Constantine VI, was patriarch of Constantinople and revered for his acts of charity.

26 **Nestor**, bishop, was tortured and crucified when he refused to recant his obedience to God and submit to the Emperor Decius.

27 **Gabriel Possenti** promised that if he recovered from an illness, he would serve God. He did so — but it took until the second time around. The patron of youth, students, and the clergy, he was canonized in 1920.

28 **Antonia of Florence** ruled the monastery of Corpus Christi under the strict rule of St. Clare. She had visions and at times was seen to be in ecstasy and rise from the ground.

March

1 **David** or **Dewi**, bishop, is the patron of Wales and perhaps the most celebrated of British saints.

2 **Chad** or **Ceadda** was one of four brothers, all of whom became priests and of whom two — including Chad — became bishops. Once a bishop, Chad traveled not by horseback but on foot, in the manner of the apostles.

3 **Nonnita, Non,** or **Nonna**, born of noble birth, lived in a convent and was seduced by Sant, a local chieftain. The child of that union was St. David.

4 **Casimir**, a son of King Casimir III of Poland, is the patron of Poland, Russia, Lithuania, and the ill.

5 **Kieran** or **Ciaran of Saighir** is known as Ireland's firstborn saint. Legend has it that when St. Kieran returned to Ireland from Italy, St. Patrick recruited him as one of twelve bishops to help him in evangelizing the country.

6 **Colette**, christened Nicolette in honor of St. Nicholas of Myra, was known for restoring the original strict observance of St. Clare throughout France, Savoy, and Flanders. She had a great fondness for children and animals.

7   **Felicity**, along with **Perpetua**, was a victim of Christian persecution in Carthage.

8   **John of God**, founder of the Brothers Hospitallers, began his dedication to God by peddling sacred pictures and books. He is the patron of printers and booksellers, as well as of the sick.

9   **Dominic Savio** was the youngest nonmartyr to receive canonization and is the patron of boys, juvenile delinquents, Pueri Cantors, and choirboys.

10 **Anastasia Patricia**, it is believed, was martyred under Diocletian. Her popularity is due to the fact that her memory is associated with the second Mass at Christmas. She is the patron of weavers.

11 **Aurea**, a nun from Spain, lived her life as a solitary, without material possessions, and was rewarded by the vision of her patron saints, who assured her of God's favor.

12 **Seraphina** or **Fina** lived her life in poverty and pain. When illnesses left her paralyzed, she lay on a plank of wood, in the same position, for six years. When she died and her body was taken off the rotted wood, it is said that the wood was covered in white violets. The white violets that bloom during this feast day in St. Seraphina's town of San Geminiano are called "Santa Fina's flowers."

13 **Roderic** or **Rudericus** was betrayed by his Moslem brother, who falsely claimed Roderic had renounced Christ. Imprisoned, Roderic still refused to deny his Christianity and was eventually beheaded.

14 **Matilda**, also known as **Mechtildis** and **Maud**, was queen of Germany and noted for her holiness and charitable works.

15 **Louise de Marillac** became a nun and, with St. Vincent de Paul, founded the Sisters of Charity, which provides education, hospitals for the poor, and homes for abandoned children. She is the patron of social workers.

16 **Abraham Kidunaia** is revered for converting an entire town of pagans to Christianity.

17 **Patrick**, archbishop, was born in Scotland but was captured by pirates and taken to Ireland. After six years he escaped, returned home, and vowed to go back and organize the Irish Church. His success made him the patron of Ireland and of Nigeria (whose people were converted to Christianity primarily by Irish clergy).

18   **Cyril of Jerusalem**, archbishop and Doctor of the Church, was erroneously charged with wrongful deeds and spent years in exile. He was noted for his great gentleness and reasonableness.

19   **Joseph**, husband of the Virgin Mary and foster father of Jesus Christ, is the patron of the Universal Church, social justice, carpenters, doubters, travelers, Austria, Bohemia, Canada, Belgium, Mexico, Peru, Russia, and South Vietnam. St. Joseph is also a protector of working men and viewed as a good role model for fathers.

20   **Herbert**, a disciple and close friend of St. Cuthbert, asked that he not be abandoned but be "taken" at the same time as his friend, since they had both served God together in their earthly life. A year later both saints died — on the same day.

21   **Serapion** was called "the Scholastic" because of his great knowledge in matters both sacred and secular.

22   **Nicholas von Flue** was a religious figure of major import in Swiss history; he helped prevent civil war. He is Switzerland's patron.

23   **Victorian**, one of Carthage's wealthiest citizens, was appointed proconsul by Huneric, Arian King of the Vandals. During Huneric's persecution of Catholics, Huneric urged Victorian to convert to Arianism. Victorian refused and was tortured to death.

24   **Catherine of Sweden**, the daughter of St. Bridget, is called upon for protection against abortion — perhaps because of her state of chastity despite her marriage.

25   **Margaret Clitherow** used her home as a refuge for England's fugitive priests and is one of the Forty Martyrs of England and Wales.

26   **Marcartan** or **Aedh MacCairthinn**, bishop, has little known about his life, although many outstanding miracles are attributed to him.

27   **John of Egypt** was one of the most famous of desert hermits because of his wisdom, his miracles, and his ability to read the minds of others, thus discovering their secret sins.

28   **Tutilo** was a monk of all trades: a master of poetry, painting, architecture, sculpture, and metalworking. He was also a musician, orator, and composer.

29   **Rupert of Salzburg** helped rebuild the old town Juvavum,

which he renamed Salzburg. Considered the first bishop of Salzburg, he died on March 29 — Easter Sunday.

30 **Leonard Murialdo** was devoted to educating poor boys and began Italy's first Catholic worker movement. He was canonized in 1970 by Pope Paul VI.

31 **Benjamin**, a deacon preaching Christianity in Persia, clung to his faith even while being tortured to death.

April

1 **Macarius the Wonder-Worker**, baptized Christopher, was known for his miracles of healing. He was imprisoned, tortured, and eventually exiled for his opposition to iconoclasm.

2 **Francis of Paola** is the patron of sailors, naval officers, and navigators.

3 **Irene** and her sisters **Agape** and **Chionia** were sentenced to death for owning and protecting copies of the Holy Scriptures.

4 **Isidore of Seville**, bishop, Doctor of the Church, and one of the most learned men of his time, is thought of as the last of the ancient Christian philosophers. He is the patron of Madrid and farmers.

5 **Gerald**, confessor, and founder of the abbey of Sauve-Majeure (Silver Major) near Bordeaux, was noted for his preaching.

6 **William of Eskill**, abbot, is known for the reforms he made at monasteries in Denmark.

7 **John Baptist de la Salle**, the patron of teachers, revolutionized the art of teaching with his many schools, which included a boys' reformatory and a school for adult prisoners.

8 **Julia Billiart**, devoted to helping the sick and the poor, helped found the Institute of the Sisters of Notre Dame. Paralyzed for twenty-two years, Julia was suddenly able to walk on the Feast of the Sacred Heart after a priest bade her to.

9 **Hugh of Rouen** is said to have used family connections to help him become bishop of Rouen, Paris, and Bayeux, and abbot of Fontenelle and Jumieges. He then used his family's money to benefit the churches, promoting both piety and learning.

10   **Fulbert**, bishop, was a poet and author of many hymns. An influential scholar for his day, he was regarded as another Socrates or Plato.

11   **Gemma Galgani**, plagued with physical pain and supernatural manifestations, underwent many extraordinary religious experiences, including the stigmata. She was canonized in 1940.

12   **Julius I**, the pope who succeeded Pope Mark, was involved with the controversy between the Catholics and the Arians. He was also responsible for building several basilicas and churches in Rome.

13   **Martin I**, unfairly tried for treason, was flogged, imprisoned, and then exiled. He was the last pope to die a martyr.

14   **Lambert of Lyons**, raised at the court of King Clotaire III, became a monk at Fontenelles and then the abbot. He founded the abbey of Donzère and then became archbishop of Lyons.

15   **Anastasia** and **Basilissa**, disciples of St. Peter and St. Paul, are said to have buried the bodies of two executed saints. Both women lost their lives for doing so.

16   **Bernadette**, baptized Marie Bernarde, had eighteen visions of the Virgin Mary beside the River Gave in Lourdes. As a result, a chapel, which is now the most-visited pilgrimage site in modern Europe, was built there. She is the patron of shepherds.

17   **Kateri Tekákwitha**, known as "the Lily of the Mohawks," was the first Native American proposed for sainthood. She is Blessed.

18   **Laserian, Laisren**, or **Molaisse**, named bishop and papal legate for Ireland by Pope Honorius I, was sent to Rome to settle the dispute between Roman liturgical usages and the Celtic practices. He decreed in favor of the Roman practices.

19   **Leo IX**, born Bruno, was quite a military man, both before he became a man of the cloth and while he was pope. He was responsible for proposing that popes be elected only by cardinals, a procedure still in effect to this day.

20   **Marcian** or **Marian** is famed for his great rapport with wild and domestic animals.

21   **Anselm**, archbishop of Canterbury and Doctor of the Church, was known for his patience and gentleness. He was a superior theologian, called "the Father of Scholasticism."

22 **Alexander of Lyons** was persecuted by Marcus Aurelius; he was crucified when he stood fast by his faith.

23 **George the Great**, according to legend, slew the dragon and saved the princess. It's no wonder he's the patron of the Boy Scouts, as well as of England, Istanbul, Aragon, Portugal, Germany, Genoa, and Venice. He can be called on to defend against syphilis, leprosy, and the plague. His feast day is kept as a holy day of obligation.

24 **Fidelis of Sigmaringen**, born Mark Rey, championed the rights of the poor, earning him the nickname "the Poor Man's Lawyer."

25 **Mark**, evangelist, wrote the Second Gospel. He is patron of secretaries, notaries, Venice, and Egypt.

26 **Stephen of Perm**, a Russian bishop, translated the Liturgy and part of the Bible into a language for which he had invented the alphabet. He was a missionary as well as a champion of the downtrodden.

27 **Zita**, who often visited the sick, the poor, and prisoners, is the patron of housewives and servants.

28 **Louis Mary of Montfort**, in addition to being a hospital chaplain in Poitiers, was named missionary apostolic by Pope Clement XI. Through his emotional sermons and his writing of "The True Devotion to the Blessed Virgin," he fostered devotion to Mary and to the rosary.

29 **Catherine of Siena**, Doctor of the Church, was the youngest of twenty-five children and an extremely effective arbitrator who could end feuds. Referred to as "La beata popolaria," meaning "the blessed popular one," she experienced the stigmata and is the patron of Italy, Italian nurses, and fire prevention.

30 **James**, deacon, and **Marian** lector, were imprisoned and tortured, along with hundreds of others, during Emperor Valerian's persecution of the Christians.

May

1 **Amator** or **Amatre** is thought to be the bishop who ordained St. Patrick.

2 **Athanasius**, bishop and Doctor of the Church, has been named in history as "the Father of Orthodoxy," "Pillar of the Church," and "Champion of Christ's Divinity."

3   **James the Less**, a first cousin of Jesus and the first bishop of Jerusalem, was surnamed "the Just" for the great esteem in which he was held. He is the patron of the dying (because he forgave his murderers on his deathbed).

4   **Florian** surrendered during Diocletian's persecution of Christians and was tortured and thrown into the River Enns with a rock tied around his neck. He is the patron of Austria and Poland, and of those in danger from water, floods, and drowning.

5   **Angelo** is said to be the son of Jews from Jerusalem who converted to Christianity after a vision of the Virgin Mary. In Sicily, he successfully converted many Jews to Christianity, and it was there he suffered martyrdom.

6   **Edbert** or **Eadbert**, bishop, was a biblical scholar known for his generosity to the poor.

7   **Serenus** or **Senericus** was a renowned miracle worker credited with ending a plague and a horrendous drought through the power of prayer. Those nearby remarked that they heard celestial music while St. Serenus was on his deathbed.

8   **Victor Maurus** converted to Christianity at an early age and served as a Christian officer in the Roman army. Later on he was arrested under Emperor Maximilian and tortured to death. He is one of the patrons of Milan.

9   **Gregory Nazianzen**, a Doctor of the Church and archbishop of Constantinople, is often referred to as "the Theologian" for his eloquent sermons and masterful defense of the orthodoxy.

10 **Solangia**, sometimes called **St. Genevieve**, is the patron of the province of Berry in France. She had a way with animals and a great gift of healing. During her prayers and meditation a star was said to shine over her head.

11 **Walter of L'Esterp**, abbot, was noted for his ability to convert sinners and perform miracles.

12 **Dominic of the Causeway** was so named because he built a road, bridge, and hospice in the dangerous wilderness through which pilgrims had to pass to get to the shrine of St. James.

13 **Andrew Hubert Fournet** went from a frivolous life-style to a meaningful and pious one. It is said that prayers to St. Andrew bring an abundance of food to needy nuns and those under their care.

14 **Matthias**, apostle, was chosen by Christ to take the place of the traitor Judas Iscariot.

15 **Dympna**, or **Dymphna**, is the patron of the mentally ill and of nurses. She protects against possession by the Devil and sleepwalking (which was thought, in the Middle Ages, to be a form of possession).

16 **Brendan**, one of the most popular Irish saints, wrote the epic saga "Navigatio Sancti Brendani Abbatis," meaning "Abbot Brendan, Holy Navigator," about his seven-year journey to the promised land. Because of his many missionary voyages he is the patron of sailors.

17 **Paschal Baylon**, originally a poor shepherd, is the patron of shepherds, the Eucharist, and Italian women.

18 **Eric IX of Sweden** did a lot to establish Christianity as king of Sweden and was considered the principal patron of Sweden until the Protestant Reformation.

19 **Dunstan**, archbishop of Canterbury, is said to have been an excellent painter, embroiderer, harpist, and metal-worker. He is the patron of locksmiths, goldsmiths, and jewelers.

20 **Basilla** or **Basilissa** was promised in childhood to Pompeius, a Roman patrician. But when she converted to Christianity, she consecrated herself to the Lord and reneged on her commitment to marry. Emperor Gallienus gave her a choice of marriage or death by the sword; the virgin martyr was beheaded.

21 **Godric** was taught songs during visions of Virgin Mary; they remain today as the oldest surviving pieces of English verse with rhyme and meter. He also foresaw — and then prayed for — ships in danger of shipwreck.

22 **Rita of Cascia**, married at twelve to an abusive man, is the patron of those in desperate situations, of parenthood, and against infertility. In Spain she is the patron of matrimonial difficulties.

23 **Ivo of Chartres**, bishop, taught Scripture, theology, and canon law. He wrote abundantly, and many of his letters and sermons still survive.

24 **David I of Scotland**, son of King Malcolm Canmore and St. Margaret, succeeded his brother as king of Scotland. During his reign he founded many monasteries, established Norman law, and was known for his justice, charities, and religious devotion.

25   **Madeleine Sophie Barat** was one of the first members of the Society of the Sacred Heart of Jesus — the female counterpart of the Jesuits. Even though, at twenty-three, she was the youngest member of the group, she was named superior of the convent and school, and held that post for sixty-three years. By the time of her death, she had opened more than one hundred houses and schools in twelve countries.

26   **Philip Neri** was said to be a witty but gentle man who loved practical jokes. His ability to read consciences eased his conversion of many people. He is the patron of Rome and is called "the Second Apostle of Rome."

27   **Austin** or **Augustine of Canterbury**, the first archbishop of Canterbury, was a man of great patience. He was also known as "the Apostle of England."

28   **Germain** or **Germanus** was named bishop of Paris by King Childebert I, whom he miraculously cured of a fatal illness.

29   **Raymund**, along with eleven other members of Pope Gregory IX's Order of Preachers, were preaching the faith in Toulouse when they were driven out by the Albigensians. In good faith, they accepted an offer of lodging in a local castle, but during the night were massacred by soldiers.

30   **Joan of Arc**, also known as "the Maid of Orleans," was a young girl who heard the voices of Sts. Michael, Catherine, and Margaret encouraging her to help the king of France regain his kingdom. As a military leader she was captured, imprisoned, and trapped into making damaging statements. Condemned to death, she was burned at the stake. Thirty years later she was exonerated. She is the patron of France and French soldiers.

31   **Angela Merici**, a tertiary of St. Francis at thirteen years of age, established the first teaching order of women in the Church. She was possibly one of the first to grasp the changed role of women in a society transformed by the Renaissance.

June

1   **Justin Martyr** or **Justin the Philosopher**, the first great Christian philosopher, was beheaded when he refused to sacrifice to the pagan gods. He is the patron of philosophers and apologists.

2   **Elmo**, also known as **Erasmus**, is the patron of sailors. The

bluish electrical charges seen around a ship's mast before or after a storm are thought to be a sign of his protection and are called St. Elmo's Fire. Because of his martyrdom (in which his intestines were drawn out), he is called upon for help with the pain of cramps, childbirth, and colic in children.

3 **Kevin**, also known in Ireland as **Coemgen** or **Caoimhghin**, had many sensational miracles attributed to him, such as feeding his community with the salmon brought to him by an otter. He is the patron of Dublin.

4 **Francis Caracciolo**, at age twenty-two, had a severe skin disease that was thought incurable. He vowed that if he recovered, he would devote his life to God and to serving others. He did recover and thereafter spent his life doing God's wishes.

5 **Dorotheus of Tyre**, scholar, author, priest, and bishop, was beaten to death when he was 107 for defending his faith against the persecution of Julian the Apostate.

6 **Norbert** was, at thirty-three, a handsome young man living a worldly life, when he was struck by lightning. While he was unconscious, a voice supposedly told him to reform his life. He did so and soon thereafter was ordained.

7 **Robert of Newminster**, abbot, is credited for his supernatural gifts, visions, and encounters with demons. It is said that his soul ascended to Heaven like a ball of fire.

8 **Medard**, bishop, is called upon to help cure toothaches and is the patron of corn and grape harvesting. It is said that if it rains on his feast day, the next forty days will be wet; if it's fair weather, the next forty days will also be good.

9 **Colum**, **Columba**, or **Colm**, was later called **Columcille**, which seems to refer to the numerous *cells* or religious foundations he established. He is patron of Ireland.

10 **Landry** or **Landericus of Paris**, bishop, was known for his kindness to the poor. During a famine, it is said, he sold church vessels and furniture to provide the poor with food. He erected his city's first real hospital.

11 **Barnabas**, born Joseph, was given the name Barnabas, meaning "man of encouragement" or "son of consolation," by the apostles. He is considered an apostle by the Church, although he is not one of the Twelve. He is the patron of Cyprus.

12 **Ternan** worked as a missionary among the Picts and founded the abbey of Culross, in Scotland.

13   **Anthony of Padua**, Doctor of the Church, is the patron of barren women, Flemish men, harvests, and Padua. He is called upon to help find lost articles. One of the greatest preachers of all time, Anthony was also called "the Living Ark of the Covenant" because of his marvelous memory for Scripture.

14   **Rufinus** and **Valerius** were thought to be part of a group of missionaries sent from Rome to evangelize Gaul. They were eventually tortured and beheaded for their faith.

15   **Alice** or **Aleydis** asked, at the tender age of seven, to live with the nuns in a convent. While still young, she contracted leprosy and had to be isolated. Although she suffered greatly, she also experienced visions and ecstasies and is credited with several miracles.

16   **Guy** or **Guido Vignotelli of Cortona** was known for his holiness and his miracles, which included resuscitating a little girl who had drowned.

17   **Harvey** or **Hervé** is a very popular saint in Brittany, and his name is very common for Breton boys. He was known for his exorcisms and is called upon for help with eye problems.

18   **Gregory Barbarigo**, bishop and cardinal, was compassionate and kind, although demanding when it came to himself. He worked to reconcile the Churches of the East and West.

19   **Juliana Falconieri** became a Servite tertiary when she was sixteen. Eventually she headed, and drew up a rule for, a group of women dedicated to prayer and charity. The rule was approved 120 years later, and St. Juliana is now considered the founder of the Servite nuns.

20   **Silverius**, pope, incurred the wrath of Empress Theodora and the Byzantines when he stood steadfast by his principles; his stance eventually cost him his life.

21   **Aloysius Gonzaga** is the patron of Catholic youth and the protector of Jesuit college students.

22   **Thomas More**, a brilliant scholar, lawyer, and writer, was in favor of the education of women. He disagreed with Henry VIII's efforts to divorce Catherine of Aragon and later proclaimed, "I am the King's good servant but God's first." Eventually he was beheaded and his head exhibited on London Bridge. He is the patron of lawyers.

23   **Audrey**, or **Etheldreda**, abbess, was married twice—for a total of fifteen years—but remained chaste, claiming she had consecrated herself to God.

24 **John the Baptist** is so called because he baptized many Jews. He was beheaded (without trial) and his head handed on a silver platter to Salome, simply because she requested it. He is the patron of monks because of his spartan and solitary life-style. His feast day is celebrated on his birthday, rather than on the day of his death, because he was born free of original sin.

25 **Adalbert of Egmond** successfully converted many nonbelievers because of his holiness, patience, and gentleness.

26 **Anthelm** or **Anthelmus**, bishop, set out to reform the noncelibate clergy and cared for lepers. Upon his death, a miracle occurred; when he was being lowered into his tomb, a lamp used only for important festivals lit spontaneously.

27 **Cyril of Alexandria**, bishop and "the Doctor of the Incarnation," is considered the most brilliant theologian of Alexandrian tradition.

28 **Irenaeus of Lyons**, bishop, was the first great ecclesiastical writer of the West. His writings stress the unity of the Gospels and the importance of both the Old and the New Testaments.

29 **Paul**, born Saul, originally persecuted Christians. But when Jesus spoke to him, he converted and became one of the apostles. He is the patron of the lay apostolate, Catholic Action, Malta, and Greece.

30 **Bertrand**, bishop, founded a monastery, a hospice, and a church and was known for his interest in grape-growing, the development of land, and other forms of agriculture.

July

1 **Oliver Plunket** was the last Catholic to suffer martyrdom at Tyburn, a place of public execution in England. In 1975, he became the first Irish saint to be canonized since 1226.

2 **Otto** served as the mediator between Henry V and the pope. His most noted accomplishment was leading a group of missionaries to eastern Pomerania, to convert and baptize over twenty thousand people.

3 **Aaron** and **Julius** were two Britons executed for keeping the faith during Diocletian's persecution of Christians.

4 **Elizabeth of Portugal**, queen, was known in Portugal as **Isabella**, the Spanish version of the name. Because of her skills

as an arbitrator, she prevented wars and was thus known as "the Peacemaker."

5   **Antony Mary Zaccaria** founded a congregation whose goal was to resurrect spirituality in the Church.

6   **Maria Goretti**, a twelve-year-old martyr, forgave her eighteen-year-old murderer right before her death. She is the patron of teenagers — especially girls — and the Children of Mary.

7   **Felix of Nantes**, bishop, was known for helping the poor and for building the cathedral at Nantes.

8   **Sunniva**, according to Norse legend, was the daughter of an Irish king. She fled to a cave on an island off Norway to escape her marriage. When she and her companions were entombed by a landslide, it is said that only her body remained intact and uncorrupt.

9   **Veronica Giuliana**, born Ursula, changed her name when she became a Capuchin nun in Umbria. She experienced visions of Christ as well as the stigmata.

10 **Rufina** and **Secunda**, daughters of a Roman senator, were each engaged to be married. During Emperor Valerian's persecution of Christians, their fiancés abandoned the faith. The sisters refused to do the same and fled from Rome but were captured, tortured, and beheaded for their Christianity.

11 **Benedict** is the patron of Europe, monks, farm workers, Italian speleologists (cave specialists), engineers, and architects. He is called upon for help against poison and death.

12 **Jason** welcomed St. Paul into his home on his second missionary journey. Greek legend says Jason was the bishop of Tarsus who evangelized Corfu, while Syrian legend says he evangelized the area around Apamea and was martyred there by being thrown to wild beasts.

13 **Mildred of Thanet**, abbess, was one of the most popular saints in medieval England. She was noted for her piety and for aiding the poor and the afflicted. Her sisters and her brother were also saints.

14 **Camillus de Lellis** contracted a painful disease in his leg. His horrible hospital experiences led him to revolutionize nursing and patient care.

15 **Donald**, on the death of his wife, formed a religious group with his nine daughters. Many hills, wells, and other natural features of Scotland are named Nine Maidens, in memory of St. Donald's daughters.

16 **Mary Magdalen Postel**, baptized Julia Frances Catherine, opened a school for girls when she was eighteen. When the school was closed during the French revolution, she and three other teachers founded the Sisters of the Christian Schools of Mercy. She was named superior, and it was then that she took the name Mary Magdalen.

17 **Alexis**, the son of a wealthy Roman senator, led a life of extreme poverty and virtue, and was known for a long time as "the Man of God."

18 **Frederick of Utrecht**, bishop, was noted for his holiness and sacred learning. When he helped mediate the emperor's family matters, he alienated Empress Judith. He was stabbed to death by assassins who, many speculated, were hired by the empress.

19 **Arsenius the Great** is said to have cried so much for his shortcomings and those of others that he wore away his eyelashes.

20 **Margaret** or **Marina**, said to be one of the "voices" that Joan of Arc heard, is patron of pregnant women, childbirth, and death. She is one of the most popular virgin martyr saints of the Middle Ages.

21 **Angelina of Marsciano**, Blessed, was married at fifteen, widowed at seventeen, and became a Franciscan tertiary. Accused of sorcery for preaching about celibacy to young women, she was exiled from her community. In Assisi, she founded an enclosed monastery. It was so successful that she established fifteen more in her lifetime.

22 **Philip Evans**, a Jesuit, was ministering to the Catholics of south Wales when he was arrested. When no evidence could be produced linking him or fellow prisoner John Lloyd with the Titus Oates plot, both were convicted of being priests illegally in England and executed. St. Philip was canonized in 1970 by Pope Paul VI.

23 **Susanna** or **Anne** fled to Leucadia, where she lived as a hermit, to escape the persecution of a rejected suitor. Since Leucadia is also known as Maura, this saint is also known as St. **Maura**.

24 **Boris** and **Gleb**, also known as **Romanus** and **David**, were the sons of the first Christian prince in Russia and were honored for being "passion bearers": blameless men who did not wish to die but who had refused to defend themselves. In this

sense they had submitted to death just like Christ. St. Boris is the patron of Moscow.

25 **James the Greater**, the first martyr among the apostles, was beheaded by King Herod. He is the patron of pilgrims, Spain, Guatemala, and Nicaragua.

26 **Anne** or **Hannah** and her husband, **Joachim**, were childless. When an angel told Anne that she would have a child, Anne promised that the child would serve God for all its life. Her child was Mary, the mother of Jesus. St. Anne is patron of housewives, childless women, cabinetmakers, and miners.

27 **Natalia**, a convert, attended the churches of Cordova with her face unveiled, thus giving away her identity. She and husband **Aurelius** were beheaded.

28 **Samson**, after recovering from an attempt on his life by two nephews jealous of his ordination, lived as a hermit. Then he became a bishop, an abbot, a missionary, and the founder of many monasteries and churches.

29 **Martha**, the sister of Mary Magdalene, is the patron of housewives, servants, waiters, and cooks.

30 **Julitta of Caesarea**, a wealthy widow in the time of Emperor Diocletian, fell victim to his edicts against Christians. Unprotected by the law, she had to go to court to defend her estates from a neighbor's claims. When she would not offer sacrifice to the pagan gods, she was put to death and her estates given to her opponent.

31 **Justin de Jacobis**, bishop, overcame persecution, imprisonment, and extreme hardships. He managed to convert over twelve thousand Africans.

August

1 **Faith**, age twelve, **Hope**, ten, and **Charity**, nine, were the daughters of Divine Wisdom (known in the Roman Martyrology as Sophia). During Hadrian's persecution of Christians, the girls were beheaded. Three days later their mother died while praying at their graves.

2 **Alphonsus Mary Liquori**, bishop and Doctor of the Church, is the patron of confessors and moral theologians.

3 **Peter Julian Eymard** established the Servants of the Blessed Sacrament, founded the Priests' Eucharistic League, organized the Confraternity of the Blessed Sacrament, and wrote

many books on the Eucharist. He was canonized by Pope John XXIII in 1962.

4 **Molua** or **Lughaidh**, a cowherd who became a monk, founded many monasteries. It is said that he never killed any living thing and that when he died, the birds wept.

5 **Nonna** converted her husband, Gregory 'Nazianzen (the Elder), to Christianity, and had three sons who became saints: St. Gregory Nazianzen the Divine, St. Caesarius, and St. Gorgonia.

6 **Justus**, age thirteen, and his brother **Pastor**, nine, were executed in Spain for proclaiming their faith as Christians. They are the patrons of Alcala and Madrid.

7 **Gaetano** or **Cajetan** helped institute pawnshops, which gave loans to the poor. He is thought of as one of the great Catholic reformers.

8 **Dominic**, the first domestic theologian for the pope, laid the foundation for the Dominican order.

9 **Romanus**, a Roman soldier, was baptized in prison by St. Laurence. When Romanus announced his conversion, he was beheaded.

10 **Laurence of Rome**, who met a fiery death, is the patron of cooks.

11 **Blane** or **Blaan**, bishop, is credited with several miracles, including striking fire from his fingernails to rekindle the church lights that had gone out.

12 **Clare of Assisi** helped found and lead the Poor Clares, the most austere of any female order. She is the patron of embroiderers and patron against sore eyes, and was made the patron of television in 1958 by Pope Pius XII.

13 **Cassian of Imola**, a teacher, refused to sacrifice to pagan gods during the persecution of the Catholics. His students were ordered to bring his life to an end — which they did.

14 **Maximilian Mary Kolbe**, baptized Raymond, harbored over fifteen hundred Jews and three thousand Polish refugees during the German occupation of Poland. After his arrest he voluntarily took the place of another man who was condemned to death in Auschwitz.

15 **Hyacinth**, born in Poland, joined the Dominicans in Rome and preached in Scandinavia, Prussia, and Lithuania. He is credited with many miracles and is revered as an apostle of Poland.

16   **Stephen of Hungary**, born Vaik, worked as the king of Hungary to establish sees and prohibit pagan customs in his land. He is the patron of Hungary.

17   **Joan Delanoue**, Blessed, received messages from God through a widow. They inspired her to turn to a religious, austere life of helping others and performing miracle healings.

18   **Helena** was kind to the poor, to soldiers, and to prisoners. St. Helena, an island in the Atlantic, was named after her because Spanish sailors had discovered it on her feast day.

19   **Louis of Anjou**, the son of the imprisoned King Charles II of Naples and Sicily, was traded for his father's release and only freed after seven years. When he refused to marry the sister of King James II, he gave up all rights to the throne. He chose to be ordained instead and thereafter lived a life of great austerity.

20   **Bernard of Clairvaux**, abbot and Doctor of the Church, was an eloquent and witty speaker, known as "the Honeysweet Doctor." He is considered one of the founders of the Cistercian Order, and his writings influenced medieval mysticism. He is the patron of Gibraltar.

21   **Abraham of Smolensk**, a biblical scholar and charismatic preacher, cared for the sick and the poor, but his preaching and his popularity offended the authorities. He was charged with heresy and deprived of his priestly duties. After five years he was completely exonerated and reinstated.

22   **Andrew of Fiesole** founded a monastery, rebuilt a church, and was known for his holiness.

23   **Owen**, whose name is the English translation of **Eoghan**, was kidnaped along with two other boys and sold into slavery in Britain. Legend has it that one day the slave master found the boys reading while angels ground their corn for them. The boys were released and returned to Ireland.

24   **Bartholomew**, apostle, is the patron of tanners, bookbinders, and plasterers.

25   **Patricia** fled from Constantinople to escape marriage and, while in Rome, took vows to consecrate her virginity to God. She is the patron of Naples.

26   **Teresa of Jesus Jornet E Ibars**, founder of the Little Sisters of the Aged Poor, is the patron of the elderly.

27 **Monica** prayed for the conversion of her dissolute son, Augustine, for nine years; finally he was converted, and eventually he became a saint. A model for Christian mothers because of her concern for her son, she is the patron of married women and mothers.

28 **Austin** or **Augustine of Hippo**, the first archbishop of Canterbury, was St. Monica's son. Called "the Doctor of Grace," he was known as one of the greatest intellects of the Catholic Church. He is the patron of theologians.

29 **Sabina** was converted to Christianity by Serapia, her Syrian servant. During Emperor Hadrian's persecution of Christians, Serapia suffered martyrdom for her faith; a month later, Sabina did, too.

30 **Rose of Lima**, baptized Isabel, was said to rub her face with pepper to disguise her beauty. It is thought that her prayers saved Lima from an earthquake. Known as "the Flower of Lima," she is the patron of florists and gardeners. She is also the patron of Peru, Central and South America, the Philippines, and India.

31 **Aidan** or **Aedan of Lindisfarne**, bishop, was a learned man, an eloquent preacher, and a miracle worker who was kind to the poor.

September

1 **Giles**, or **Aegidius**, abbot, is one of the Fourteen Holy Helpers. His shrine attracted a great number of medieval pilgrimages. He is the patron of beggars, the lame, and blacksmiths.

2 **Castor** founded the Mananque monastery near Apt in Provence, France, and became its first abbot. He then became the bishop of Apt.

3 **Gregory the Great**, the last of the traditional Latin Doctors of the Church, nicknamed himself "Servant of the Servants of God." This pope made magnificent contributions to the Liturgy. He is the patron of music and is called upon for protection against the plague.

4 **Ida of Herzfeld**, granddaughter of Charlemagne, is said to have put food for the poor in a stone coffin made for her; she did this to remind herself, on a daily basis, of her own mortality and her responsibility to others.

5   **Bertinus** was a missionary who, with St. Mommolin and St. Bertrand, founded a monastery in Sithiu, France. They evangelized whole areas that were totally downtrodden.

6   **Eve** is the patron of Dreux, France, where she is honored as a martyr.

7   **Regina** or **Reine**, whose pagan mother died at her birth, was raised by her nurse as a Christian. Upon discovering this, her father disowned her. She lived as a shepherdess until a disgruntled suitor persecuted her to death.

8   **Adrian of Nicomedia** was condemned to die for his faith by burning, but a violent storm put out the flames. He was then beheaded. He is called upon for help against the plague and is the patron of prison guards and butchers.

9   **Isaac the Great**, bishop, was responsible for the launching of Armenian literature and is considered the founder of the Armenian Church.

10   **Ambrose Barlow**, bishop and Doctor of the Church, stressed the importance of the independence of church and state and was extremely influential in bringing St. Augustine back to the faith. He is the patron of beekeepers and bishops.

11   **Theodora of Alexandria** reportedly left her husband to do penance for her sins and went to live, disguised as a man, as a monk in a monastery. Until her death no one knew she was a woman.

12   **Guy of Anderlecht**, born of poor parents, devoted his life to helping the poor, and invested what little he had in a business venture to earn more money to give to the poor. When he lost everything, he made a pilgrimage on foot to Rome, then to Jerusalem. After his death, miracles were reported at the grave of "the Poor Man of Anderlecht," as he was called.

13   **Amatus**, also known as **Amé**, was a Benedictine monk who converted Romaric, a nobleman who then founded a double monastery at Habendum. Amatus was its first abbot.

14   **Cormac**, King of Munster and the first bishop of Cashel in Ireland, was responsible for the creation of the book of psalms called the Cashel Psalter.

15   **Catherine of Genoa**, originally called **Caterinetta**, received communion daily for the rest of her life after she repented her sins. She wrote many impressive documents in the field of mysticism.

16   **Cyprian**, also known as **Thascius**, was a bishop, a pioneer of

Latin Christian literature, and the patron of North Africa and Algeria.

17 **Robert Francis Romulus Bellarmine**, bishop, cardinal, and Doctor of the Church, is the patron of seminarians.

18 **Joseph of Cupertino** experienced ecstasies and was known for his supernatural abilities, especially his power of levitation, which earned him the nickname of "the Flying Friar." He is the patron of students, aviators, and astronauts.

19 **Januarius**, bishop, became most famous after his martyrdom; a solid red substance — supposedly his blood — that is still stored in a vial in the Naples cathedral suddenly liquefies and bubbles up several times a year — including on his feast day. He is the patron of Naples.

20 **Andrew Kim Taegon** was the first Korean priest and pastor to give up his life for his faith.

21 **Maura of Troyes** dedicated her life to prayer, fasting, and helping the poor. She was noted for her piety and the miracles credited to her intercession.

22 **Thomas of Villanova**, bishop, was called "the Almsgiver" because of all that he gave the poor. He was said to have the power not only to multiply food, but to heal. He is the patron of Valencia.

23 **Adamnan**, or **Eunan**, abbot, was responsible for the principle that neither women nor children should be taken prisoner or slaughtered during times of war. This philosophy was thereafter called Adamnan's Law. He also wrote about the life of St. Columba. One of the most outstanding hagiographical documents in existence, it's also the most complete and important biography from the early Middle Ages.

24 **Mercedes**, from *merces,* meaning "mercy," is a name in honor of the Blessed Virgin Mary and her title "Our Lady of Mercy."

25 **Barry, Bairre**, or **Finbar**, bishop, was baptized Lochan, but the Irish monks called him Fionnbharr — or "white head" — because of his blond hair. He is the patron of Cork, Barra, and the Outer Hebrides.

26 **Damian** and **Cosmas** were brothers who practiced medicine without ever charging for their services. They are the patrons of doctors, surgeons, chemists, pharmacists, barbers, and the blind.

27 **Vincent de Paul** was one of the greats of the French Church.

He is patron of charitable organizations, Madagascar, hospitals, and prisoners.

28 **Wenceslaus** became king of Bohemia at age eighteen, and in that capacity he ended his country's persecution of Christians. He is patron of Bohemia.

29 **Michael**, **Gabriel**, and **Raphael** are three of the seven archangels said to stand closest to God; all three share the same feast day.

   Michael, the chief of the archangels, is patron of battle, policemen, paratroops, Brussels, banking, radiologists, death, cemeteries, England, Germany, Papua New Guinea, the Solomon Islands, the sick, and those possessed by the Devil.

   Gabriel, as a deliverer of messages, is the patron of telecommunications, television, radio, postal services, and philatelists. And, because he was thought of as "God's ambassador," he is patron of Argentinian ambassadors and of Spain's and Argentina's diplomatic services.

   Raphael is the patron of travelers, safe journeys, young people leaving home, pharmacists, health inspectors, and the blind, and patron against eye diseases.

30 **Jerome**, Doctor of the Church, spent thirty years preparing the Latin Vulgate translation of the Bible; it is still in use today. He is patron of students and librarians.

October

1 **Teresa of the Child Jesus of Lisieux** was baptized Marie-Françoise-Thérèse. She wrote *The Story of a Soul,* one of the most popular of modern spiritual autobiographies. Nicknamed "the Little Flower," she is the patron of florists and flower growers, foreign missions, Russia, and France.

2 **Leger** or **Leodegarius**, bishop, was an effective mediator and reformer and was concerned for the poor.

3 **Gerard of Brogne**, abbot, renounced his military life for a religious life and spent twenty years reforming the abbeys in Flanders, Lorraine, and Champagne.

4 **Francis of Assisi**, baptized John, abandoned his affluent lifestyle to embrace extreme poverty. He holds claim to the first certain recorded incidence of stigmata, and started the Fran-

ciscan movement. He is the patron of Italy, Italian merchants, and ecology.

5 **Flora of Beaulieu** was noted for her many mystical experiences, including levitation, prophecies, and visions.

6 **Bruno** chose the life of a hermit and began the Carthusian Order, referred to as "the angels of the earth." Due to the Carthusians' aversion to publicity, Bruno was never canonized, but Pope Leo X gave permission to keep his feast.

7 **Rosaria**, from "rosary," is a name in honor of the Blessed Virgin Mary and her title "Our Lady of the Rosary."

8 **Demetrius**, a soldier martyred for his faith, is, along with St. George, patron of the Crusaders and Christian fighting men.

9 **Denis** is thought of as the first bishop of Paris. He is the patron of Paris and France and is called upon for help against headaches.

10 **Daniel** accompanied six Franciscan friars as their superior to Africa. Before they could accomplish their mission and evangelize the Mohammedans, they were arrested in Morocco. Since they refused to renounce their faith, they were beheaded.

11 **Kenneth** or **Canice**, abbot, converted numerous pagans in Ireland and Scotland and founded the church at Kilkenny, Ireland. He is the patron of Kilkenny.

12 **Wilfrid**, bishop, championed the replacing of Celtic practices with Roman ways in northern England.

13 **Edward the Confessor**, king of England for twenty-three years, was known for his goodness and fairness and for solving problems with wisdom rather than warfare.

14 **Angadrisma** was promised in marriage but wanted to become a nun. She asked God to make her physically repulsive, so that her fiancé would no longer want her. Her wish was fulfilled when she got leprosy. Once she became a nun, her leprosy disappeared, and she became known for her holiness and beauty.

15 **Teresa of Avila** was the first female Doctor of the Church. She is the patron of headache sufferers, Spanish Catholic writers, and the Spanish army.

16 **Gerard Majella** earned his reputation as "the most famous wonder-worker of the eighteenth century"; he was supposedly able to read minds, exert power over inanimate ob-

jects, and be in two places at one time. He is the patron of expectant mothers and childbirth.

17 **Richard Gwyn**, born in Wales, was raised Protestant and converted to Catholicism. When his presence at Anglican services was missed, he was arrested, tortured, and convicted of trumped-up charges of treason. He was hanged, drawn, and quartered. He was canonized by Pope Paul VI in 1970 and is the protomartyr of Wales.

18 **Luke**, evangelist, is the patron of doctors, artists, sculptors, painters, lacemakers, notaries (as a result of his account of Christ's life), and butchers.

19 **Paul of the Cross**, one of the most esteemed preachers of his time, brought faith back to the biggest of sinners and the most hardened of criminals. He is said to have had the gifts of prophecy and healing.

20 **Bertilla Boscardin**, christened Anne Frances, was given the unkind nickname "Goose." When she was accepted by the Sisters of St. Dorothy at Vicenza, she said, "I'm a poor thing, a goose. Teach me. I want to become a saint." She worked hard by caring for the sick, and eventually reached her goal.

21 **Ursula**, believed to have been martyred at Cologne, is the patron of schoolteachers.

22 **Donatus**, legend has it, was on his way from Rome to Ireland when he stopped off at Fiesole. As he entered the town's cathedral — where its congregants had gathered to elect a new bishop — the church bells rang and the candles spontaneously ignited. Donatus was immediately declared bishop.

23 **Romanus**, bishop, worked to root out idolatry and ministered to criminals sentenced to death.

24 **Mark** or **Martin**, as a hermit on Mount Marsicus in Campagnia, is said to have performed many miracles.

25 **Daria** was a priestess of Minerva who married Chyrsanthus when she agreed to convert and have a chaste marriage. The couple then converted many Romans, but when word of it reached the ears of Emperor Numerian, he ordered everyone's execution.

26 **Lucian** and **Marcian** practiced black magic but publicly burned their magic paraphernalia and converted to Christianity when they found their witchery had no effect on a Christian maiden.

27 **Abraham**, often called "the Poor" or "the Child," was a disci-

ple of St. Pachomius. He chose the eremitic life and lived in a cave for seventeen years.

28 **Jude**, also called **Thaddeus** or **Lebbeus**, was an apostle and is the patron of those in hopeless situations.

29 **Narcissus**, a Greek who was a bishop in Jerusalem, wrought miracles and was said to have been 119 when he died.

30 **Alphonsus Rodriguez** went back to grade school in his forties, was then admitted to the Jesuits as a lay brother, and took his final vows at age fifty-four. He was consulted on many spiritual matters because of his wisdom.

31 **Quentin**, or **Quintinus**, was tortured and killed for his faith. He is called on for help against coughs.

November

1 **Marcellus**, as bishop of Paris, defended his city against barbarian attacks. He was noted for his holiness and miracles.

2 **Tobias**, a Christian soldier stationed in Armenia, was burned at the stake because he would not participate in a pagan sacrifice.

3 **Martin de Porres**, known as "the Father of Charity" by his Lima, Peru, community, nursed the sick, cared for animals, and founded both an orphanage and a foundling hospital. He is the patron of race relations; social justice; Peru's public education, TV, and health services; Spanish trade unionists; and people of mixed race.

4 **Charles Borromeo**, bishop and cardinal, was important in the Counter-Reformation and a great supporter of learning and the arts. He is the patron of seminarians.

5 **Elizabeth** and **Zachary** had reached a childless middle age when an angelic vision told Zachary that the couple would have a son, who should be named John. Zachary was skeptical and so lost his power of speech. At the baby's birth, Zachary regained his voice and named the baby John. Thus Zachary and Elizabeth became the parents of John the Baptist.

6 **Leonard of Noblac**, abbot, was a favorite saint of Western Europe in the late Middle Ages. He is patron of childbirth, prisoners, and those in danger from robbers and thieves.

7 **Ernest**, a Benedictine abbot of South Germany, participated in the Crusades, then stayed in Palestine to preach the Gospel. When he moved on through Arabia, he was put to death by the Moslems at Mecca.

8   **Godfrey**, bishop of Amiens, was unrelentingly strict, making him unpopular with the less diligent clergy.

9   **Benen** or **Benignus** became St. Patrick's disciple, companion, and confidant, and eventually succeeded him as chief bishop of Ireland.

10   **Leo I the Great**, pope and Doctor of the Church, created stability in a time of chaos and is historically known for convincing Attila the Hun not to attack Rome. His actions affected the concept of the papacy for centuries to come.

11   **Martin of Tours**, bishop, is the patron of soldiers, beggars, France, horses and their riders, and wine makers.

12   **Josaphat**, bishop, was born in Poland and was the first Eastern saint to be formally canonized (in 1867).

13   **Frances Xavier Cabrini**, born in Italy, founded the Missionary Sisters of the Sacred Heart. When she was thirty-nine, she went to New York to work with Italian immigrants. In less than three decades, her congregation spread across the U.S. and established more than fifty hospitals, schools, orphanages, and convents. She became an American citizen in 1909 and was the first U.S. citizen to be canonized (in 1946). She is the patron of emigrants and migrants.

14   **Laurence O'Toole**, archbishop of Dublin and a strict disciplinarian, was responsible for many clerical reforms.

15   **Albert the Great**, bishop and Doctor of the Church, is called "the Universal Doctor" and is ranked as one of the first — and greatest — natural scientists. He is the patron of scientists.

16   **Gertrude of Helfta** experienced revelations and is one of the most outstanding of medieval mystics. She is the patron of the West Indies.

17   **Hilda**, as abbess of a double monastery in England, was noted for her great spiritual wisdom.

18   **Odo of Cluny** was known for his hymns, treatises on morality, and an epic poem on the Redemption.

19   **Elizabeth of Hungary**, daughter of the king of Hungary, founded a Franciscan convent and provided for helpless children. She is the patron of Catholic charities.

20   **Edmund the Martyr** became the king of East Anglia at the young age of fourteen. He ruled wisely for fifteen years, until the Danes invaded and beheaded him.

21 **Gelasius I** was a pope known for his holiness, justice, charity, and learning.

22 **Cecilia** or **Cecily** is the patron of music and musicians. Supposedly when the organ played she sang only to God.

23 **Clement I**, pope, is the patron of marble workers, lighthouses, and lightships.

24 **Flora**, whose father was a Mohammedan, was secretly raised Christian by her mother. She was then betrayed by her own brother.

25 **Catherine of Alexandria**, one of the "voices" heard by Joan of Arc and one of the Fourteen Holy Helpers, is the patron of philosophy, learning, students, young women, nurses, Christian apologists, librarians, and wheelwrights.

26 **Leonard Casonova of Port Maurice**, baptized Paul Jerome, set up nearly six hundred Stations of the Cross throughout Italy and is the patron of parish missions.

27 **Fergus**, an Irish bishop surnamed "the Pict," founded several churches in Scotland in honor of St. Patrick.

28 **Simeon Metaphrastes**, one of the most celebrated medieval Greek writers, recorded the legends and stories of the Byzantine saints for Emperor Constantine VII Porphyrogenitus. His feast day is observed by the Byzantine or Orthodox Church but is not recognized in Rome.

29 **Radbod**, bishop, wrote hymns and was known for helping the poor.

30 **Andrew**, apostle, was a fisherman and Christ's first disciple. He is the patron of fishermen, Scotland, Greece, and Russia.

December

1 **Florence** was a hermit who practiced much penance and fought against the temptations of the Devil.

2 **Viviana**, or **Bibiana**, legend has it, suffered under Emperor Julian the Apostate and was a martyr.

3 **Francis Xavier**, called "the Apostle of the Indies and Japan," is credited with more than 700,000 conversions. He is the patron of foreign missions, India, Pakistan, and Outer Mongolia.

4 **Barbara** took secret instruction in Christianity and was baptized. Her conversion cost her her life at the hand — and

ax — of her father. She is the patron of firemen, mathematicians, and carpenters.

5   **Cyran**, also known as **Sigiramnus**, broke his engagement to a nobleman's daughter to enter the religious life. When Cyran's father died, Cyran gave all his family's wealth to the poor. Authorities initially thought him insane and imprisoned him. When he was released, he made a pilgrimage to Rome, founded monasteries, and was known for helping criminals as well as the poor.

6   **Nicholas**, bishop, is one of the most popular saints of all time and the patron of children. The idea of "St. Nick" being representative of Santa Claus may have started when children were given gifts on St. Nick's feast day. He is also the patron of brides, unmarried women, bakers, pawnbrokers, perfumers, travelers, sailors, Russia, Greece, Sicily, Lorraine, Apulia, and of many cities, dioceses, and churches.

7   **Ambrose**, bishop and Doctor of the Church, is the patron of bishops, bees and their keepers, candlemakers, and domestic animals.

8   **Lilian**, **Lillian**, or **Lily** are names given in honor of the Blessed Virgin; her symbol is a white lily, for purity. This day is celebrated as the Immaculate Conception of the Blessed Virgin Mary.

9   **Peter Fourier** worked toward free education for the poor.

10 **Eulalia of Mérida** was burned at the stake; legend has it that a white dove flew out of her mouth as she died.

11 **Damasus I**, pope, poet, and biblical scholar, is the patron of archaeologists. In his lifetime he was the patron of St. Jerome, who commissioned him to revise the Latin text of the Bible, resulting in the Vulgate version.

12 **Jane Frances Fremiot de Chantal**, under the spiritual tutelage of St. Francis de Sales, founded sixty-five convents. According to St. Vincent de Paul, she was "one of the holiest souls I have ever met."

13 **Lucy of Syracuse**, one of the most illustrious of the virgin martyrs, is the patron of sufferers of eye diseases, hemorrhages, and throat infections.

14 **John of the Cross**, Doctor of the Church and one of Spain's most celebrated poets, wrote masterpieces of Spanish literature and Catholic mysticism. He is the patron of mystics.

15 **Christiana** (so called in the Roman Martyrology) or **Nino** (so

called by Georgians in Russia) performed miracles of healing, which she claimed were the work of Christ.

16 **Adelaide**, called "the Peacemaker of Europe," restored monasteries and strove to convert the Slavs.

17 **Olympias**, a deaconness of the Church, was extremely generous to the poor and gave shelter to expelled monks.

18 **Gatian** was thought to be the first bishop of Tours.

19 **Urban V**, born William de Grimoard, was elected pope, succeeding Innocent VI. He is best known for working to move the papacy from Avignon to Rome, instituting more clerical discipline, and reviving religion.

20 **Dominic of Silos**, abbot, was known for his miraculous healings. It is believed that the invocation of his name helped rescue Christian slaves from the Moors.

21 **Peter Canisius**, Doctor of the Church and "the Second Apostle of Germany," is thought to have led the Catholic Counter-Reformation in southern Germany.

22 **Chaermon** was an Egyptian bishop who took to the Arabian mountains to avoid persecution and was never seen again.

23 **Anatolia** and **Victoria** were responsible for many conversions and many miracles, respectively. Suitors whom they had rejected instigated their executions when the women refused to denounce their faith.

24 **Adela** or **Adele** and **Irmina**, daughters of the king of Germany, founded a convent in which they lived a holy and charitable life. Adele was a disciple of St. Boniface.

25 **Anastasia** is said to have ministered to persecuted Christians. She is the patron of weavers.

26 **Stephen the Deacon** was the first martyr and is the patron of stonemasons (as he was stoned to death) and deacons. He is called upon for help against headaches.

27 **John the Evangelist** was the only apostle present at the foot of Christ's cross and the only apostle not to suffer martyrdom. He is the patron of Asia Minor and of protection against poison.

28 **Theodore** and his brother Theophanes, tortured for opposing Emperor Theophilus's iconoclasm, had twelve lines of verse branded on their foreheads. After they were banished to Apamea, Theodore died.

29 **Thomas Becket** went from riches to rags when he was elected archbishop of Canterbury. After one of many major disagree-

ments with the archbishop, King Henry II ordered the death of his longtime friend, and Thomas was murdered in his own church, at the foot of his altar.

30   **Anysia** used her inheritance to help the poor. She lost her life to a soldier while defending her faith.

31   **Melania the Younger** was one of the great religious philan-thropists of all time, freeing over eight thousand slaves.

Names from Mythology

Myths are the creative imaginings of primitive people in a pre-scientific world. Their stories of how the world began, along with its early history and its evolvement, are studded with the deeds of heroes, knights, nymphs, magicians, maidens, muses, titans, warriors, royalty, gods, and goddesses.

Although we attempted to eliminate from the following list the names of those mythological characters — Phaedra, for example — who were responsible for extremely mean-spirited acts, some, undoubtedly, slipped by us. (In case you're wondering, Phaedra caused the death of her stepson Hippolytus by falsely accusing him of rape.)

And talk about Hippolytus. . . . We're not going to! We've also excluded complex names like his which would be "myth-pronounced" more often than not.

That leaves us with a variety of names, all possessing strength, beauty, and intrigue. The more we researched, the more we saw that no two mythographers agree on the details of the lives of these mythical characters. Therefore we decided that along with each name, we would give you only *one* very brief version of his or her identity.

Most of the names we've selected have their origins in Greek and Roman mythology simply because they are the ones most like our Anglicized names, and therefore the most usable.

We've adopted the spellings from familiar current usage, and, in some rare instances, we've included the pronunciation we think sounds best.

Without further ado or adon't, here is a compendium of these classical beauties.

FEMALE MYTHOLOGICAL NAMES

Anteia (An-tay'-uh) — Greek: Wife of the sea god Proetus, she tried to convince the Corinthian hero Bellerophon (who killed the fire-breathing Chimaera) to elope with her.

Ariadne — Greek: Daughter of Minos who gave Theseus the thread by which he escaped from the labyrinth. After being deserted by him on the island of Naxos, she married Dionysus, the god of fertility, wine, and drama.

Artemis — Greek: Goddess of the moon; virgin goddess of the hunt; twin sister of the sun god Apollo.

Astraea (As-tray'-uh) — Greek: Goddess of justice; daughter of Zeus and Themis, the Titaness. After witnessing too much of the world's wickedness, Astraea returned to heaven and became the constellation Virgo.

Athena — Greek: Goddess of wisdom, arts and crafts, fertility, and warfare.

Aurora — Roman: Goddess of the dawn.

Camilla — Roman: Loved and protected by Diana, the daughter of Metabus, king of the Volsci, was able to run through grain without trampling it beneath her and cross the sea without wetting her feet.

Cassandra — Greek: Daughter of Priam, king of Troy; twin sister of Helenus. She was endowed by Apollo with the gift of prophecy, but when she wouldn't return his love, he ensured that henceforth, nobody would believe her prophecies. She was sometimes called Alexandra. The Hellenistic poet Lycophron made her the star of his epic poem *Alexandra.*

Castalia (Kuh-stal'-yuh) — Greek: Wife of King Delphus (the hero who gave his name to Delphi); mother of Castalius, who ruled over Delphi after his father died.

Chloris — Greek: The only surviving daughter of Niobe and Amphion, a couple who had anywhere from two sons and three daughters to ten sons and ten daughters, depending on which mythographer you follow. When Niobe bragged about her brood to Leto, who had just one son and one daughter (they were, respectively, Apollo and Artemis), Leto asked her children to get revenge. And so Apollo killed all but one of Niobe's sons, Artemis all but one of Niobe's daughters. The surviving daughter was pallid with terror and took the name Chloris, which means "green."

Clementia — Roman: Goddess of pity; depicted in statues with a goblet in one hand to refresh the weary and a lance in the other to defend the oppressed.

Clio — Greek: The muse of history.

Cybele — An Asiatic goddess who found acceptance in both Greece and Rome. She took responsibility for every phase of her worshipers' well-being, including extending to them a promise of immortality. Cybele was often identified by the Greek mythographers with Rhea.

Daphne — Greek: A nymph who, when pursued by an amorous Apollo, was saved by being changed into a laurel tree.

Diana — Roman name for Artemis.

Dione (Die-oh′-knee) — Greek: Titan goddess; believed to be the mother of Aphrodite.

Doris — Greek: Daughter of Oceanus and Tethys; sea goddess who married Nereus and then had fifty sea nymphs called the Nereids.

Echo — Greek: A nymph of the trees and springs whose love for Narcissus was unrequited. She faded away until all that remained was her voice . . . her voice . . . her voice. . . .

Elissa — Greek: As Dido she was the queen of Carthage. When she lived in Tyre, she was called Elissa. She killed herself when abandoned by Aeneas, hero of Vergil's *Aeneid*.

Eris — Greek: Goddess of discord.

Evadne — Greek: Daughter of Poseidon and Pitane, she was raised by Aepytus, ruler of Arcadia. She was loved by Apollo and they had a son.

Feronia — Roman: A goddess of springs and woods, she is said to be the mother of Erylus, a hero who had three bodies and three separate lives.

Flora — Roman: Goddess of flowers.

Freya (Fray'-ha) — Norse: Daughter of Njord, god of fertility; goddess of love, beauty, and reproduction, she is the second most important Norse goddess. (The first is Frigg, mother of the gods.)

Galatea (Gal'-uh-tee'-uh) — Greek: An ivory statue of a beautiful maiden that Aphrodite brought to life to answer the fervent prayers of its sculptur, Pygmalion, who had fallen in love with his creation.

Harmonia — Greek: Some say she was the daughter of Ares and Aphrodite, while others claim her parents were Zeus and Electra. All seem to agree, however, that she was the wife of the Phoenician prince Cadmus, who founded Thebes.

Helen (of Troy) — Greek: Daughter of Zeus and Leda; the incredibly beautiful wife of the Spartan king, Menelaus. Her abduction by Paris is said to have been the cause of the Trojan War.

Hera — Greek: Queen of Olympus; goddess of marriage and childbirth. She is both the sister and wife of Zeus, the supreme deity of the ancient Greeks.

Hestia — Greek: Goddess of the hearth; sister of Zeus.

Iris — Greek: Goddess of the rainbow; a messenger for Zeus and Hera who rode the rainbows between heaven and earth.

Juno — Roman name for Hera.

Lara — Roman: Daughter of the River Tiber, this nymph — whose real name is Lala, "the Gossip" — was loved by Mercury, a Roman god who was also messenger of the gods. Their union begot the Lares, the Roman guardian gods.

Larissa — Greek: No two sources agree on this heroine's story. Some say she was from Argos; others claim Thessaly as her birthplace. Some say she was the mother of Pelasgus by Zeus, others say by Poseidon; still others believe she was the *daughter* of Pelasgus. The only thing *not* arguable is that her name is pretty! It's also the name of a Greek city in the eastern part of Thessaly.

Lavinia — Greek: Second wife of Aeneas, the Trojan hero and star of Vergil's *Aeneid.*

Lucina — Roman: Goddess of childbirth.

Macaria (Ma-kair'-ee-uh) — Greek: Virgin daughter of Heracles (a.k.a. Hercules) and Deianira. When an oracle pronounced that for victory over Eurystheus (the ruler of Tiryns, Mycenae, and Midea) a human sacrifice was necessary, she ensured that victory by offering herself up as the sacrifice.

Maia (May'-uh or My'uh) — Greek: One of the seven daughters of Atlas. According to the Roman: Goddess of spring; daughter of the ancient woodland deity Faunus (Pan); wife of Vulcan.

Marica (Ma-reek'-uh) — Roman: A nymph whom Vergil described as the mother of Latinus, king of the Aborigines, and wife of Faunus, protector of shepherds and their flocks. Marica is thought to be Circe deified.

Megara (Meg'-uh-ruh) — Greek: Daughter of Cron of Thebes, and wife of Heracles (Hercules).

Melia (Meh-lee'-ah) — Greek: The nymph daughter of Oceanus, the Titan god of the outer sea encircling the earth. After an affair with Apollo, she gave birth to two sons, one of whom was Tenerus, the famous soothsayer and king of Thebes.

Melissa — Greek: Nursemaid to the infant Zeus. She taught humankind the value of using honey.

Nanna — Norse: Wife of Baldur, who was the son of Odin and Frigg and the most gentle and best loved of the gods.

Nike (Nigh'-key) — Greek: Goddess of victory.

Penelope — Greek: The faithful wife of Odysseus, king of Ithaca and star of Homer's *Odyssey,* who turned away many suitors while awaiting Odysseus's return from ten years of wandering.

Phyllis — Greek: Daughter of King Phyleus of Thrace. Legend has it that Phyllis was metamorphosed into a leafless almond tree. When Demophon, her lover, embraced the tree, it grew leaves. At that moment, the Greek word for leaves changed from *petala* to *phylla.*

Rhea — Greek: A Titaness, she is the daughter of Uranus, the personification of Heaven and ruler of the world; and Gaea, goddess of the earth. Also wife of the Titan Cronus, who dethroned Uranus; and mother of Zeus, Poseidon, Hera, Hestia, Hades, and Demeter. (Also see: Cybele)

Selene — Greek: The Greek mythological sun and moon pair is Helios (god of the sun) and his sister, Selene (goddess of the moon). She loved Endymion, who is kept immortally beautiful and youthful through eternal sleep.

Sibyl — Greek and Roman: The name given to all prophetesses, probably thanks to a young girl named Sibyl who had the gift of prophecy and earned a great reputation as a soothsayer. She was the daughter of Dardanus, who was the son of Zeus and Electra.

Thalia (Thuh-lie'-uh, Thayl'-ya, or Thuh-lee'-yuh) — Greek: The muse of comedy and pastoral poetry.

Timandra — Greek: Daughter of Tyndareus, a hero at Sparta, and Leda. She married Echemus, defender of the Peloponnese, but allowed herself to be abducted by Phyleus, who gave up the throne of Elis to take part in the Calydonian boar hunt.

Vesta — Roman name for Hestia.

MALE MYTHOLOGICAL NAMES

Adonis — Greek: The beloved of Aphrodite, the goddess of beauty and love. His name has become synonymous with masculine beauty. According to Near East mythology, Adonis, known as Tammuz, embodies the spirit of the fruitful year.

Andreus — Greek: Son of the River Peneius, which flows through a region in ancient Greece.

Apollo — Greek: God of the sun, manly beauty, prophecy, music, healing, and poetry; twin brother of Artemis.

Arion — Greek: A musician who was thrown overboard by pirates and saved by a dolphin.

Auster — Roman: The south wind.

(The) Cabiri (Kuh-beer'-ee) — Greek: The gods of fertility. Said to be four in number, they were worshiped in Phrygia, an ancient country in west-central Asia Minor.

Cadmus — Greek: A Phoenician prince, married to Harmonia. He introduced writing and founded Thebes with the warriors who sprang from the dragon's teeth he had planted.

Dymas (Dee'-mahs) — Greek: King of Phrygia in ancient Greece and father of Hecate, a goddess of the earth.

Eryx (Ehr'-ix) — Greek: Son of Aphrodite and Poseidon. He gave his name to Mount Eryx in Sicily, where he built the Temple of Aphrodite Erycina.

Evander — There are several mythological Evanders: the son of Sarpedon; one of Priam's sons; and the one we favor, who is said to be the son of Hermes and an Arcadian nymph. As founder of Pallantium (which would later become Rome), he was a benevolent ruler who taught writing, music, and other then-unknown skills to his people.

Geb — Egyptian: Earth god; father of Osiris, the king and judge of the dead.

Hermes — Greek: Herald and messenger of the gods; god of roads, commerce, invention, cunning, and theft. The Romans called him Mercury.

Janus — Roman: God of gates, doorways, and beginnings. Usually depicted with two back-to-back bearded faces looking in opposite directions. His festival month is January.

Jason — Greek: Heroic leader of the Argonauts who, with the help of Medea, retrieved the Golden Fleece. He married Medea, the sorceress-daughter of the king of Colchis, but then deserted her for Creüsa. Medea sent her rival a gift: a wedding dress dipped in poison that would make the wearer's veins burn violently.

Linus — Greek: A musician and poet; the inventor of rhythm and melody.

Maron — Greek: According to Euripides, he was the son of Dionysus, god of the vine, of wine, and of mystic ecstasy.

Myles — Greek: Son of Lelex, king of Laconia, whom Myles later succeeded. Myles is said to have invented the corn mill.

Nestor — Greek: King of Pylos; noted most for his wise counsel in the Trojan War.

Orion (Oh-rye′-un) — Greek: Giant-size hunter; lover of Aurora. Slain by Artemis, he was then placed in the sky near Gemini and Taurus as a constellation.

Paris — Greek: Son of King Priam and Hecuba; prince of Troy whose abduction of Helen caused the Trojan War.

Priam (Pry′-em) — Greek: King of Troy; father of many children (some mythographers say he had as many as fifty sons). Three of his most acknowledged offspring are Paris (see above), Cassandra, and Hector, the much-loved leader of the Trojan army. Priam was killed when his city fell to the Achaeans.

Regin — Norse: In the *Volsunga Saga:* A blacksmith; brother of Fafnir who raised Sigurd and encouraged him to kill Fafnir.

Sigmund — Norse: In the *Volsunga Saga:* Son of Volsung, king of Hunland, and Liod; father of Sigurd, who performed heroic deeds.

Syrus — Greek: The Syrians got their name from him. He is credited with inventing arithmetic and introducing the doctrine of metempsychosis, the transmigration of souls.

Talos (Tay′-lohss) — Greek: A bronze, robotlike giant who was created by the god Hephaestus to protect Minos's island of Crete. And protect it he did, until Medea's magic pierced his one vulnerable vein and destroyed him.

Thor — Norse: God of thunder, rain, and farming, and the son of Odin and Frigg. Thor, the hammer-hurler, is usually represented wielding his hammer Miölnir (or Mjollnir) as he rides a goat-drawn chariot.

Zeus — Greek: Last, but certainly not least, is the presiding and greatest god of the Greek pantheon, Zeus! He is ruler of the heavens; god of light, clear skies, and thunder; father of other gods and mortal heroes; and protector of strangers and guests.

Names Foreign Wide:
Popular Names from Foreign Countries

For those of you who have a special feeling about or a link to a particular country of the world, you might want to consider a name for your baby that will reflect that ethnic connection.

The following lists offer a sampling of popular, contemporary names from twenty-eight different cultures. There are many different ways to pronounce these names, but we've given you some help by including the standard pronunciations of those names hardest to figure out.

To get in the mood, sip a cup of Chinese tea and grab some Swiss cheese on Italian bread with Russian dressing and a side of French fries — and then pretend you're lunching at the United Nations as you thumb through the lists.

AFRICA

Swahili Names for Eastern and Central Africa, including Kenya

Girl Names

Asha (Ah'-shah) — Life
Aziza (Ah-zee'-zah) — Precious
Dalila (Dah-lee'-lah) — Gentle
Hadiya (Hah-dee'-yah) — Gift
Jamila (Jah-mee'-lah) — Beautiful
Marjani (Mahr-jah'-knee) — Coral
Ramla (Rahm'-lah) — One who predicts the future
Rashida (Rah-shee'-dah) — Righteous
Safiya (Sa-fee'-yah) — Pure
Zalika (Zah-lee'-kah) — Well born

Boy Names

Abasi (Ah-bah'-see) — Stern
Bakari (Bah-kah'-ree) — Of noble promise
Jabari (Jah-bah'-ree) — Brave
Khalfani (Khal-fah'-knee) — Destined to rule
Masud (Mah-sood') — Fortunate
Nuru (Noo'-roo) — Born during the day
Sadiki (Sah-dee'-kee) — Loyal, true
Salim (Sah-leem') — Peace
Shomari (Sho-mah'-ree) — Forceful
Sudi (Soo'-dee) — Luck

ARABIC NAMES

Girl Names

Alima (Ah'-lee-mah) — Wise
Anan (A-nahn') — Clouds
Basimah (Bah-see'-mah) — Smiling

Hayat (Ha-yaht') — Life
Lateefah (Lah-tee'-fah) — Gentle
Malak (Mah'-lak) — Angel
Nawal (Na-wahl') — Gift
Sabirah (Sah-bee'-rah) — Patient
Thana (Thah'-nah) — Gratitude
Yasmin (Yahs-meen') — Jasmine

Boy Names

Ahmad (Ah'-mahd) — Worthy
Ali (Ah-lee') — Form of Allah, the supreme being of the Mohammedan religion
Faris (Fah'-rees) — Knight
Jabir (Zhah-beer') — Comforter
Kadar (Kah'-dahr) — Powerful
Muhammad (Muh-hahm'-mud) — Praised one
Nadir (Nah-deer') — Rare
Rashid (Rah-sheed') — Divinely faithful
Tabari (Tah'-bah-ree) — Famous Muslim historian
Zaid (Zah'-eed) — To add to

ARMENIA

Girl Names

Anoush (Ah-nush') — Sweet
Astrid — Star
Elmas (El-mahss') — Diamond
Gadar (Gah-dahr') — Purity, perfection
Lucine (Loo-seen') — Moon
Ohanna (Oh-hahn'-nah) — God's gracious gift
Perouze (Pair-ooze') — Turquoise
Shoushan (Shoe-shahn') — Lily
Siran (Seer-ahn') — Alluring
Zagir (Zah-geer') — Flower

Boy Names

Ara — Heroic Armenian king
Armen — Armenian
Avedis (A-vee'-dis) — Good news
Bedros (Be-drohs') — Rock
Dareh — Rich man
Haig — Famous Armenian forefather
Nishan (Nee'-shan) — Sign
Raffi — Noted nineteenth-century writer
Yervant (Yer-vahnt') — An Armenian king
Zeroun (Zer-oon') — Elderly sage

CHINA

Girl Names

An (Ahn) — Peace
Chow — Summer
Chyou (Chee-oh) — Autumn
Eu-meh (You'-meh) — A great beauty
Guan-yin (Kwah-yin') — Goddess of mercy
Hua (Hwah) — Flower
Jun (Joon) — Truth
Lian (Lee-ahn) — Graceful willow
Lien (Lee-en) — Lotus
Tao (Tau) — Peach (symbol of long life)

Boy Names

Chen — Great, expansive
Chung — Intelligent
Gan (Gahn) — Bold, courageous
Li (Lee) — Strength
Manchu (Mahn'-choo) — Pure
Park — Cypress tree
Quon — Bright
Shen — Spiritual, deep-thinking
Wang (Wahng) — Hope
Wing — Glory

CZECHOSLOVAKIA

Girl Names

Anezka (Ah'-nez-kah) — Gentle, pure
Dana (Dah'-nah) — God is my judge
Emilie (Em-meel'-lee) — Industrious
Jana (Yah'-nah) — God's gracious gift
Katrina, Katra — Pure
Ludmila (Lood'-mill-ah) — Beloved by the people
Marjeta (Mahr'-jee-tah) — Pearl
Nadia (Nahd'-ya) — Hope
Pavla (Pavh'-lah) — Little
Velika (Vel'-lee-kah) — Great one

Boy Names

Evzen (Ev'-zen) — Of noble birth
Ivan (Ee'-vahn) — God's gracious gift
Jan (Yahn) — God's gracious gift
Jiri (Yir'-zee) — Farmer
Karel (Kahr'-el) — Strong, virile
Risa (Ree'-shah) — Strong and rich ruler
Stanislav (Stahn'-yih-slav) — Glory of the camp
Tomas (Toe'-mahs) — Twin
Vladimir (Vlad'-eh-meer) — World prince
Wenzel — To know

DENMARK

Girl Names

Agneta (Ahg-neh'-tah) — The chaste
Dagmar — Glory of the Danes
Dagny — Dane's happiness
Dania — God is my judge
Grette (Gret'-tah) — Pearl
Hanne (Hahn'-uh) — Gracious

Inger — Daughter of a hero
Kirsten (Keer′-sten) — Christian
Laila (Lah′-ee-la) — Night
Saffi — Wisdom

Boy Names

Bo — Commanding
Diederik (Dee′-dah-rick) — Ruler of the people
Henerik — Landlord
Jorgen (Your′-gehn) — Farmer
Klaus — Victory of the people
Lief (Life) — Descendant
Mikkel (Mee′-kel) — Who is like God?
Nils — Champion
Peder — Stone
Roeland — Fame of the land

FRANCE

Girl Names

Félicité (Fay-liss-i-tay′) — Fortunate
Françoise (Fran-swahs′) — Free
Ghislaine (Zhees-layn′) — Sweet pledge
Joelle — God is willing
Lisette — Consecrated to God
Mignon (Me-nyown′) — Delicate, petite
Monique — Advisor
Odile (Oh-deal′) — Rich
Solange (So-lahnje′) — Rare jewel
Sylvie — From the forest

Boy Names

Alain — Handsome
Bernard — Courage of a bear

Clément — Merciful
Donatien (Dough-nah-tyen') — Gift
Grégoire (Greh-gwah') — Vigilant
Jacques/Jaques — Supplanter
Luc (Lewk) — Light
Maxime (Max-eem') — Greatest
Philippe — Lover of horses
Yves (Eve) — Little archer

GERMANY

Girl Names

Antje (Ahnt'-yeh) — Grace
Berta — Glorious
Didrika (Did-ree'-kah) — People's rule
Franziska (Fran-sees'-kah) — Free
Heidi — Kind
Katherina — Pure
Katja (Cot'-yah) — Pure
Rebekka — Servant of God
Tamara — Palm tree
Ursula — Little bear

Boy Names

Bernhard — Courage of a bear
Christian — Christian
Gunther — War
Hagan — Strong defense
Johann (Yo'-hahn) — God's gracious gift
Konrad — Honest counselor
Lothar — Famous warrior
Matz — Gift of God
Otto — Prosperous
Tobias — God is good

GREECE

Girl Names

Aleka — Defender of humankind
Athena — Goddess of wisdom
Charis (Kahr'-iss) — Love
Euphemia (You-fem-ee'-yah) — Well known
Irene — Peace
Kalliope (Kahl-ee-oh'-pee) — Beautiful voice
Sofi — Wisdom
Stefania (Stef-an-ee'-ah) — Crown
Theodosia (Tay-oh-do-see'-ah) — Gift of God
Zoe — Life

Boy Names

Apostolos — Apostle
Christos — Christ
Cosmo — Well ordered
Demetrios — For Demeter, goddess of the harvest
Nicholas — People's victory
Soterios — Savior
Stavros — Crowned with laurels
Stefanos — Crown
Thanos (Tahn'-os) — Noble
Vasilis (Vah-see'-lees) — Kingly

HAWAII

Girl Names

Alani (Ah-lah'-knee) — Orange tree
Haunani (Ha-oo-nah'-knee) — Beautiful dew
Kalea (Kuh-lay'-uh) — Bright
Lahela (Lah-he'-lah) — Innocence of a lamb
Luana — Enjoyment

Malu (Ma'-loo) — Peace
Nani — Beautiful
Oliana (Oh-lee-ahn'-ah) — Oleander
Pualani (Poo-ah-lah'-knee) — Heavenly flower
Wanika (Wah-knee'-kah) — God's gracious gift

Boy Names

Alika (Ah-lee'-kah) — Defender of humankind
Havika (Ha-vee'-kah) — Beloved
Kalani (Kah-lah'-knee) — The heavens
Kapono (Kah-pone'-oh) — Righteous one
Keoni (Kee-own'-ee) — God's gracious gift
Lani (Lah'-knee) — Sky
Makani (Ma-kah'-knee) — The wind
Manu (Man'-oo) — Bird
Nohea (No-he'-ah) — Handsome
Palani (Pah-lah'-knee) — Free man

INDIA

Girl Names

Aruna (A-roo'-nah) — Radiance
Chandra — Moon
Guri — Goddess of abundance
Kalinda — Sun; place name — Kalinda Mountains
Lalasa (Lah-lah'-sah) — Love
Latika (Lah-tea'-kah) — Name of a god
Ramya — Beautiful, elegant
Sarisha — Charming
Tulsi — Sacred tulasi plant
Vidya (Vee'-dyah) — Knowledge and education

Boy Names

Anand — Happiness
Chander — Moon

Jafar (Jah-fahr) — Little stream
Kamal (Kah-mahl') — Name of a god
Mohan — Delightful
Ravi — Sun god
Sahir — Friend
Taj — Crown
Vadin (Vah'-dean) — Speaker
Vishnu — Protector

IRELAND

Girl Names

Briana — Strong
Caitlin (Cat'-leen) — Pure
Deirdre — Young girl; in Irish legend, she was a princess of Ulster who eloped to Scotland
Erlina — Girl from Ireland
Glynis — Valley
Keara — Name of a saint
Meara — Merry
Pegeen — Pearl
Sheena — God's gracious gift
Treasa — Strong

Boy Names

Aidan — Fiery
Bevan — Youthful warrior
Cullan — Handsome
Darby — Free man
Éamon (Eh'-mon) — Happy warrior
Ferris — Rock
Keefe — Well-being
Nolan — Noble, famous
Shane — Gracious gift of God
Torin — Chief

ISRAEL

Girl Names

Aleeza — Joy
Davida (Dah-vee′-dah) — Beloved
Edrea (Ed′-ree-uh) — Mighty
Jaffa or Yaffa (Yah′-fah) — Beautiful
Malka (Mahl′-kah) — Queen
Nira — Of the loom
Ora, Orah — Light
Rena (Ree′-nah) — Joyous song
Shoshana — Rose
Ziva (Zee′-vah) — Aglow, splendor

Boy Names

Akiva (Ah-kee′-vah) — Supplanter
Dov (Dove) — Bear
Elan (E-lahn′) — Tree
Gedalya (Geh-dahl′-yah) — God is great
Namir (Nah-meer′) — Leopard
Ravid (Rah-veed′) — Wander
Sasson (Sahs′-son) — Joy
Tovi (Toe-vee′) — Good
Uri (Oo′-ree) — My light
Zelig (Seh′-leeg) — Blessed

ITALY

Girl Names

Benedetta — Blesses
Carmelina — Vineyard
Fiorenza — Flower
Giovanna — God's gracious gift

Grazia (Grah'-tsee-ah) — Grace
Lucia (Loo-chee'-ah) — Light
Oriana — Golden
Pia — Pious
Renata — Reborn
Serafina — Seraph (angel)

Boy Names

Angelo — Messenger
Carmine — Vineyard
Donato (Dough-not'-oh) — Gift
Fabiano (Fah-bee-ah'-no) — Bean farmer
Georgio — Farmer
Guiseppe (Joe-sehp'-ah) — God will add
Guido (Gwee'-dough) — Life
Luciano (Loo-chee-ah'-no) — Light
Sergio (Sehr'-gee-oh) — Attendant
Vincenzo (Veen-chenz'-oh) — Conqueror

JAPAN

Girl Names

Akina — Spring flower
Cho — Butterfly
Etsu (Et'-sue) — Delight
Hoshi (Ho'-she) — Star
Kohana — Little flower
Mika — New moon
Nami — Wave
Sachi — Bliss
Takara — Treasure
Yori — Trustworthy

Boy Names

Akira — Intelligent
Hiroshi (Here-oh'-she) — Generous

Joji (Joe'-gee) — Farmer
Kiyoshi (Kee-oh'-she) — Quiet
Masao — Righteous
Naoko (Nay-oh'-ko) — Honest
Ringo — Peace be with you
Taro — First son
Tomi — Rich
Yukio (You-kee'-oh) — Gets his heart's desire

KOREA

Girl Names

Cho — Beautiful
Dae — Greatness
Hea (Hay'-ah) — Grace
Jin — Jewel
Kyon — Brightness
Min — Cleverness
Soo — Long life
Sun — Goodness
Yon — Lotus blossom
Young — Flower

Boy Names

Bae — Inspiration
Chin — Precious
Doh — Accomplishment
Gi (Gee) — Brave
Ho — Goodness
Ki (Key) — Vigor
Kwan — Strong
Sam — Achievement
Sook — Light
Yong — Bravery

NIGERIA

Girl Names

Abeo (Ah-beh-o') — Happy she was born
Akanke (Ah-kahn-keh') — To know her is to love her
Ayo (Ah'-yo) — Joy
Bayo (Bah'-yo) — To find joy
Fayola (Fah-yo'-lah) — A healthy baby is joyous
Ifama (Ee-fah'-mah) — Everything is fine
Jumoke (Jew-mo'-keh) — Everyone loves the baby
Nayo (Nah'-yoh) — We are elated
Omolara (O-mo'-lah-rah) — Born at the right time
Urbi (Oor'-bee) — Princess

Boy Names

Ajani (Ah-jah'-nee) — Winner
Akin (Ah-keen') — Hero
Banjoko (Ban'-jo-ko) — Stay with me forever
Chi (Chee) — Personal guardian angel
Jaja (Jah'-jah) — Honored
Kayin (Kah-yeen') — Celebration of long-awaited baby
Mongo (Mon'-go) — Famous
Ola (Aw'-lah) — Great wealth
Osaze (Oh-sah'-zeh) — Loved by God
Tor — King

NORTH AMERICAN INDIAN

Girl Names

Alaqua (Ah-lah'-qwah) — Sweet-gum tree
Chumani (Chew-mahn'-ee) — Dewdrops
Eyota (Ee-yoh'-ta) — Greatest one
Halona (Ha-loan'-ah) — Fortunate
Koko — Night

Kwanita — God is gracious
Nita — Bear
Satinka — Magic dancer
Tehya (Tay'-yah) — Precious
Winona — Generous

Boy Names

Anoke (Ah-no'-kee) — Actor
Delsin — Truthful one
Dyami (Die-ahm'-ee) — Eagle
Halian (Hah-lee-ahn') — Youthful
Kuruk (Koo'-rook) — Bear
Kwam — God's gracious love
Makya (Mahk'-yah) — Eagle hunter
Motega (Mo-teh'-gah) — New arrow
Quanah (Kwan'-ah) — Fragrant
Takoda (Ta-kode'-ah) — Friend to all

NORWAY

Girl Names

Andras (Ahn'-drahs) — Breath
Erika — Ever powerful
Kelsey — From the ship's island
Liv (Leev) — Life
Magna (Mahg'-nah) — Strength
Mathea (Mah-teh'-ay) — Gift of God
Nora — Light
Siv (Seev) — Kinship; wife of the Norse god Thor
Sonja (Son'-yah) — Wisdom
Trine (Tree'-neh) — Pure one

Boy Names

Aksel (Ahk'-sel) — Father of peace
Anders — Masculine, virile

Bjarne or Bjorn (Byarn or Byuhrn) — Bear
Borg — From the castle
Canute — Knot
Dag (Dahg) — Day
Erik — Ever powerful
Ivar (Ee'-vahr) — A Norse god; archer
Lars (Larss) — Laurel
Vidar (Vee'-dahr) — Tree-warrior

PHILIPPINES

Girl Names

Amalia — Industrious
Corazon — Heart
Imelda — Industrious
Julita — Youth
Malaya (Mah-lay'-ah) — Free
Milagros (Me-lah'-gross) — Miracles
Paz (Pahz) — Peace
Rosario — Rosary
Soledad (So-lee-dahd') — Health
Victoria — Victory

Boy Names

Arturo — Noble
Bayani (Bay-ahn'-ee) — Hero
Ferdinand — Courageous
Gregorio — Vigilant
Juan — God's gracious gift
Manuel — God is with us
Matalino — Bright
Pacifico — Peaceful
Renato — King
Salvador — Savior

POLAND

Girl Names

Basha (Bosh'-ah) — Stranger
Felcia (Fehl'-shah) — Lucky
Gita (Gee'-tah) — Pearl
Helenka (Hel-ehnk'-ah) — Little Helen, light
Jolanta (Yo-lahn'-tah) — Violet blossoms
Lilka — Famous warrior-maiden
Lucyna (Loot'-sih-nah) — Bringer of light
Marya (Mar'-yah) — Bitter
Tola — Priceless
Zosia (Zo'-shah) — Wise

Boy Names

Bazyli (Bah-zih'-lee) — Of royalty
Dobry (Do'-bree) — Good
Gerik (Gehr'-ik) — Prosperous spearman
Hilary — Cheerful
Karol — Strong, virile
Ludwik (Lood'-vik) — Famed warrior
Marek (Mah'-rek) — Warlike
Stasio (Stah'-shyo) — Stand of glory
Tymon (Tee'-mon) — Honoring God
Ziven (Zie'-ven) — Alive, energetic

PORTUGAL AND BRAZIL

Girl Names

Antonia — Priceless
Bibiana — Lively
Carlota — Womanly
Elzira (Ehl-see'-rah) — Consecrated to God

Laurinda — Praise
Palmeira — Palm tree
Paula — Little
Rosa — Rose
Susana — Lily
Vidonia — Vine branch

Boy Names

Alexio — Defender of humankind
Antonio — Priceless
Carlos — Strong, virile
Enrique (Ehn-ree'-keh) — Ruler of an estate
Fernando — Courageous, adventurous
Francisco — Free
Gilberto — The will to be bright
Julio (Zhool'-yo) — Youthful
Ramiro — Great judge
Silvino — Forest

RUSSIA

Girl Names

Dasha (Dahsh'-ah) — Gift of God
Galina — God has redeemed
Kira — Light
Larisa — Cheerful
Marina (Mah-ree'-nah) — Sea maiden
Natasha — Born on Christmas
Olga — Holy
Sonya — Wisdom
Svetlana (Svet-lah'-nah) — Star
Tatyana (Taht-yah'-nah) — Fairy queen

Boy Names

Alexei — Defender of humankind
Anatolii/Anatoly — From the East

Boris — Warrior
Fyodor — Divine gift
Gavril (Gav-reel') — Man of God
Igor — Farmer
Nicolai — Victory of the people
Vanya — God's gracious gift
Vladimir — World prince
Youri/Yuri/Yurii/Yury — Farmer

SCOTLAND

Girl Names

Coleen — Girl
Elspeth — Consecrated to God
Fiona — White, fair
Gillian (Jill'-ee-an) — Youth
Glynis — Valley
Lorna — Crowned with laurel
Moira — Great
Robina — Robin
Sibyl — Wise woman
Vanora — White wave

Boy Names

Alister, Alaster — Defender of humankind
Blair — Child of the fields
Colin — Child
Fergus — Strong man
Gawain — Hawk of battle
Grant — Great
Lawren — Laurel
Murdoch — Sea protector
Nairn — Place name in Scotland; from the river narrows
Payton — Pastor or guardian

SPAIN

Girl Names

Aldonza — Sweet
Carmen — Song
Esperanza (Ess-pier-ahn'-zah) — Hope
Guadalupe (Gwah-dah-loo'-pay) — Virgin Mary
Ines (Ee-nehss') — Gentle
Jacinta (Jah-seen'-tah) — Hyacinth
Monica — Advisor
Paloma — Dove
Rocío (Ro-see'-oh) — Dewdrops
Solana — Sunshine

Boy Names

Alfredo — Wise counselor
Carlos — Manly
Emilio — Winning one
Esteban (Ehs-tay'-vahn) — Crown
Fernando — Brave
Gilberto — Noteworthy pledge
José — God will increase
Luis — Renowned warrior
Placido — Serene
Tajo (Tah'-ho) — Day

SWEDEN

Girl Names

Annika (Ah-knee'-kah) — Grace
Brigitta — Strength
Erika — Powerful
Gala — Singer
Inga — Hero's daughter

Kerstin (Care′-sten) — Christian
Lena — Light
Maj (My) — Pearl
Sigrid — Victorious counselor
Ulla (Oo′-lah) — Will

Boy Names

Anders (Ahn′-dersh) — Strong, macho
Bjorn (Bee-orn′) — Bear
Gunnar — War
Hans — God's gracious gift
Ingmar — Famous son
Kalle (Kahl′-uh) — Powerful, manly
Lars — Laurel
Magnus — Strength
Nils — Champion
Ulf — Wolf

VIETNAM

Girl Names

Am — Of the moon
Be (Bay) — Doll
Cam — Sweet
Cara — Precious gem
Hanh (Han) — Faithful, moral
Hoa (Hwah) — Peace
Kim — Needle, gold
Le (Le′-ah) — Pearl
Thanh (Tan) — Brilliant
Thuy (Two′-ee) — Gentle

Boy Names

Antoan (An′-twan) — Safe, protected
Cadao (Ka-dah′-oh) — Folk song

Chim (Kim) — Bird
Gan — Close to
Hy (Hee) — Hope
Lap — Independent
Son — Mountain
Tai (Tah-ee) — Talent
Thang (Tahng) — Victory
Tuyen (Tuing) — Angel

ZIMBABWE

Girl Names

Chipo (Chee'-poh) — Gift
Dorleta (Door-lay'-tah) — A name honoring the Virgin Mary
Jendayi (Jen-dah'-yee) — Show gratitude
Kambo (Kam'-boh) — Must work for everything
Maiba (Mah'-ee-bah) — Serious
Mudiwa (Moo-day'-wah) — Beloved
Rufaro (Roo-fah'-roh) — Happiness
Sibongile (See-bon-gee-leh') — Thanks
Sitembile (See-tem-bee-leh') — Trust
Sukutai (Soo-koo-tay'-ee) — Hug

Boy Names

Banga (Bang'-gah) — Knife
Dakarai (Dah-kah'-rah-ee) — Happiness
Gamba (Gam'-bah) — Warrior
Hondo (Hoan'-doh) — War
Jabulani (Jah-boo-lah'-knee) — Be jubilant
Kokayi (Koh-kah'-yee) — Summon the people
Mashama (Mah-shah'-mah) — Surprised
Petiri (Peh'-tee-ree) — Where we are
Runako (Roo-nah'-koh) — Handsome
Zuka (Zoo-kah') — Sixpence

A Bouquet of Names:
Flowers and More

Dorothy Parker described flowers as "Heaven's masterpiece."
How appropriate, then, to give your little masterpiece a floral
name! We bet you'll be surprised to see how many lovely and
usable floral names there are. We certainly were.

However, since most of the blooming names are feminine,
we decided to include the names of herbs to make this a more
"equal opportunity" list. We broke with style here and did not
separate male and female names. We'll leave that up to you and
your good judgment.

FLOWERS AND HERBS

Amaryllis
Angelica
Aster
Azalea
Basil
Bay

Begonia
Berony
Blossom
Bryony
Burnet
Camellia

Cassia
Cicely
Cinnamon
Clove
Clover
Daffodil

Dahlia
Daisy
Fern
Geranium
Ginger
Hazel
Heather
Holly
Hyacinth
Iris
Ivy
Jasmine
Lark
Laurel

Lavender
Lilac
Lily
Linden
Lotus
Mace
Magnolia
Marguerite
Marigold
Myrtle
Olivia, Olive
Orchid
Pansy
Petunia

Poppy
Rose
Rosemary
Rue
Saffron
Sage
Tansy
Tulip
Valerian
Violet
Willow
Zinnia

The Family Jewel:
A Gem of a Name

Good name in man and woman, dear my lord,
Is the immediate jewel of their souls.
                                    WILLIAM SHAKESPEARE
                                    Othello, Act 3, Scene 3

Just as with babies, when we think of gems, the word "precious" comes to mind. Precious and semiprecious gemstones are more popular than ever, not only because of their great beauty but because these natural wonders of our earth are thought to have mystical powers. Today New Agers are practicing age-old methods of harnessing the stones' powers to supposedly attract, protect, and/or heal.

While you may not want to name your child Aquamarine, we do have a list of names from the mineral kingdom well worth considering. As in the chapter of flower and herb names, we are not dividing the list into male and female names. We're leaving gem-name-gender to your good judgment, so keep that in mind as you're mining for a name.

Also, keep in mind that when a child has a *gem* of a name, it's easy to buy him or her a gift — a piece of gemstone jewelry or, as they say in the insurance-company commercial, "a piece of the rock."

Gem	Family and/or Origin	Colors
Amber	Fossilized resin of the extinct conifer trees	Light yellow and gold to brown and red

When you rub amber against silk or wool, it becomes electrically charged. So appropriately enough, its old Greek name was *elektron,* from which the modern word *electricity* is derived. Amber's energy is believed to lift one's spirits, replacing depression with joy. In other words, it's a real upper.

Amethyst	Quartz	Pale purple to deep violet

The Greek word *amethustos* means "without drunkenness," and the stone was used, in Greco-Roman times, to prevent intoxication and protect against the discomfort caused by overeating. Now known as the tranquilizer of the mineral kingdom, the amethyst's energy supposedly restores calm and brings peace to those who are stressed out. It's also thought to bring out one's psychic ability.

Anatase	Ore of titanium	Ranges from blue to blue-black to lavender, and from yellow to brown

Because of its eight-sided crystal structure, this rare mineral is also known as octahedrite . . . a great name for an octopus, but stick with Anatase for a child. The word *anatase* is derived from the Greek *anateinein,* meaning "stretch up," as is characteristic of the gem's long crystals.

Beryl	Beryllium aluminum silicate	Usually bluish green or light yellow, some of these stones are green, gold, pink, white, or colorless. Deep green beryls are called emeralds; pale, greenish blue and transparent beryls are aquamarine.

Gem	Family and/or Origin	Colors

The beryl's energy is said to give a lazy person some needed get-up-and-go. Plus, it is believed that if you visualize a lost object while holding a beryl in your hand, you will suddenly see its whereabouts in your mind's eye.

Gem	Family and/or Origin	Colors
Carnelian	Quartz	Orange-red to orange-brown, salmon, sienna, rust, and various shades of gold

Carnelian comes from the Latin word for "flesh," probably because the stones are often salmon or flesh colored. It is thought that the Carnelian's energy helps one look at the bright side of life, clears up problems with the reproductive organs, and stimulates one's appetite.

Gem	Family and/or Origin	Colors
Cinnabar	Mercuric sulfide	Chinese red, red, reddish brown, gray, black

This abundant ore is said to protect objects (rather than living creatures).

Gem	Family and/or Origin	Colors
Coral	Calcified skeletons of marine animals	Pale to deep red, white, black, all shades of pink and orange

White coral's energy is said to strengthen self-esteem and help with the handling of family frustrations, while reddish coral's energy is said to relieve the fear of decision making. Coral is thought to be a good gemstone for small children, because of its powers to encourage growth.

Gem	Family and/or Origin	Colors
Crystal	Quartz	Clear; able to reflect every color of the rainbow

The word *crystal* comes from *krystallos,* a Greek word meaning "ice." The Greeks thought that crystal was water frozen forever by the gods. Supposedly the energy of the crystal puts one's body in harmony.

Gem	Family and/or Origin	Colors
Diamond	Carbon	Clear and colorless; blue-white; shades of blue, yellow, pink, green, red, gray, and black

The diamond's energy is thought to encourage one to follow the golden rule. It also promotes honesty with oneself, as well as with others. The diamond is supposedly of the greatest benefit when used in conjunction with other gems, as it enhances their properties.

Gem	Family and/or Origin	Colors
Emerald	Beryl	Deep green

Emerald is derived from the Persian word for "green." The emerald's energy is believed to open one's heart to wisdom and love.

Gem	Family and/or Origin	Colors
Flint	Quartz	Gray, brown, black

Prehistoric men used flint for making tools. Later on it was used to strike sparks from a piece of steel and start a fire. Those same sparks were used in early rifles to set off the powder charge. Today flint is used in Brazil for divining gold, water, gemstones, and other underground treasures.

Gem	Family and/or Origin	Colors
Galena	Lead sulphide	Gray

The most common of all lead minerals, Galena is said to bring a sense of calm to one's system.

Gem	Family and/or Origin	Colors
Garnet	Silicate minerals	Red, brown, black, green, yellow, white

The name comes from the Latin word *granatus,* meaning "seed," because of this stone's tiny, seedlike crystals. The garnet's energy is thought to help develop the patience and perseverance necessary to achieve one's goals.

Gem	Family and/or Origin	Colors
Ivory	Dentine of elephants' tusks	Off-white

Gem	Family and/or Origin	Colors

It is believed ivory provides both spiritual and physical protection.

| **Jacinth** | Zirconium silicate Zircon | Red, orange, and brown |

In ancient times, jacinth (or hyacinth) was known as "the protector stone from Heaven," and travelers wore it to assure safe passage and warm welcomes. The energy of the jacinth is believed to heal the spirit and bring inner peace.

| **Jade** | Two different opaque minerals: jadeite and nephrite | Many shades of green; black, red, pink, brown, white, cream |

Legend has it that the most powerful symbol for attracting true love is a jade butterfly. Jade's energy supposedly prevents illness, prolongs life, nurtures healthy plants, and attracts money to its wearer.

| **Jasper** | Form of quartz/opaque variety of chalcedony | Red, green, brown, mottled |

When held in the hand of a woman during childbirth, jasper is thought to relieve pain as well as protect both the mother and the child. Jasper is also thought to attract rain, which is why Native Americans call it "rainbringer."

| **Jet** | Fossilized wood millions of years old | Black (*jet* black) |

Jet's energy is absorbent and is said to rid one of negativity. It is said that when a small piece of jet is placed momentarily on a newborn baby's stomach, the stone safeguards the infant from the wickedness of the world.

Gem	Family and/or Origin	Colors
Mica	Complex aluminum silicates	Muscovite mica is light yellow, red, green, brown, or white. Phlogopite mica is yellowish brown, green, or white. Lepidolite mica is light lavender or pink. Biotite mica is dark green, brown, or black.

The energy of mica is said to expand intuitive awareness, thus giving one insight into what the future holds.

Onyx	Chalcedony-type quartz	Black and white, gray and white, black and red, white and red

The onyx's energy supposedly helps one end—and/or recover from—a negative relationship. It is also thought to improve concentration and devotion—perhaps the reason why so many rosaries are made out of onyx.

Opal	Silica or quartz	White, milky, black; shades of blue or gray. There's a great variety in the play of colors and/or iridescence of opals.

In Greco-Roman times, the opal was used to treat eye problems, and in fact, its name is derived from the Greek word *opthalmos,* meaning "eye." These days, it is believed that the opal's energy enhances inner beauty and one's psychic powers.

Pearl	Aragonite/crystallized calcium carbonate	White, cream, pink, rose, yellow, gray, blue, black

Pearls come from sea creatures and are traditionally worn by deep-sea divers as protection against the dangers of the sea. The energy of the pearl supposedly stimulates one's sense of femininity.

Gem	Family and/or Origin	Colors
Ruby	Corundum	Many shades of red, from rose to deep red to deep purplish red

From the Latin *rubeus,* meaning "red," the ruby was thought of as the king and queen of gems and was used by the ancients in wedding rings. Today it is still thought of as an expression of everlasting love. It is also believed that the strong, fiery stone energizes one's spirit and self-esteem.

Gem	Family and/or Origin	Colors
Sapphire	Corundum	All shades of blue; clear, white, pink, orange, green, purple, black. (When this corundum gemstone is red, it's a ruby.)

Believing that the world rested on a colossal blue sapphire, the ancient Persians credited the gemstone for giving the sky its color. *Sapphire* is derived from a Sanskrit word meaning "beloved of Saturn." Appropriately, the stone is the symbol for the natural sciences, astronomy, and astrology. It is believed that wearing a sapphire heightens the study of the sky, sun, moon, stars, planets, and planetary influences on human events.

Gem	Family and/or Origin	Colors
Topaz	Topaz	Yellow, colorless, white, gray, blue, pink, brown

Topaz in Sanskrit means "fire," but the gem may have gotten its name from the island Topazion in the Red Sea, off the coast of Egypt, where the stone was first found thousands of years ago. It is believed that you will bring light and warmth into your life with the energy of the sun-colored topaz, knowledge and wisdom with the energy of the clear topaz, and peace and understanding with the energy of the blue topaz.

Gem	Family and/or Origin	Colors
Turquoise	Turquoise	Shades range from greenish blue to sky blue to darker sky blue; yellow-green to apple green to greenish blue

Gem	Family and/or Origin	Colors

This is one gem that all cultures—from the Far East to the Southwestern United States—have in common, and all consider it a lucky stone. Turquoise is said to emit protective energy, but (according to some beliefs) only if given by a friend.

And when it comes to names, don't forget: There's always Jewel or Gem or Gemma.

Tennis Names, Anyone?

With the growing popularity of tennis, and the international participation of both women and men, we thought a list of the world's top-ranked players would comprise an intriguing collection of names. We think you'll agree.

VIRGINIA SLIMS/WOMEN'S TENNIS ASSOCIATION'S RANKINGS OF THE TOP FIFTY WOMEN PLAYERS

Ranking as of 10/19/92	Women Players	Birthplace
1	Monica Seles	Yugoslavia
2	Steffi Graf	Germany
3	Gabriela Sabatini	Argentina
4	Martina Navratilova	Czechoslovakia
5	Arantxa Sanchez Vicario	Spain
6	Mary Joe Fernandez	Dominican Republic
7	Jennifer Capriati	USA
8	Conchita Martinez	Spain
9	Manuela Meleeva-Fragniere	Bulgaria
10	Jana Novotna	Czechoslovakia
11	Anke Huber	Germany

Ranking as of 10/19/92	Women Players	Birthplace
12	Katerina Maleeva	Bulgaria
13	Nathalie Tauziat	France
14	Mary Pierce	Canada
15	Zina Garrison	USA
16	Helena Sukova	Czechoslovakia
17	Lori McNeil	USA
18	Amanda Coetzer	South Africa
19	Amy Frazier	USA
20	Sabine Appelmans	Belgium
21	Magdalena Maleeva	Bulgaria
22	Kimiko Date	Japan
23	Leila Meskhi	USSR
24	Julie Halard	France
25	Naoko Sawmatsu	Japan
26	Judith Wiesner	Austria
27	Natalia Zvereva	USSR
28	Radka Zrubakova	Czechoslovakia
29	Brenda Schultz	Netherlands
30	Sabine Hack	Germany
31	Barbara Rittner	Germany
32	Sandra Cecchini	Italy
33	Patricia Hy	Cambodia
34	Pam Shriver	USA
35	Andrea Strnadova	Czechoslovakia
36	Ann Grossman	USA
37	Natalia Medvedeva	USSR
38	Gigi Fernandez	Puerto Rico
39	Emanuela Zardo	Switzerland
40	Rachel McQuillan	Australia
41	Laura Gildemeister	Argentina
42	Wiltrud Probst	Germany
43	Nicole Provis	Australia
44	Karina Habsudova	Czechoslovakia
45	Patty Fendick	USA
46	Manon Bollegraf	Netherlands
47	Rosalyn Fairbank-Nideffer	South Africa
48	Pascale Paradis-Mangon	France
49	Yayuk Basuki	Indonesia
50	Catarina Lindquist	Sweden

IBM/ASSOCIATION OF TENNIS PROFESSIONALS RANKINGS
OF THE TOP FIFTY MEN PLAYERS

Rankings as of 10/19/92	Men Players	Birthplace
1	Jim Courier	USA
2	Stefan Edberg	Sweden
3	Pete Sampras	USA
4	Michael Chang	USA
5	Goran Ivanisevic	Yugoslavia
6	Petr Korda	Czechoslovakia
7	Boris Becker	Germany
8	Ivan Lendl	Czechoslovakia
9	Andre Agassi	USA
10	Wayne Ferreira	South Africa
11	Guy Forget	Morocco
12	Carlos Costa	Spain
13	Richard Krajicek	Netherlands
14	MaliVai Washington	USA
15	Alexander Volkov	USSR
16	Sergi Bruguera	Spain
17	Michael Stich	Germany
18	Thomas Muster	Austria
19	Aaron Krickstein	USA
20	Francisco Clavet	Spain
21	John McEnroe	USA
22	Karel Novacek	Czechoslovakia
23	Emilio Sanchez	Spain
24	Henrik Holm	Sweden
25	Amos Mansdorf	Israel
26	Andrei Cherkasov	USSR
27	Andrei Medvedev	USSR
28	Brad Gilbert	USA
29	Jordi Arrese	Spain
30	Omar Camporese	Italy
31	Carl-Uwe Steeb	Germany
32	Fabrice Santoro	Tahiti
33	Paul Haarhuis	Netherlands
34	Javier Sanchez	Spain
35	Arnaud Boetsch	France

Rankings as of 10/19/92	Men Players	Birthplace
36	Alberto Mancini	Argentina
37	Wally Masur	England
38	Andrei Chesnokov	USSR
39	Magnus Larsson	Sweden
40	Franco Davin	Argentina
41	Guillermo Perez-Roldan	Argentina
42	Marc Rosset	Switzerland
43	Jeff Tarango	USA
44	Gabriel Markus	Argentina
45	Jakob Hlasek	Czechoslovakia
46	Cedric Pioline	France
47	Renzo Furlan	Italy
48	Jaime Yzaga	Peru
49	Magnus Gustafsson	Sweden
50	Mark Woodforde	Australia

Run with It!
Names of Marathon Runners

Marathon running has come into its own during the last decade. As with tennis, there's international participation for women as well as men. And there are some intriguing names among the participants.

Author and runner Dr. George Sheehan said of the New York Marathon, "We are here to be heroes. It shows the extraordinary powers of ordinary people."

Here are the names of the first fifty men and women heroes to cross the finish line during the 1992 New York Marathon.

Place	Female Runners	Country
1	Lisa Ondieki	Australia
2	Olga Markova	Russia
3	Yoshiko Yamamoto	Japan
4	Kamila Gradus	Poland
5	Bettina Sabatini	Italy
6	Gordon Bloch	USA (New York)
7	Suzanna Ciric	Serbia
8	Sally Eastoll	Great Britain
9	Irina Bogacheva	Kyrghizstan

Place	Female Runners	Country
10	Kerstin Pressler	Germany
11	Maria Lelut-Rebelo	France
12	Alevtina Naumova	Russia
13	Franca Fiacconi	Italy
14	Sissel Grottenberg	Norway
15	Jane Weizel	USA (Colorado)
16	Gillian Horovitz	USA (New York)
17	Jean C. Chodnicki	USA (New Jersey)
18	Odile M. Leveque	France
19	Petra Sander	Germany
20	Radka Patkovo	Czechoslovakia
21	Anita A. Anderson	Sweden
22	Maria A. Anderson	Sweden
23	Nancy S. Stanley	USA (Nebraska)
24	Judith Hine	New Zealand
25	Djamila Hellal	France
26	Corinne Gerard	France
27	Brooke Skulski	USA (New York)
28	Eliana Reinert	Brazil
29	Janet E. Jordan	USA (Oregon)
30	Ulrice Jansson	USA (New York)
31	Stephanie C. Leroy	France
32	Gabriele Schmidt	Germany
33	Stephanie W. Kessler	USA (New York)
34	Mariley A. Da Silva	Brazil
35	Scherezada Alvear	Chile
36	Truus De Maare Van Duin	Netherlands
37	Joanne L. Baxter	Canada
38	Teresa Gomez	USA (New York)
39	Mary E. Ryzner	USA (California)
40	Sylvie Langenove	France
41	Jennifer A. Reda	USA (New York)
42	Beth A. Powell	USA (New York)
43	Laurie Jones Sawyer	USA (New York)
44	Laura M. Roman	USA (Connecticut)
45	Antonia Antini	Italy
46	Anna Magrethe Trave	Norway
47	Dominique Dubart	France
48	Rosemaria S. Vuoso	USA (Florida)
49	Kathleen A. Coughlin	USA (New York)
50	Annamaria Racca	Italy

Place	Male Runners	Country
1	Willie Mtolo	South Africa
2	Andras Espinoza	Mexico
3	Wan-Ki Kim	South Korea
4	Osmiro Silva	Brazil
5	Antoni Niemczak	Poland
6	Walter Durbano	Italy
7	Luca Barzaghi	Italy
8	Driss Dacha	Morocco
9	David Lewis	Great Britain
10	Steve Brace	Great Britain
11	Ed Eyestone	USA (Utah)
12	Risto Ulmala	Finland
13	Faustina Reynoso	Mexico
14	Severino Bernardini	Italy
15	Jesus Herrera	Mexico
16	Dominique Chauvalier	France
17	Sammy Lelei	Kenya
18	Dick Tesselaar	Netherlands
19	Regis Ancel	France
20	Marcos Barreto	Mexico
21	Mohamed Idris	USA (New York)
22	Pierre Levisse	France
23	Peter K. Whitehead	England
24	Jesus De Grado	Spain
25	Lameck Aguta	Kenya
26	Daniel Mbuli	South Africa
27	Jean-Michel Charbonnel	France
28	Nivaldo Filho	Brazil
29	Miguel Rios	Spain
30	Roberto Barbi	Italy
31	Juan Samuel Lopez	Mexico
32	Luca Foglia	Switzerland
33	Nempo Luis	Chile
34	Ryszard Marczak	Poland
35	Joseph Chiaramonte	France
36	Patrick Joannes	France
37	Sam Ngatia	USA (Texas)
38	Mark D. Lindrud	USA (New York)
39	David N. Payne	England
40	Juan Antonio Garcia Tineo	Spain
41	Luis Lopez	Costa Rica
42	Thomas Greger	Germany
43	Orjan Hemstrom	Sweden

Place	Male Runners	Country
44	Christian Jocher	Italy
45	Jean-Baptiste Protais	France
46	Christopher D. Wiggs	USA (New Mexico)
47	Patrick Mercier	France
48	Robert B. Finz	USA (New York)
49	Larry C. Austin	England
50	Christian Dargnat	France

Names of Your Favorite Soap Stars

The soap opera is an American art form, bringing to the lives of its viewers romance, intrigue, fantasy, adventure, thrills, suspense, laughter, and the overall feeling of "And I thought *I* had problems!"

Since the 1970s, the soaps have come into their own in terms of popularity and sophistication. Most are on for an hour a day, five days a week. Many are very real reflections of life and deal with issues of the day. In many ways the soaps make an impact on their viewers' lives. They influence styles of dress and hair; they help with problem-solving and, yes, even with naming babies!

Imaginative and distinctive names used on soap operas show up on health departments' "most popular name" lists. Tiffany and Nicole are just two examples of those names whose origins can be traced to characters on daytime serials.

With the assistance of *Soap Opera Digest,* we've compiled a list of the most interesting soap opera characters' names from both past and present. Last names change quite often on the soaps, so please forgive us if-and-when we're not totally up-to-date.

Ready to take a look at how these names rate for your little character?

Lights! Camera! Action!

ALL MY CHILDREN

Female Characters

Brooke English
Hayley Vaughan
Ceara Connor Hunter
Claudette Montgomery
Mimi Reed
Opal Cortlandt
Angelique Marick
Erica Kane
Leora Sanders
An Li (pronounced "on lee")
   Chen
Noelle Keaton
Livia Frye
Dixie Larson
Marestella LaTour
Devon Shepherd
Margo Flax
Daisy Cortlandt
Silver Kane
Skye Patterson
Bianca Montgomery
Galen Henderson
Taylor Roxbury-Cannon

Male Characters

Trevor Dillon
Trask Bodine
Jeremy Hunter
Kent Bogard
Derek Frye
Palmer Cortlandt
Dimitri Marick
Travis Montgomery
Wade Matthews
Terrence Frye

Lars Bogard
Lucas Barnes
Thadeus (Tad) Martin
Wyatt Coles
Brandon Kingsley
Langley Wallingford
Nigel Fargate
Jackson Montgomery
Adam Chandler
Edmund Grey
Jesse Hubbard
Victor Borelli

AS THE WORLD TURNS

Female Characters

Jade Sullivan
Courtney Baxter
Dawn Stewart
Iva Snyder
Lucinda Dixon

Male Characters

Darryl Crawford
Nels Andersson
Duncan McKechnie
Kent Bradford
Holden Snyder

Female Characters	*Male Characters*
Connor Jamison	Gavin Kruger
Cricket Montgomery	Gunnar Stenbeck
Dana Lambert	Kirk Andersson
Ariel Aldrin	Linc Lafferty
Charmane McColl	Tucker Foster
Lily Walsh	Dustin Donovan
Sierra Estaben	Tad Channing
Sabrina Hughes	Earl Mitchell
Taylor Baldwin	Tonio Reyes
Olivia Wycroft	Grant Colman
Lyla Montgomery Peretti	Gar Kramer

THE BOLD AND THE BEAUTIFUL

Female Characters	*Male Characters*
Felicia Forrester	Ridge Forrester
Macy Alexander	Jake MacLaine
Darla Dinkle	Clarke Garrison
Margo Lynley Spencer	Blake Hayes
Brooke Logan	Thorne Forrester
Kristen Forrester	Storm Logan
Faith Roberts	Saul Feinstein
Julie DeLorean	Zack Hamilton
Taylor Hayes	Pierre Jourdan

DAYS OF OUR LIVES

Female Characters	*Male Characters*
Glynnis Turner	Marcus Hunter
Calliope Jones	Tanner Scofield
Carly Kiriakis	Victor Kiriakis
Savannah Wilder	Bo Brady
Marlena Evans-Brady	Roman Brady
Daphne DiMera	Stefano DiMera
Trista Evans	Speed Selejko
Jeri Clayton	Shane Donovan
Brooke Hamilton	Kellam Chandler
Delia Abernathy	Maxwell Jarvis
Kayla Brady	Woody King
Nikki Wade	Hart Bennett

Female Characters	*Male Characters*
Tess Janings	Howie Hoffstedder
Valery Grant	Shawn Brady
Desiree McCall	Brett Fredricks

GENERAL HOSPITAL

Female Characters	*Male Characters*
Kira Faulkner	Harlan Barrett
Felicia Cummings Jones	Mitch Williams
Lila Quartermaine	Noah Drake
Dominique Taub	Cesar Faison
Jade Soong	Blackie Parrish
Tiffany Hill Donely	Connor Olivera
Robin Scorpio	Duke Lavery
Ruby Anderson	Frisco Jones
Jessie Brewer	Chase Murdock
Augusta McLeod	Gordon Grey
Dorne Fleming	Finian O'Toole
Holly Sutton Scorpio	Cameron Faulkner
Tanya Roskov Jones	Derek Barrington
Lesley Webber	Lord Rama
Monica Quartermaine	Grant Putnam
Louisa (Lou) Swenson	Luke Spencer
Celia Quartermaine	Crane Tolliver

GUIDING LIGHT

Female Characters	*Male Characters*
Chelsea Reardon	Ross Marler
Nadine Cooper Lewis	Dylan Shayne Lewis
Violet Penfield	Quinton Chamberlain
Eleni Andros	Warren Andrews
Reva Shayne Lewis	Hart Jessup
Harley Cooper	Kyle Sampson
India von Halkein	Hawk Shayne
Holly Lindsey	Clay Tynan
Roxie Shayne	Fletcher Reade
Blake Thorpe	Jackson Freemont
Maeve Stoddard	Hampton Speakes
Gilly Grant	Dean Blackford

Female Characters	*Male Characters*
Kit Vested	Justin Marler
Linell Conway	Logan Stafford
Viola Stapleton	Derek Colby
Hillary Bauer	Cameron Stewart
Brandy Shelooe	Rusty Shayne
Calla Matthews	Floyd Parker

LOVING

Female Characters	*Male Characters*
Shana Vochek	Dane Hammond
Trisha Alden	Cabot Alden
Bethel Ford	Austin Cushing
Tessa Saxton	Flynn Reilley
Gwyneth Alden	Bentley Saxton
Carly Rescott	Clay Alden
Merrill Vochek	Rio Domecq
Noreen Vochek Donovan	Rhett Saxton
Lorna Forbes	Desmond Hamilton
Isabelle Alden	Curtis Alden

ONE LIFE TO LIVE

Female Characters	*Male Characters*
Cassie Callison	Brad Vernon
Meri Lynn Dennison	Troy Nichols
Rika Price	Victor Lord
Dorian Cramer Lord Callison	Cord Roberts
Clover Wilde	Talbot Huddleston
Lana McClain	Asa Buchanan
Luna Moody	Marco Dane
Didi O'Neill	Hudson King
LeAnn Demerest	Marcello Salta
Sadie Gray	Hunter Guthrie
Gwendolyn Abbott	Carlo Hesser
Edwina Lewis	Rafe Garretson
Gretel Cummings	Cain Rogan
Katrina Karr	Trent Chapin
Courtney Wright	Clint Buchanan
Jinx Rollins	Giles Morgan
Delilah Ralston Buchanan Garretson	Alec Lowndes

SANTA BARBARA

Female Characters	*Male Characters*
Santana Andrade	Dash Nichols
Halley Benson	Brick Wallace
Augusta Lockridge	Kirk Cranston
Dylan Hartley	Mason Capwell
Cassandra Benedict	Cruz Castillo
Kelly Capwell	Amado Alvarez
Minx Lockridge	Brandon Demott
Marissa Perkins	Channing Capwell, Jr.
Ginger Jones	Carmen Castillo II
Eden Capwell Castillo	Lionel Lockridge
Summer Blake	Reuben Andrade
Laken Lockridge	Cain Garver
Tori Lane	Craig Hunt

THE YOUNG AND THE RESTLESS

Female Characters	*Male Characters*
Cricket Blair Romalotti	Clint Radison
Leanna Newman	Rex Sterling
Lauralee Brooks	Jazz Jackson
Salena Wiley	Miguel Rodriguez
Dina Abbott	Jared Markson
Mamie Johnson	Nathan Hastings
Drucilla Barber	Snapper Foster
Boobsie Caldwell	Brock Reynolds
Nikki Newman	Warner Wilson
Casey Reed	Jed Andrews
April Stevens	Lance Prentiss
Faren Connor	Brent Davis

Names of Fictional Characters

While working on this chapter, we noticed that many of the classics, as well as popular literature and Broadway plays and musicals, have been made into movies. So, when there is a movie based on a book or play, we've listed the name of the fictional character, followed by the actor or actress who played the part. That way, if you're interested in a character's name for your baby, you'll know there's a film you can rent to see and hear the name in action.

Of course, in the case of the classics, you can always get a copy of the book and read it. That's what fourteen-year-old Susan Weaver was doing — reading F. Scott Fitzgerald's *Great Gatsby* for her English class — when she came across a name that she felt truly embodied her personality. So right then and there, at the Ethel Walker School, a prestigious all-girl boarding school in Simsbury, Connecticut, the young woman changed her name to Sigourney Weaver.

Demi Moore and Bruce Willis named their daughter Scout, the name of one of Atticus Finch's daughters in *To Kill a Mockingbird*. John Travolta's son is Jett, the name of the character played by James Dean in *Giant*. We're guessing that the fictional characters inspired these celebrities when they named their children. We hope they'll inspire you, too.

NOTE: There's *no way* we can include all of literature's greatest classics, or all the best movies. So we've included here our favorite names, books, plays, and movies. Hope they work for you as well!

"A" IS FOR ALIBI, by Sue Grafton
    Kinsey Millhone (female detective)

THE ACCIDENTAL TOURIST, based on the novel by Anne Tyler
    Macon Leary . . . William Hurt
    Muriel Pritchett . . . Geena Davis

THE AGE OF INNOCENCE, by Edith Wharton
    Newland Archer

ALIEN, screenplay by Dan O'Bannon
    Ripley . . . Sigourney Weaver

ALL ABOUT EVE, based on a novel by Mary Orr
    Eve Harrington . . . Anne Baxter
    Margo Channing . . . Bette Davis
    Addison De Witt . . . George Sanders

ANNIE HALL, screenplay by Woody Allen and Marshall Brickman
    Annie Hall . . . Diane Keaton
    Alvy Singer . . . Woody Allen

AROUND THE WORLD IN 80 DAYS, based on a novel by Jules Verne
    Phileas Fogg . . . David Niven
    Aouda . . . Shirley MacLaine

BACK TO THE FUTURE, screenplay by Robert Zemeckis and Bob Gale
    Marty McFly . . . Michael J. Fox

BATMAN, based on the characters created by Bob Kane
    Bruce Wayne (Batman) . . . Michael Keaton
    Jack Napier (the Joker) . . . Jack Nicholson

BEACHES, based on the novel by Iris Rainer Dart
C. C. Bloom . . . Bette Midler
Hillary Whitney . . . Barbara Hershey

BELL, BOOK AND CANDLE, based on the play by James Van Druten
Shepherd Henderson . . . James Stewart
Gilliam Holroyd . . . Kim Novak

BEVERLY HILLS COP, screenplay by Daniel Petrie
Axel Foley . . . Eddie Murphy

BIG, screenplay by Anne Spielberg and Gary Ross
Josh Baskin . . . Tom Hanks

BORN YESTERDAY, based on the play by Garson Kanin
Billie Dawn . . . Judy Holiday

BREAKFAST AT TIFFANY'S, based on the novel by Truman Capote
Holly Golightly . . . Audrey Hepburn

BRIGADOON, based on the musical by Alan Jay Lerner
Fiona Campbell . . . Cyd Charisse

THE BROTHERS KARAMAZOV, based on the novel by Fyodor Dostoyevski
Dmitri Karamazov . . . Yul Brynner
Fyodor Karamazov . . . Lee J. Cobb
Alexey Karamazov . . . William Shatner
Katya . . . Claire Bloom

BUS STOP, based on the play by William Inge
Cherie . . . Marilyn Monroe
Bo . . . Don Murray
Virgil . . . Arthur O'Connell

BUTTERFIELD 8, based on the novel by John O'Hara
Gloria Wandrous . . . Elizabeth Taylor
Weston Liggett . . . Laurence Harvey
Bingham Smith . . . Jeffrey Lynn

THE CARPETBAGGERS, based on the novel by Harold Robbins
Jonas Cord . . . George Peppard
Nevada Smith . . . Alan Ladd

CASABLANCA, based on an unproduced play by Murray Burnett
and Joan Allison
    Rick Blaine . . . Humphrey Bogart
    Ilsa Lund Laszlo . . . Ingrid Bergman

CAT BALLOU, based on the novel by Roy Chanslor
    Cat Ballou . . . Jane Fonda
    Kid Shelleen/Strawn . . . Lee Marvin
    Clay Boone . . . Michael Callan

CAT ON A HOT TIN ROOF, based on the play by Tennessee
Williams
    Maggie . . . Elizabeth Taylor
    Brick . . . Paul Newman

CATCHER IN THE RYE, by J. D. Salinger
    Holden Caulfield
    Phoebe Caulfield

CHARADE, based on a story by Peter Stone and Marc Behm
    Alexander Dyle, Adam Canfield, Peter Joshua, and Bryan Cruik-
        shank . . . Cary Grant
    Reggie Lampert . . . Audrey Hepburn
    Hamilton Bartholomew . . . Walter Matthau

CIMARRON, based on the novel by Edna Ferber
    Yancey Cravat . . . Richard Dix
    Sabra Cravat . . . Irene Dunne

THE COLOR PURPLE, based on the novel by Alice Walker
    Celie . . . Whoopi Goldberg
    Sofia . . . Oprah Winfrey
    Shug Avery . . . Margaret Avery

CONAN THE BARBARIAN, screenplay by John Milius and Oliver
Stone
    Conan . . . Arnold Schwarzenegger
    Thulsa Doom . . . James Earl Jones
    Valeria . . . Sandahl Bergman
    Rexor . . . Ben Davidson

CYRANO DE BERGERAC, based on Brian Hooker's translation of
the play by Edmond Rostand
    Cyrano de Bergerac . . . Gerard Depardieu
    Roxanne Robin . . . Anne Brochet

DADDY LONG LEGS, based on the play and novel by Jean Webster
  Jervis Pendleton . . . Fred Astaire
  Julie . . . Leslie Caron

DIAMONDS ARE FOREVER, based on the novel by Ian Fleming
  James Bond . . . Sean Connery
  Tiffany Case . . . Jill St. John
  Plenty O'Toole . . . Lana Wood

THE DIRTY DOZEN, based on the novel by E. M. Nathanson
  Tassos Bravos . . . Al Mancini
  Victor Franko . . . John Cassavetes
  Glenn Gilpin . . . Ben Carruthers
  Robert Jefferson . . . Jim Brown
  Pedro Jiminez . . . Trini Lopez
  Roscoe Lever . . . Stuart Cooper
  Archer Maggott . . . Telly Savalas
  Vernon Pinkley . . . Donald Sutherland
  Samson Posey . . . Clint Walker
  Seth Sawyer . . . Colin Maitland
  Joseph Wladislaw . . . Charles Bronson

DOCTOR ZHIVAGO, based on the novel by Boris Pasternak
  Lara . . . Julie Christie
  Yuri . . . Omar Sharif
  Tonya . . . Geraldine Chaplin

DRIVING MISS DAISY, based on the play by Alfred Uhry
  Daisy Werthan . . . Jessica Tandy
  Hoke Colburn . . . Morgan Freeman

EAST OF EDEN, based on the novel by John Steinbeck
  Cal . . . James Dean
  Abra . . . Julie Harris

E.T. — THE EXTRA-TERRESTRIAL, screenplay by Melissa Mathison
  Elliott . . . Henry Thomas
  Gertie . . . Drew Barrymore

ETHAN FROME, by Edith Wharton
  Ethan Frome
  Zenobia (Zeena) Frome

THE EXORCIST, based on the novel by William Peter Blatty
   Regan MacNeil . . . Linda Blair

THE FALCON AND THE SNOWMAN, based on the novel by Robert Lindsey
   Daulton Lee . . . Sean Penn
   Christopher Boyce . . . Timothy Hutton

FEAR OF FLYING, by Erica Jong
   Isadora Wing

FLAMINGO ROAD, based on the play by Robert Wilder and Sally Wilder
   Lane Bellamy . . . Joan Crawford
   Fielding Carlisle . . . Zachary Scott
   Titus Semple . . . Sydney Greenstreet

FATAL ATTRACTION, screenplay by James Dearden
   Alex Forrest . . . Glenn Close
   Dan Gallagher . . . Michael Douglas

FORT APACHE, suggested by the story "Massacre" by James Warner Bellah
   Kirby York . . . John Wayne
   Owen Thursday . . . Henry Fonda
   Philadelphia Thursday . . . Shirley Temple

FOR WHOM THE BELL TOLLS, based on the novel by Ernest Hemingway
   Robert Jordan . . . Gary Cooper
   Maria . . . Ingrid Bergman
   Pilar . . . Katrina Paxinon
   Pablo . . . Akim Tamiroff

GHOST, screenplay by Bruce Joel Rubin
   Molly Jensen . . . Demi Moore
   Sam Wheat . . . Patrick Swayze
   Oda Mae Brown . . . Whoopi Goldberg

GHOSTBUSTERS, screenplay by Dan Akroyd and Harold Ramis
   Peter Venkman . . . Bill Murray
   Raymond Stantz . . . Dan Ackroyd
   Egon Spangler . . . Harold Ramis
   Dana Barrett . . . Sigourney Weaver

GIANT, based on the novel by Edna Ferber
  Leslie Lynnton Benedict . . . Elizabeth Taylor
  Bick Benedict . . . Rock Hudson
  Jett Rink . . . James Dean
  Luz Benedict . . . Mercedes McCambridge

GONE WITH THE WIND, based on the novel by Margaret Mitchell
  Rhett Butler . . . Clark Gable
  Scarlett O'Hara . . . Vivien Leigh
  Ashley Wilkes . . . Leslie Howard
  Melanie Hamilton . . . Olivia De Havilland
  India Wilkes . . . Alicia Rhett

THE GREAT GATSBY, based on the novel by F. Scott Fitzgerald
  Nick Carraway . . . Sam Waterston
  Daisy Buchanan . . . Mia Farrow
  Tom Buchanan . . . Bruce Dern
  Jay Gatsby . . . Robert Redford
  Jordan Baker . . . Lois Chiles
  Myrtle Wilson . . . Karen Black

GREEN CARD, screenplay by Peter Weir
  Bronte Mitchell . . . Andie MacDowell

GREEN MANSIONS by W. H. Hudson
  Rima

GUYS AND DOLLS, based on the musical by Jo Swerling and Abe Burrows, from a story by Damon Runyon
  Sky Masterson . . . Marlon Brando
  Sarah Brown . . . Jean Simmons

HARVEY, based on the play by Mary C. Chase
  Elwood P. Dowd . . . James Stewart
  Veta Louise Simmons . . . Josephine Hull

HAWAII, based on the novel by James A. Michener
  Jerusha Bromley . . . Julie Andrews
  Rafer Hoxworth . . . Richard Harris

HOME ALONE, screenplay by John Hughes
  Kevin McCallister . . . Macauley Culkin

THE HOUSE OF SEVEN GABLES, by Nathaniel Hawthorne
  Hepzibah Pyncheon
  Clifford Pyncheon
  Jaffrey Pyncheon
  Phoebe Pyncheon

INDIANA JONES AND THE TEMPLE OF DOOM, screenplay by
Willard Huyck and Gloria Katz
  Indiana Jones . . . Harrison Ford
  Willie Scott . . . Kate Capshaw

IN HARM'S WAY, based on the novel by James Bassett
  Rockwell Torrey . . . John Wayne

KINGS ROW, based on the novel by Henry Bellamann
  Randy Monoghan . . . Ann Sheridan
  Parris Mitchell . . . Robert Cummings
  Drake McHugh . . . Ronald Reagan
  Cassandra Tower . . . Betty Field

KLUTE, screenplay by Andy K. Lewis and Dave Lewis
  Bree Daniel . . . Jane Fonda

THE LAST PICTURE SHOW, based on the novel by Larry McMurtry
  Sonny Crawford . . . Timothy Bottoms
  Duane Jackson . . . Jeff Bridges
  Jacy Farrow . . . Cybill Shepherd

THE LITTLE FOXES, by Lillian Hellman
  Regina Giddens

THE LITTLE MERMAID, screenplay by John Musker and Ron Clements
  Ariel . . . animated mermaid

LITTLE WOMEN, by Louisa May Alcott
  Meg March . . . Frances Dee
  Jo March . . . Katharine Hepburn
  Beth March . . . Jean Parker
  Amy March . . . Joan Bennett

THE LITTLEST REBEL, based on the play by Edwin Burke
  Virgie Cary . . . Shirley Temple

LONESOME DOVE, by Larry McMurtry
Augustus McCrae
Woodrow Call
Jake Spoon
Lorena Wood
Clara Allen

LOVE STORY, based on the novel by Erich Segal
Jenny Cavilleri . . . Ali MacGraw
Oliver Barrett IV . . . Ryan O'Neal

LOVING, by Danielle Steele
Bettina Daniels
Ivo Stewart

THE MAN WHO CAME TO DINNER, based on the play by George
S. Kaufman and Moss Hart
Sheridan Whiteside . . . Monty Woolley

THE MARK OF ZORRO, based on the story "The Curse of Capis-
trano" by Johnston McCulley
Diego Vega . . . Tyrone Power
Lolita Quintero . . . Linda Darnell
Esteban Pasquale . . . Basil Rathbone
Inez Quintero . . . Gale Sondergaard
Fray Felipe . . . Eugene Pallette

THE MISFITS, screenplay by Arthur Miller
Gay Langland . . . Clark Gable
Roslyn Taber . . . Marilyn Monroe
Perce Howland . . . Montgomery Clift

MOONSTRUCK, screenplay by John Patrick Shanley
Loretta Castorini . . . Cher

THE MUSIC MAN, based on the musical by Meredith Willson
Harold Hill . . . Robert Preston
Marian Paroo . . . Shirley Jones
Marcellus Washburn . . . Buddy Hackett
Eulalie Mackechnie Shinn . . . Hermione Gingold
Amaryllis . . . Monique Vermont
Winthrop Paroo . . . Ronny Howard

NATIONAL VELVET, based on the novel by Enid Bagnold
Velvet Brown . . . Elizabeth Taylor
Mi Taylor . . . Mickey Rooney

NINE TO FIVE, screenplay by Colin Higgins and Patricia Resnick
  Judy Bernley . . . Jane Fonda
  Violet Newstead . . . Lily Tomlin
  Doralee Rhodes . . . Dolly Parton

ON THE BEACH, based on the novel by Nevil Shute
  Dwight Towers . . . Gregory Peck
  Moira Davidson . . . Ava Gardner

PAPER MOON, based on the novel *Addie Pray* by Joe David Brown
  Moses Pray . . . Ryan O'Neal
  Addie Loggins Pray . . . Tatum O'Neal
  Trixie Delight . . . Madeline Kahn

THE PHILADELPHIA STORY, based on the play by Philip Barry
  Dexter Haven . . . Cary Grant
  Tracy Lord . . . Katharine Hepburn

PRETTY WOMAN, screenplay by J. F. Lawton
  Vivian Ward . . . Julia Roberts
  Edward Lewis . . . Richard Gere

THE PRINCE OF TIDES, based on the novel by Pat Conroy
  Savannah Wingo . . . Melinda Dillon
  Sallie Wingo . . . Blythe Danner
  Lila Wingo . . . Kate Nelligan
  Chandler Wingo . . . Brandlyn Whitaker

REQUIEM FOR A HEAVYWEIGHT, screenplay by Rod Serling
  Mountain Rivera . . . Anthony Quinn
  Maish Rennick . . . Jackie Gleason

THE RETURN OF THE NATIVE, by Thomas Hardy
  Diggory Venn
  Damon Wildeve
  Thomasin Yeobright
  Clement (Clym) Yeobright
  Eustacia Vye

ROCKY, screenplay by Sylvester Stallone
  Rocky Balboa . . . Sylvester Stallone
  Adrian . . . Talia Shire
  Apollo Creed . . . Carl Weathers

SABRINA, based on the play *Sabrina Fair* by Samuel Taylor
  Sabrina Fairchild . . . Audrey Hepburn
  Linus Larrabee . . . Humphrey Bogart

THE SANDS OF TIME, by Sidney Sheldon
  Lucia
  Graciella
  Megan
  Teresa

THE SCARLET LETTER, by Nathaniel Hawthorne
  Hester Prynne

SCRUPLES, by Judith Krantz
  Billy Winthrop Orsini, born Wilhelmina Hunnenwell Winthrop
  Spider Elliot, born Peter Elliot
  Valentine O'Neill
  Maggie MacGregor, born Shirley Silverstein

SEASON OF PASSION, by Danielle Steele
  Kaitlin (Kate) Harper
  Felicia (Licia) Norman
  Tygue Harper (male)

SEVEN BRIDES FOR SEVEN BROTHERS, based on the story "The
Sobbin' Women" by Stephen Vincent Bent
  Alice . . . Nancy Kilgas
  Dorcas . . . Julie Newmeyer
  Liza . . . Virginia Gibson
  Milly . . . Jane Powell
  Ruth . . . Ruta Kilmonis
  Martha . . . Norma Doggett
  Sarah . . . Betty Carr
  Adam . . . Howard Keel
  Benjamin . . . Jeff Richards
  Caleb . . . Matt Mattox
  Daniel . . . Marc Platt
  Ephraim . . . Jacques d'Amboise
  Frank . . . Tommy Rall
  Gideon . . . Russ Tamblyn

SHOW BOAT, based on the novel by Edna Ferber and the musical
by Oscar Hammerstein II and Jerome Kern
  Magnolia Hawks . . . Kathryn Grayson
  Gaylord Ravenal . . . Howard Keel

THE SILENCE OF THE LAMBS, based on the novel by Thomas Harris
 Hannibal Lecter . . . Anthony Hopkins
 Clarice Starling . . . Jodie Foster

A STAR IS BORN, based on a story by William A. Wellman and Robert Carson
 Vicki Lester, born Esther Blodgett . . . Judy Garland
 Norman Maine . . . James Mason

STAR WARS, screenplay by George Lucas
 Luke Skywalker . . . Mark Hamill
 Princes Leia . . . Carrie Fisher
 Han Solo . . . Harrison Ford
 Obi-wan Kenobi . . . Alec Guinness
 Darth Vader . . . David Prowse, with voice of James Earl Jones

STEEL MAGNOLIAS, based on the play by Robert Harling
 M'Lynn Eatenton . . . Sally Field
 Truvy Jones . . . Dolly Parton
 Ouiser Boudreaux . . . Shirley MacLaine
 Annelle Dupuy Desoto . . . Darryl Hannah
 Claree Belcher . . . Olympia Dukakis
 Shelby Eatenton Latcherie . . . Julia Roberts

THE SUN ALSO RISES, based on the novel by Ernest Hemingway
 Jake Barnes . . . Tyrone Power
 Brett Ashley . . . Ava Gardner

SWEET BIRD OF YOUTH, based on the play by Tennessee Williams
 Chance Wayne . . . Paul Newman
 Heavenly Finley . . . Shirley Knight

TEENAGE MUTANT NINJA TURTLES, screenplay by Todd W. Langen and Bobby Herbeck
 Raphael . . . Josh Pais
 Michelangelo . . . Michelan Sisti
 Donatello . . . Leif Tilden
 Leonardo . . . David Forman
 April O'Neil . . . Judith Hoag

TERMS OF ENDEARMENT, based on the novel by Larry McMurtry
 Aurora Greenway . . . Shirley MacLaine
 Emma Horton . . . Debra Winger

Garrett Breedlove . . . Jack Nicholson
Flap Horton . . . Jeff Daniels

THE THORN BIRDS, based on a novel by Colleen McCullough

(This is the cast of the ABC-TV Mini-Series)
Meggie Cleary . . . Rachel Ward
Fiona 'Fee' Cleary . . . Jean Simmons
Ralph de Bricassart . . . Richard Chamberlain
Rainer Hartheim . . . Ken Howard
Luddie Miller . . . Earl Holliman
Justine O'Neill . . . Mare Winningham
Luke O'Neill . . . Bryan Brown
Dane O'Neill . . . Philip Anglim
Vittorio Contini-Verchese . . . Christopher Plummer

THE THREE SISTERS, by Anton Chekhov
Olga
Masha
Irina

TO KILL A MOCKINGBIRD, based on the novel by Harper Lee
Atticus Finch . . . Gregory Peck
Scout Finch . . . Mary Badham
Jem Finch . . . Philip Alford
Dill Harris . . . John Megna

UNCLE BUCK, screenplay by John Hughes
Buck Russell . . . John Candy
Tia Russell . . . Jean Kelly
Maizy Russell . . . Gaby Hoffman
Miles Russell . . . Macauley Culkin
Chanice Kobolowski . . . Amy Madigan

VALLEY OF THE DOLLS, based on the novel by Jacqueline Susann
Neely O'Hara . . . Patty Duke
Lyon Burke . . . Paul Burke

THE WIZARD OF OZ, adapted from the novel by L. Frank Baum
Dorothy . . . Judy Garland
Hunk (Scarecrow) . . . Ray Bolger
Zeke (Cowardly Lion) . . . Bert Lahr
Hickory (Tin Woodman) . . . Jack Haley
Glinda . . . Billie Burke
Oz . . . Frank Morgan

WORKING GIRL, screenplay by Kevin Wade
  Tess McGill . . . Melanie Griffith
  Jack Trainer . . . Harrison Ford
  Katherine Parker . . . Sigourney Weaver

WUTHERING HEIGHTS, based on the novel by Emily Brontë
  Heathcliff . . . Laurence Olivier
  Catherine . . . Merle Oberon
  Nellie . . . Flora Robson
  Hindley . . . Hugh Williams

ZORBA THE GREEK, based on the novel by Nikos Kazantzakis
  Alexis Zorba . . . Anthony Quinn

Something to Sing About:
Lyrical Names

> "She has eyes that men adore so
> And a torso, even more so."
> —From "Lydia, the Tattooed Lady"

Okay, okay, so "Lydia, the Tattooed Lady" isn't a beautiful ballad that opens the floodgates of one's most romantic memories. But from experience, I can tell you that I love it when I'm introduced to someone and they sing that song to me. It means they know my name—and it becomes unlikely that they'll forget it. Plus, not only is it a good icebreaker, but I get more attention than people whose names are not associated with songs.

> —Lydia Hope Wilen

So there you have it . . . an unsolicited testimonial in favor of giving your child a name worth singing about!

With the help of the Billboard Research Service, here are all the songs we uncovered to start you thinking (and singing!) about the right name for your child. When you go through the list, be prepared for a sentimental stream of memories to flow

149

by as you spot some of your old favorites. Whenever possible, we've listed one or more of the song's recording artists to make it easier for you to find the song in your local music store. And now, you're ready to play "Name That Tune with a Name!"

SONGS WITH GIRLS' NAMES

Song	*Recording Artist*
Sweet ADELINE	
ALICE Blue Gown	
ALICE in Wonderland	Neil Sedaka
ALLISON	Elvis Costello
AMANDA	Boston; Waylon Jennings
AMAPOLA	Helen O'Connell
Once in Love with AMY	Ray Bolger
ANASTASIA	Pat Boone; Roger Williams
ANGIE	Rolling Stones
ANGIE Baby	Helen Reddy
ANNIE	(from Broadway show of same title)
ANNIE's Song	John Denver
Dreamboat ANNIE	Heart
AUBREY	Bread
BARBARA Polka	
BARBARA ANN	Beach Boys; Regents
BERNADETTE	Four Tops
BERNADINE	Pat Boone
BESS You Is My Woman	(from Broadway show *Porgy and Bess*)
BETH	Kiss
Sweet BETSY from Pike	
BETTY Co-Ed	
My Girl BILL	Jim Stafford
BILLIE JEAN	Michael Jackson
BOBBIE SUE	Oak Ridge Boys
BONNIE Came Back	Duane Eddy
I've Got BONNIE	Bobby Rydell
My BONNIE	Beatles and Tony Sheridan
BRANDY	Scott English
CANDIDA	Dawn
CANDY	Iggy Pop & Kate Pierson
CANDY's Room	Bruce Springsteen

Song	Recording Artist
CAROL	Chuck Berry
Oh, CAROL	Neil Sedaka
CAROLINE, No	Brian Wilson
Sweet CAROLINE	Neil Diamond
CARRIE	Europa; Cliff Richards
CARRIE ANN	Hollies
CATERINA	Perry Como
Close to CATHY	Mike Clifford
CECILIA	Simon & Garfunkel
Sweet CHARITY	(from Broadway show of same title)
Hush, Hush Sweet CHARLOTTE	(from film of same title)
CHARMAINE	
CHERRY, CHERRY	Neil Diamond
CHLOE	Elton John
CINDY's Birthday	Johnny Crawford
CINDY, Oh, CINDY	Eddie Fisher; Vince Martin
CINNAMON	Derek
CLAIR	Gilbert O'Sullivan
CLAUDETTE	Everly Brothers
CLEMENTINE	Bobby Darin; Weavers
Oh My Darling CLEMENTINE	
CORINNA, CORINNA	Ray Peterson
DAISY, DAISY	
DAISY JANE	America
Darlin' DANIELLE Don't	Henry Lee Summer
DELILAH	Tom Jones
Modern Day DELILAH	Van Stephenson
DELTA DAWN	Helen Reddy
DENISE	Randy & the Rainbows
DIANA	Paul Anka
DIANE	Bachelors
Little DIANE	Dion
DINAH	Danny Kaye
Hello, DOLLY!	(from Broadway show of same title); Louis Armstrong
DOMINIQUE	
DONNA	Ritchie Valens
DOTTIE	Danny & the Juniors
Come On EILEEN	Derek & the Dominos
I Still See ELISA	(from Broadway show *Paint Your Wagon*)
ELVIRA	Oak Ridge Boys

Song	Recording Artist
EMILY	(from film *The Americanization of Emily*)
For EMILY	Simon & Garfunkel
EMMA	Hot Chocolate
FANNIE (Be Tender with My Love)	Bee Gees
FANNIE MAE	Buster Brown
FANNY	(from film of same title)
FRANCENE	ZZ Top
GEORGY Girl	(from film of same title)
GIGI	(from film of same title)
GINA	Johnny Mathis
GINNY Come Lately	Brian Hyland
GLORIA	Shadows of Knight; Laura Branigan; Them; Doors
Amazing GRACE	
GUINNEVERE	
Hard Hearted HANNAH	
Hi Hi HAZEL	Gary & the Hornets
Hooray for HAZEL	Tommy Roe
HEATHER Honey	Tommy Roe
HELENA Polka	
HONEY (I Miss You)	
HONEY (I'm in Love with You)	
IDA, Sweet as Apple Cider	Eddie Cantor
Goodnight, IRENE	Weavers
JAMIE	Eddie Holland; Ray Parker, Jr.
JANE	Jefferson Starship
JANET	Commodores
The Ballad of JAYNE	L.A. Guns
JEAN	Oliver
JEANNIE with the Light Brown Hair	
JEANNIE's Packin' Up	(from Broadway show *Brigadoon*)
Little JEANNIE	Elton John
JENNIE LEE	Jan & Arnie
JENNY	Danny Kaye
JENNY, JENNY	Little Richard
JEZEBEL	Frankie Laine
JILL	Gary Lewis & the Playboys
JO ANN	Playmates
JOANNA	Kool & the Gang

Song	Recording Artist
JOANNE	Michael Nesmith
JOLENE	Dolly Parton
JOSEPHINE	Bill Black's Combo
My Girl JOSEPHINE	Fats Domino
JOSIE	Steely Dan
JUDY in Disguise (with Glasses)	John Fred & His Playboy Band
Suite: JUDY Blue Eyes	Crosby, Stills & Nash
JULIA	Beatles
JULIE, Do Ya Love Me	Bobby Sherman
Oh, JULIE	Crescendos
O KATHARINA	
Sister KATE	
I'll Take You Home Again, KATHLEEN	
KATHY-O	Diamonds
K-K-K-KATY	
LAURA	(from film of same title)
Think of LAURA	Christopher Cross
LAURIE (Strange Things Happen . . .)	Dickey Lee
LEAH	Roy Orbison
LEILA	Eric Clapton
Sweet LEILANI	
LILI MARLENE	
LILY of the Valley	
I Saw LINDA Yesterday	Dickey Lee
LINDA	Jan & Dean, or Buddy Clarke
LOLA	Kinks
Whatever LOLA Wants	(from Broadway show *Damn Yankees*)
Sweet LORRAINE	Kay Starr
LOUISE	Maurice Chevalier
LUCILLE	Everly Brothers; Kenny Rogers
LUCY in the Sky with Diamonds	Beatles; Elton John
Watch Out for LUCY	Eric Clapton
LULU's Back in Town	
LYDIA, the Tattooed Lady	Groucho Marx; Burl Ives
MABEL's Waltz Song	(from operetta *The Pirates of Penzance*)
MAGGIE	Redbone
When You and I Were Young, MAGGIE	

Song	Recording Artist
MAME	(from Broadway show of same title)
MANDY	Barry Manilow; Johnny Mathis
MARGIE	
MARIA	(from Broadway shows *The Sound of Music; West Side Story*)
MARIA ELENA	Los Indios Tabajaras
MARIAN the Librarian	(from Broadway show *The Music Man*)
C'mon MARIANNE	Four Seasons; Donny Osmond
MARIANNE	Hilltoppers; Terry Gilkyson
MARIE	Bachelors
MARLENA	Four Seasons
Mostly MARTHA	Crew Cuts
Along Comes MARY	Association
MARY's a Grand Old Name	
MARY's Prayer	Danny Wilson
Proud MARY	Creedence Clearwater Revival
Take a Message to MARY	Everly Brothers
MARY ANN	
MARY JANE	Rick James
MARY LOU	Ronny Hawkins
MATILDA	Harry Belafonte
Twistin' MATILDA	Jimmy Soul
Waltzing MATILDA	
Sweet MAXINE	Doobie Brothers
MELINDA	
MICHELLE	Beatles; David & Jonathan
Thoroughly Modern MILLIE	(from film of same title)
Good Golly Miss MOLLY	Little Richard; Swinging Blue Jeans
MONA LISA	Conway Twitty; Nat "King" Cole
NADIA's Theme	(from soap opera *The Young and the Restless*)
NADINE (Is It You)	Chuck Berry
NANCY with the Laughing Face	Frank Sinatra
No, No NANETTE	(from Broadway show of same title)
Wait Till the Sun Shines, NELLIE	
NELLY Was a Lady	
NOLA	Billy Williams
PAMELA	Toto

Song	Recording Artist
PATRICIA	Perez Prado
Hey PAULA	Paul & Paula
PEG	Steely Dan
PEG o' My Heart	
PEGGY SUE	Buddy Holly
POLLY Wolly Doodle	Burl Ives
RAMONA	Nat "King" Cole
REBECCA Came Back from Mecca	Burl Ives
Walk Away RENEE	Four Tops
Help Me RHONDA	Beach Boys
RIKKI Don't Lose That Number	Steely Dan
Lovely RITA	Beatles
RONI	Bobby Brown
RONNIE	Four Seasons
ROSALIE	
ROSANNA	Toto
Honeysuckle ROSE	
My Wild Irish ROSE	
Rambling ROSE	
ROSE of Washington Square	Barbra Streisand
Second Hand ROSE	Barbra Streisand
ROSEMARIE, I Love You	
ROSIE, You Are My Posie	
ROXANNE	Police
ROXIE	(from Broadway show *Chicago*)
RUBY	Ray Charles
RUBY Baby	Dion
RUBY ANN	Marty Robbins
SADIE, SADIE, Married Lady	(from Broadway show and film *Funny Girl*)
My Gal SAL	
Lay Down SALLY	Eric Clapton
SALLY	Grand Funk Railroad
Long Tall SALLY	Pat Boone; Little Richard
SANDY	Ronny & the Daytonas; Larry Hall; Dion
SANDY's Song	Dolly Parton
SARA	Fleetwood Mac; Starship
SARA Smile	Daryl Hall & John Oates
SHANNON	Henry Gross
Oh SHEILA	Ready for the World
SHEILA	Tommy Roe
Oh SHERRIE	Steve Perry

Song	Recording Artist
Letter from SHERRY	Dale Ward
SHERRY	Four Seasons
STELLA by Starlight	
Sweet SUE, Just You	
SUSAN	Buckinghams
O, SUSANNA	
If You Knew SUSIE	Eddie Cantor
Wake Up Little SUSIE	Everly Brothers; Simon & Garfunkel
SUZANNE	Journey
TAMMY	Debbie Reynolds
JUSTINE	Righteous Brothers
TARA's Theme	(From the film *Gone with the Wind*)
TINA MARIE	Perry Como
TRACY	Cuff Links
TRACY's Theme	Spencer Ross
VALERIE	Steve Winwood
VENUS	Bananarama; Shocking Blue
VERONICA	Elvis Costello
VICTORIA	Kinks
I'm Coming VIRGINIA	
WENDY	Beach Boys

SONGS WITH BOYS' NAMES

Song	Recording Artist
You Can Call Me AL	Paul Simon
ALEXANDER's Ragtime Band	
ALFIE	Cher; Dionne Warwick
ARTHUR's Theme	Christopher Cross
BEN	Michael Jackson
BILL	(from Broadway show *Show Boat*)
He's Just My BILL	
Soliloquy (My Boy BILL)	(from Broadway show *Carousel*)
Ode to BILLIE JOE	Bobby Gentry
BILLY	Kathy Linden
BILLY Boy	
BRIAN's Song	(from TV film of same title)
BRUCE	Rick Springfield
CHARLIE Is My Darling	Carmen McRae

Song	Recording Artist
CHARLIE My Boy	
DANIEL	Elton John
DANNY Boy	
DUNCAN	Paul Simon
EDDIE My Love	Teen Queens, Chordettes
ELI's Coming	Three Dog Night
ELMER's Tune	
FERNANDO	Abba
FRANKIE	Connie Francis
FREDERIC's Song	(Operetta: *Pirates of Penzance*)
Blow, GABRIEL, Blow	
I'm Just Wild About HARRY	
Dance with Me, HENRY	Georgia Gibbs
Hit the Road JACK	Ray Charles & the Raelets
JESSE	Roberta Flack; Carly Simon
JIMMY	(from Broadway show of same title)
Go, JIMMY, Go	Jimmy Clanton
Ragtime Cowboy JOE	David Seville & the Chipmunks
JOEY	Concrete Blonde
Big Bad JOHN	Jimmy Dean
Where Do You Work-A, JOHN?	
JOHNNY Loves Me	Shelley Fabares
JOHNNY One Note	Judy Garland
Oh JOHNNY, Oh JOHNNY Oh!	Bonnie Baker
When JOHNNY Comes Marching Home	
Who's JOHNNY	El DeBarge
JOSHUA Fit the Battle of Jericho	Traditional
Hey JUDE	Beatles; Wilson Pickett
Hats Off to LARRY	Del Shannon
Mr. LEE	Bobbettes
Meet Me in St. Louis, LOUIS	Judy Garland
MACK the Knife	Bobby Darin
Message to MICHAEL	Dionne Warwick
MICHAEL	Highwaymen
MICHAEL, Row the Boat Ashore	Weavers
MICKEY	Toni Basil
Go Down, MOSES	
NORMAN	Sue Thompson
OLIVER	(from Broadway show of same title)
Tall PAUL	Annette

Song	Recording Artist
QUENTIN's Theme	Charles Randolph Greane Sound
ROCKY	Austin Roberts
RUDY's Rock	Bill Haley & His Comets
Lovin' SAM (The Sheik of Alabam)	
SAM	Olivia Newton-John
Watching SCOTTY Grow	Bobby Goldsboro
A Boy Named SUE	Johnny Cash
SUNNY	
Ready TEDDY	Little Richard
TEDDY	Connie Francis
TIMOTHY	Buoys
Little WALTER	Tony! Toni! Tone!
Little WILLY	Sweet
ZORBA the Greek	Herb Alpert & the Tijuana Brass

Celebrities . . .
Their Names, Once Upon a Time

Would Maurice Micklewhite have won an Academy Award in 1986 if he hadn't changed his name to Michael Caine? Would Steveland Morris be the sunshine of your life if he hadn't changed his name to Stevie Wonder? Would a film called *Pal Come Home* have been a box office hit if Pal's owner hadn't changed the dog's name to Lassie? On a scale from one to ten, how would you rate Mary Cathleen Collins? Would she be a ten if she hadn't changed her name to Bo Derek? In other words, would the celebrities who changed their names have "made it" *without* changing their names? Of course there's no way of knowing, but what you can find out from the list below is who was who, and what their name of choice currently is.

Professional Name	*Name at Birth*
Alan Alda	Alphonse D'Abruzzo
Muhammad Ali	Cassius Marcellus Clay, Jr.

Professional Name	*Name at Birth*
Woody Allen	Allen Stewart Konigsberg
June Allyson	Ella Geisman
Ann-Margret	Ann-Margret Olsson
Beatrice Arthur	Bernice Frankel
Lauren Bacall	Betty Joan Perske
Anne Bancroft	Annemarie Italiano
Brigitte Bardot	Camille Javal
Warren Beatty	Henry Warren Beaty
Tony Bennett	Antonio Dominick Benedetto
Robby Benson	Robert Segal
Bono (U2's lead singer)	Paul Hewson
Victor Borge	Borge Rosenbaum
Beau Bridges	Lloyd Vernet Bridges III
Charles Bronson	Charles Buchinsky
Mel Brooks	Melvin Kaminsky
George Burns	Nathan Birnbaum
Raymond Burr	William Stacey Burr
Michael Caine	Maurice Joseph Micklewhite
Dyan Cannon	Samille Diane Friesen
Kate Capshaw	Kathleen Sue Nail
Diahann Carroll	Carol Diahann Johnson
Ray Charles	Ray Charles Robinson
Cher	Cherilyn Sarkisian La Piere
Alice Cooper	Vincent Furnier
Elvis Costello	Declan Patrick McManus
Tom Cruise	Thomas Cruise Mapother IV
John Denver	Henry John Deutschendorf, Jr.
Bo Derek	Mary Cathleen Collins
Angie Dickinson	Angeline Brown
Bo Diddley	Elias McDaniel
Kirk Douglas	Issur Danielovitch Demsky
Patty Duke	Anne Marie Duke
Faye Dunaway	Dorothy Faye Dunaway
Bob Dylan	Robert Zimmerman
Dale Evans	Frances Octavia Smith
Jodie Foster	Alicia Christian Foster
Redd Foxx	John Elroy Sanford
Zsa Zsa Gabor	Sari Gabor
James Garner	James Baumgarner
Crystal Gayle	Brenda Gail Webb
Whoopi Goldberg	Caryn Johnson
Elliot Gould	Elliot Goldstein
Lee Grant	Lyova Haskell Rosenthal

Professional Name	*Name at Birth*
Buddy Hackett	Leonard Hacker
Margaux Hemingway	Margot Hemingway
Audrey Hepburn	Edda van Heemstra Hepburn-Ruston
Pee-Wee Herman	Paul Rubenfeld
Bob Hope	Leslie Townes Hope
Engelbert Humperdinck	Arnold Dorsey
Lauren Hutton	Mary Laurence Hutton
Mick Jagger	Michael Phillip Jagger
Elton John	Reginald Kenneth Dwight
Tom Jones	Thomas Jones Woodward
Diane Keaton	Diane Hall
Lassie	Pal
Spike Lee	Shelton Jackson Lee
Jay Leno	James Leno
Jerry Lewis	Joseph Levitch
Sophia Loren	Sofia Scicolone
Madonna	Madonna Louise Ciccone
Karl Malden	Mladen Sekulovich
Walter Matthau	Walter Matuschanskayasky
Tony Orlando	Michael Anthony Orlando Cassavitis
Mike Nichols	Michael Igor Peshkowsky
Jack Nicholson	John Joseph Nicholson
Jack Palance	Walter Palahnuik
Minnie Pearl	Sarah Ophelia Colley Cannon
Gregory Peck	Eldred Gregory Peck
Michelle Phillips	Holly Michelle Gilliam
Jane Powell	Suzanne Burce
Robert Redford	Charles Robert Redford, Jr.
Della Reese	Deloreese Patricia Early
Burt Reynolds	Burton Leon Reynolds, Jr.
Debbie Reynolds	Mary Frances Reynolds
Ginger Rogers	Virginia McMath
Roy Rogers	Leonard Slye
Mickey Rooney	Joe Yule, Jr.
Mickey Rourke	Philip André Rourke
Telly Savalas	Aristoteles Savalas
Omar Sharif	Michael Shalhoub
Charlie Sheen	Carlos Estevez
Dinah Shore	Frances Rose Shore
Neil Simon	Marvin Neil Simon
O. J. Simpson	Orenthal James Simpson
Sissy Spacek	Mary Elizabeth Spacek
Mickey Spillane	Frank Morrison

Professional Name	Name at Birth
Ringo Starr	Richard Starkey
Cat Stevens	Steven Georgion
Connie Stevens	Concetta Ann Ingolia
Shadoe Stevens	Terry Ingstad
Sting	Gordon Matthew Summer
Meryl Streep	Mary Louise Streep
Barbra Streisand	Barbara Jean Streisand
Donna Summer	La Donna Andrea Gaines
Marlo Thomas	Margaret Thomas
Lily Tomlin	Mary Jean Tomlin
Tina Turner	Annie Mae Bullock
Twiggy	Lesley Hornby
Conway Twitty	Harold Lloyd Jenkins
Mike Wallace	Myron Wallace
Gene Wilder	Jerry Silberman
Stevie Wonder	Steveland Morris
Jane Wyman	Sarah Jane Fulks
Tammy Wynette	Virginia Wynette Pugh

What the Celebrities
Name Their Kids

Kathie Lee and Frank Gifford named their son Cody after the
Cleveland Browns' tackle Cody Risien. After this, you're on
your own when it comes to why the rest of the celebrities
mentioned in this chapter chose the names they did for their
children.

Meryl Streep, whose real name is Mary Louise Streep, took
the traditional approach, naming her children Grace, Henry,
Mary, and Louisa. As to the opposite of traditional—that's
what Frank Zappa went for when he zapped his kids with the
names Moon Unit, Dweezil, Ahmet Emuukha Rodan, and Diva.

As you'll see when you go through our extensive list, most
celebs chose names for their children that are closer to traditional than way out.

NOTE: To the celebrities who have more children than we have
listed, our apologies. Next time, send us an announcement!

To get you started, here's a Pop Quiz and a Mom Quiz. See
how many celebs you can match up with the name(s) of their
children. (Correct answers can be found on the following pages,
under the celebrities' names, which are listed alphabetically.)

163

POP QUIZ

1) Woody Allen	a) Sam
2) Corbin Bernsen	b) Annie, Joe, and Lily
3) Kevin Costner	c) Sydney Brooke (girl)
4) Michael Douglas	d) Katherine Eunice and Christina Aurelia
5) Michael J. Fox	e) Cameron Morrell (boy)
6) Mel Gibson	f) Oliver and twins Henry and Angus
7) Nick Nolte	g) Sage Moon Blood (boy), Seth, and Seargeoh (boy)
8) O. J. Simpson	h) Brawley King
9) Arnold Schwarzenegger	i) Satchel O'Sullivan
10) Sylvester Stallone	j) Hannah, William, and twins Christian and Edward

MOM QUIZ

1) Valerie Bertinelli	a) Annie Maude
2) Lisa Bonet	b) Nayib (boy)
3) Glenn Close	c) Wolfgang
4) Gloria Estefan	d) Gaston and Spencer Margaret
5) Goldie Hawn	e) Sophie Frederica Alohilani
6) Reba McEntire	f) Rumer Glenn and Scout LaRue (two girls)
7) Bette Midler	g) Zoe
8) Demi Moore	h) Shelby (boy)
9) Cybill Shepherd	i) Kate Garry, Oliver, and Wyatt
10) Jaclyn Smith	j) Clementine and twins Molly Ariel and Cyrus Zachariah

CELEBRITIES' CHILDREN'S NAMES

Brooke Adams	Josie Lynn
Alan Alda	Eve, Elizabeth, and Beatrice
Kim Alexis	Jamie (boy)
Debbie Allen	Vivian
Kirstie Alley and Parker Stevenson	William
Harry Anderson	Dashiell and Eva Fay
Ursula Andress and Harry Hamlin	Dimitri
Prince Andrew and Sarah (Fergie), the Duchess of York	Beatrice Elizabeth Mary and Eugenie Victoria Helena

Julie Andrews — Emma Kate

Arthur Ashe and Jeanne Moutoussamy (a photographer) — Camera (girl)

Ed Asner — Kathryn, twins Liza and Matthew, and Charlie

Lauren Bacall and Humphrey Bogart — Stephen and Leslie Howard (girl)

with Jason Robards, Jr. — Sam

Kevin Bacon and Kyra Sedgwick — Travis Sedg and Sosie Ruth

Mikhail Baryshnikov and Lisa Rinehart — Peter and Anna Katerina

with Jessica Lange — Alexandra (Sasha)

Ellen Barkin and Gabriel Byrne — Jack

Meredith Baxter-Birney and David Birney — Kate and twins Mollie Elizabeth and Peter David Edwin

Ed Begley, Jr. — Amanda and Nick

Harry Belafonte — Adrienne, Shari, Gina, and David

Annette Bening and Warren Beatty — Kathlyn

Tony Bennett — D'Andrea (boy), Daegal (boy), Joanna, and Antonia

Robby Benson & Karla DeVito — Lyric (girl) and Zephyr (boy)

Marisa Berenson — Starlite Melody

Candice Bergen and Louis Malle — Chloe

Corbin Bernsen and Amanda Pays — Oliver and twins Henry and Angus

Valerie Bertinelli and Eddie Van Halen — Wolfgang

Lisa Bonet — Zoe

Sonny Bono — Chesare

with Cher — Chastity

Debbie Boone — twins Dustin (girl) and Gabrielle, Jordan Alexander, and Tessa

Bjorn Borg — Robin (boy)

Timothy Bottoms — Bartholomew

David Bowie and Angela Burnett — Zowie (now known as Joey)

Bruce Boxleitner — Lee Davis and Sam

Marlon Brando — Christian Devi, Miko (boy), Rebecca, Tehoto (boy), and Cheyenne Tarita (girl)

Jeff Bridges — Hayley Rose, Isabelle, and Jessica

Christie Brinkley and Billy Joel — Alexa Ray

Garth Brooks — Taylor Mayn Pearl (girl)

Mel Brooks — Stefanie, Nicholas, and Edward

with Anne Bancroft — Maximilian

Carol Burnett	Carrie Louise, Jody Ann, Erin, and Kate
David Byrne	Malu Valentine
Kate Capshaw	Jessica
with Steven Spielberg	Sasha (girl), Sawyer (boy), and Theo
David Carradine	Calista (girl) and Kansas (girl)
with Barbara Hershey	Free, who then changed his name to Tom
Keith Carradine	actress Martha Plimpton
with Sandra Will	Cade Richmond (boy), and Sorel (girl)
Shaun Cassidy	Caitlin and John
Prince Charles and Princess Diana	William Arthur Philip Louis and Henry (Harry) Charles Albert David
Chevy Chase	Caley (girl), Emily, Cydney, and Cathalene
Cher and Greg Allman	Elijah Blue
with Sonny Bono	Chastity
Jackson Browne	Ethan
Linda Carter	James Clifford
Neneh Cherry	Tyson (girl)
Rae Dawn Chong	Morgan (boy)
Jill Clayburgh and David Rabe	Lily and Michael
Glenn Close	Annie Maude
Joan Collins and Anthony Newley	Tara and Anthony
with Ron Kass	Katherine
Phil Collins	Lillie
Alice Cooper	Calico
Jimmy Connors	Aubree (girl) and Brett David
Bill Cosby	Erika Ranee, Erinn Charlene, Ennis William, Ensa Camille, and Evin Harrah
Kevin Costner	Annie, Joe, and Lily
Lindsay Crouse and David Mamet	Willa
Billy Crystal	Jennifer and Lindsay
Jane Curtin	Tess
Jamie Lee Curtis and Christopher Guest	Annie
Willem Dafoe and Elizabeth LeCompte	Jack
Roger Daltrey	Rosie Lea and Willow Amber
Tyne Daly and Georg Stanford Brown	Beatris, Elizabeth, and Kathryne

Faith Daniels	Andrew Steven and Alyx Ray (girl)
Jeff Daniels	Ben
Blythe Danner	Jake
Ted Danson	Alexis and Kate
Tony Danza	Catherine Ann and Emily Lynn
Pam Dawber and Mark Harmon	Sean and Ty Christian
Jonathan Demme	Ramona
Catherine Deneuve and Marcello Mastroianni	Chiara-Charlotte
Robert De Niro	Raphael Eugene
Brian DePalma and Gale Ann Hurd	Lolita
John Denver	Anna Kate and Jessie Belle
Rick Derringer	Mallory Loving
Danny DeVito and Rhea Perlman	Grace, Jacob, and Lucie
Joan Didion and John Gregory Dunne	Quintana Roo
Kirk Douglas	Michael, Joel, Peter, and Eric
Michael Douglas	Cameron Morrell (boy)
Lesley-Anne Down and William Friedkin	Jack
Richard Dreyfuss	Benjamin, Emily and Harry
Patrick Duffy	Padraic (boy) and Connor (boy)
Faye Dunaway and Terry O'Neill	Liam
Britt Ekland and Slim Jim Phantom	Thomas Jefferson
Nora Ephron and Carl Bernstein	Jacob Walker and Max Ephron
Louise Erdrich and Michael Dorris	Pallas (girl) and Persia (girl)
Gloria Estefan	Nayib (boy)
Emilio Estevez and Carey Salley	Paloma and Taylor Levi (boy)
Chris Evert and Andy Mill	Alex (boy)
Mia Farrow	Tam and Isaiah
with Andre Previn	Fletcher, twins Matthew Phineas and Sascha Villiers, Lark Song, Daisy, and Soon-Yi (girl)
with Woody Allen	Dylan O'Sullivan (girl), Satchel O'Sullivan (boy), and Moses Amadeus
Carrie Fisher	Billie Cathryn
Harrison Ford	Benjamin and Willard
with Melissa Mathison	Malcolm
Michael J. Fox and Tracy Pollan	Sam
Leeza Gibbons and Chris Quinten	Jordan (girl)
with Stephen Meadows	Troy Stephen

Mel Gibson	twins Christian and Edward, Hannah, and William
Kathie Lee and Frank Gifford	Cody Newton (boy)
Melissa Gilbert	Dakota Mayi (girl)
Wayne Gretzky and Janet Jones	Paulina and Ty
Melanie Griffith with Don Johnson	Alexander Dakota (boy)
George Hamilton and Alana Hamilton Stewart	Ashley Steven
Tom Hanks	Colin and Elizabeth
Mel Harris	Byron and Madeline
Goldie Hawn and Bill Hudson with Kurt Russell	Kate Garry and Oliver Wyatt
Patty Hearst	Gillian Catherine and Lydia Marie
Hugh Hefner	Marston (boy) and Cooper (boy)
Mariel Hemingway	Dree Louise and Langley Fox (girl)
Gregory Hines	Zachary, Daria, and Jessica
Dustin Hoffman and Ann Byrne with Lisa Gottsegen	Karina and Jennifer Jacob, Rebecca, Maxwell, and Alexandra
Ron Howard	twins Jocelyn and Paige
Mary Beth Hurt and Paul Schrader	Molly
William Hurt	Alex and Sam
Billy Idol	Willem Wolfe
Iman and Spencer Haywood	Zulekha (girl)
Julius Irving	Jazmin
Mick Jagger and Bianca Jagger with Marsha Hunt with Jerry Hall	Jade (girl) Karis (girl) Elizabeth Scarlett, James Leroy Augustine, and Georgia May Ayeesha
Don Johnson and Patti D'Arbanville with Melanie Griffith	Jesse (boy) Alexander
Earvin "Magic" Johnson	Earvin Johnson III
James Earl Jones	Flynn Earl
Rickie Lee Jones	Charlotte Rose
Erica Jong	Molly Miranda
Raul Julia	Benjamin and Raul Sigmund
Lainie Kazan	Jennifer
Michael Keaton	Sean
Kevin Kline and Phoebe Cates	Owen Joseph
Kris Kristofferson	Johnnie and Casey (girl)
Cheryl Ladd	Jordan Elizabeth

Christine Lahti	Wilson
Tom Landry	Thomas, Kitty, and Lisa
Jessica Lange and Mikhail (Sasha) Baryshnikov	Alexandra (Sasha)
with Sam Shepard	Hannah Jane and Samuel Rogers IV
Sugar Ray (Ray Charles) Leonard	Ray Charles
John Lithgow	Nathan and Phoebe
Kenny Loggins	Cody (boy) and Crosby (boy)
Shelley Long	Juliana
George Lucas	Katie
Susan Lucci	Andreas Martin and Liza Victoria
Joan Lunden	Jamie (girl), Lindsay (girl), and Sarah Emily
Paul and Linda McCartney	James Louis, Mary, and Stella
Reba McEntire	Shelby (boy)
Ali MacGraw and Robert Evans	Joshua
John Cougar Mellencamp	Justice (girl) and Teddi Jo (girl)
Bette Midler	Sophie Frederica Alohilani
Dennis Miller	Holden (boy)
Melba Moore	Charli (girl)
Eddie Murphy	Bria and Miles Mitchell
Bill Murray	Homer and Luke
Joe Namath	Jessica Grace
Brigitte Neilsen and Mark Gastineau	Marcus
Tracy Nelson	Remington Elizabeth
Olivia Newton-John	Chloe Rose
Jack Nicholson	Lorraine Broussard and Raymond
Nick Nolte	Brawley King
Chuck Norris	Mike and Eric
Ken Olin and Patricia Wettig	Clifford and Roxanne
Ryan O'Neal	Tatum and Griffin
with Farrah Fawcett	Redmond James Fawcett
Tatum O'Neal and John McEnroe	Kevin John and Sean Timothy
Tony Orlando	John and Jenny Rose
Marie Osmond	Stephen James
Peter O'Toole	Lorcan (boy), Pat, and Kate
Catherine Oxenberg	India (girl)
Mandy Patinkin	Isaac
Jane Pauley and Garry Trudeau	twins Rachel and Ross, and Thomas
Anthony Perkins and Berry Berenson	Elvis Brooke and Osgood Robert
Ron Perlman	Blake Amanda

John Phillips and Genevieve Waite
Michelle Phillips

Bijoux (girl) and Tamerlaine

Annie Potts
Priscilla Presley
James Danforth and Marilyn Quayle
Phylicia and Ahmad Rashad
Lynn Redgrave and John Clarke

Austin Devereux (boy) and Chynna
James Powell
Navarone Anthony
Tucker Danforth, Benjamin Eugene, and Mary Corinne
Condola Phylea
Benjamin B., Kelly B., and Annabel Lucy

Christopher Reeve and Gae Exton with Dana Morosini
Burt Reynolds and Loni Anderson
Keith Richards and Patti Hanson
John Ritter
Geraldo Rivera
Tom Robbins
Tony Roberts
Kenny Rogers
Diana Ross

Alexandra and Matthew
Owen
Quinton
Alexandria and Theodora Dupree
Carly, Jason, and Tyler
Isabella Holmes
Fleetwood Starr
Nicole
Christopher
Ross Arne (boy), Chudney Lane (girl), Rhonda Suzanne, and Tracee Joy

Isabella Rossellini
Kurt Russell and Season Hubley with Goldie Hawn
Theresa Russell and Nicholas Roeg
Bob Saget
Susan St. James

Elettra-Ingrid
Boston (boy)
Wyatt
Max and Statten Jack
Aubrey and Lara
Sunshine (girl) and Harmony (boy)

with Dick Ebersole
Susan Sarandon and Franco Amarri
with Tim Robbins

Charlie and William
Eva Maria Livia

Jack Henry and Miles Guthrie Tomalin

Caroline Kennedy Schlossberg
Arnold Schwarzenegger and Maria Shriver
Tom Selleck and Jilly Mack
Jane Seymour
Charlie Sheen
Cybill Shepherd

Rose Kennedy and Tatiana Celia
Katherine Eunice and Christina Aurelia
Hannah
Katharine Jane (Katie)
Cassandra
Clementine (Clemmy) and twins Molly Ariel and Cyrus Zachariah

Martin Short	Katherine and Oliver
Carly Simon and James Taylor	Benjamin Simon
Paul Simon	Harper (boy)
O. J. Simpson	Sydney Brooke (girl)
Grace Slick	China
Jaclyn Smith	Gaston and Spencer Margaret
Patti Smith	Jesse Paris (girl) and Jackson Frederick
Paul Sorvino	Mira, Amanda, and Michael
Sissy Spacek	Schuyler Elizabeth
Steven Spielberg and Amy Irving with Kate Capshaw	Max Samuel Sasha (girl), Sawyer (boy), and Theo
Bruce Springsteen and Patti Scialsa	Evan James and Jessica Rae
Sylvester Stallone	Sage Moon Blood (boy), Seth, and Seargeoh (boy)
Mary Steenburgen and Malcolm McDowell	Charlie and Lillie
Rod Stewart and Kelly Emberg with Alana Hamilton Stewart with Rachel Hunter	Ruby Sean Roderick and Kimberly Renee
Sting with Trudie Styler	Joe and Kate Jake, Brigitte Michael (girl, called Mickey) and Eliot (girl)
Oliver Stone	Sean
Darryl Strawberry	Diamond Nicole
Meryl Streep	Grace Jane, Henry, Mary Willa, and Louisa
Barbra Streisand and Elliot Gould	Jason Emanuel
Sally Struthers	Samantha
Donna Summer	Mimi
Kiefer Sutherland	Sarah
Meshach Taylor	Tamar, Tariq, Yasmine, and Esmé (all girls)
Philip Michael Thomas and Sheila DeWindt	India Serene and Melody
Richard Thomas	Richard Francisco and triplets Barbara Ayala, Gwyneth Gonzales, and Pilar Alma
Lea Thompson and Howard Deutch	Madeline
Charlene Tilton	Cherish
John Travolta	Jett
Alex Trebeck	Matthew Alexander

Donald and Ivana Trump	Donald, Ivanka and Eric
Tanya Tucker	Presley Tanita (girl), and Beau
Kathleen Turner	Rachel Ann
Tracey Ullman	Mabel Ellen
Lindsay Wagner	Alex and Dorian Henry
Rachel Ward and Bryan Brown	Matilda and Rosie
Billy Dee Williams	Corey Dee (boy) and Hanako (girl)
Robin Williams	Zachary, Zelda, and Cody Alan
Vanessa Williams	Melanie and Jillian
Marianne Williamson	India Emmaline
Bruce Willis and Demi Moore	Rumer Glenn (girl) and Scout LaRue (girl)
Debra Winger and Timothy Hutton	Emanuel Noah
Henry Winkler	Max and Zoe Emily
Stevie Wonder	Aisha (girl), Keita (boy), and Mumtaz (boy)
Pia Zadora and Meshulem Riklis	Christopher and Kady
Paula Zahn	Haley
Frank Zappa	Moon Unit, Ahmet Emuukha Rodan, Dweezil, and Diva

Favorites Over the Years

For centuries, America has been a melting pot of races and religions — and, therefore, names. In particular, New York City is one of the most active melting pots of the cities in the United States today. It is for that reason we're listing (in order of popularity) the most frequently chosen names for newborns according to New York City birth records. Thanks to the NYC Department of Health, we have lists of popular names for various years, starting with 1898 and ending with 1991 — the most recent list available at the time of this printing.

Girls	1898	Boys		Girls	1928	Boys
Mary		John		Mary		John
Catherine		William		Marie		William
Margaret		Charles		Annie		Joseph
Annie		George		Margaret		James
Rose		Joseph		Catherine		Richard
Marie		Edward		Gloria		Edward
Esther		James		Helen		Robert
Sarah		Louis		Teresa		Thomas

Girls	1898	Boys
Frances		Francis
Ida		Samuel

Girls	1928	Boys
Joan		George
Barbara		Lewis

Girls	1948	Boys
Linda		Robert
Mary		John
Barbara		James
Patricia		Michael
Susan		William
Kathleen		Richard
Carol		Joseph
Nancy		Thomas
Margaret		Stephen
Diane		David

Girls	1964	Boys
Lisa		Michael
Deborah		John
Mary		Robert
Susan		David
Maria		Steven
Elizabeth		Anthony
Donna		William
Barbara		Joseph
Patricia		Thomas
Ann(e)*		Christopher*
Theresa*		Richard*

Girls	1976	Boys
Jennifer		Michael
Jessica		David
Nicole		John
Melissa		Christopher
Michelle		Joseph
Maria		Anthony
Lisa		Robert
Elizabeth		Jason
Danielle		James
Christine		Daniel

Girls	1980	Boys
Jennifer		Michael
Jessica		David
Melissa		Jason
Nicole		Joseph
Michelle		Christopher
Elizabeth		Anthony
Lisa		John
Christina		Daniel
Tiffany		Robert
Maria		James

Girls	1983	Boys
Jennifer		Michael
Jessica		Christopher
Melissa		Jason
Nicole		David
Stephanie		Daniel
Christina		Anthony
Tiffany		Joseph
Michelle		John
Elizabeth		Robert
Lauren		Jonathan

Girls	1986	Boys
Jessica		Michael
Jennifer		Christopher
Stephanie		Jonathan
Nicole		Anthony
Christina		David
Amanda		Daniel
Melissa		Joseph
Tiffany		John
Danielle*		Jason
Elizabeth*		Andrew

Girls 1991 Boys

Girls	Boys
Stephanie	Michael
Ashley	Christopher
Jessica	Jonathan
Amanda	Anthony
Samantha	Joseph
Jennifer	Daniel
Nicole	David
Michelle	Matthew
Melissa	Kevin
Christina	John

*Tied

By Virtue of:
Virtuous Names

During the time of the Puritans — the 1500s and 1600s — many children (mostly baby girls) were given very meaningful names — in fact, names of virtue.

Although the trend never caught on to any great extent, some of these virtuous names remain popular to this day. My (Lydia's) middle name is Hope. When Joan went through a "feeling-cheated" phase because she didn't have a middle name, she decided to give herself a virtuous name as well. Her kid sister was Hope, so she chose Faith. It never really took, and within a short time Joan dropped the middle name. For weeks our parents joked about their daughter not wanting to *keep the Faith*.

If the thought of endowing your child with a name of virtue is an appealing one, here are the best of the batch.

Amity	Constance	Grace
Bliss	Courage	Harmony
Charity	Faith	Honor
Clarity	Felicity	Hope

Joy	Modesty	Unity
Justice	Patience	Verity
Learned	Prudence	
Mercy	Serenity	

The Way the Wind Blows:
Names of Hurricanes

The National Hurricane Center near Miami, Florida, keeps a constant watch on oceanic storm-breeding areas for tropical disturbances that may develop into hurricanes. If a disturbance intensifies into a tropical storm — with rotary circulation and wind speeds above thirty-nine miles per hour — the Center officially gives that storm a name.

According to the U.S. Department of Commerce's National Weather Service, short, distinctive names given in written — as well as in spoken — communications are quicker and less subject to error than the older and more cumbersome identification methods (which involved latitude-longitude readings). These advantages are especially important when hundreds of widely scattered stations, airports, coastal bases, and ships at sea are hurriedly exchanging detailed storm information.

For several hundred years hurricanes in the West Indies were named after the saint whose feast day it was when the hurricane developed. Before the end of the nineteenth century, an Australian meteorologist began giving women's names to tropical storms. And in 1953, our nation's weather services began using women's names for storms. Wait a second! Why should only *women* be associated with the destructive climatic forces of nature? So in the late seventies the weather service started applying men's names as well.

Come rain or come shine, your baby needs a name. The fact that these are hurricane names may appeal to you, or you may want to know these names just so that you can stay away from them. We can't *forecast* your feelings, but we can give you the names of hurricanes. (Please note that the names for the Atlantic and Eastern Pacific Storms are rotated every six years, so that the names for 1992 were also the names for 1986 and will be the names for 1998, 2004, and so forth. The names for the Central Pacific Tropical Cyclones start with the first name on List 1 and continue to the last one on List 4 — no matter how many years that may take. They then pick up the first name on List 1, and proceed onward once again. Also be aware that the National Weather Service retires names of those hurricanes, storms, or cyclones that have done terrible damage and taken lives. Two such names are Bob and Hugo.)

Since hurricanes affect other nations and are tracked by the weather bureaus of countries other than the United States, many of the names, especially the Eastern Pacific ones, have an international flavor. These more exotic names are agreed upon during international meetings of the World Meteorological Organization.

Also notice that the letters Q, U, X, Y, and Z are not used in the Atlantic Storms lists; the letters Q and U are not used in the Eastern Pacific Storms lists. The reason given by the National Weather Service is "the scarcity of names beginning with those letters." (Obviously, they haven't seen *this* book!)

Before you weather the storm, we'd like to share with you the name of the meteorologist who gave us most of this information. He is the Hurricane and Winter Storm Programs Coordinator on the national level for the U.S. National Weather Service and his name is "*Rain*er Dombrow*sky*."

ATLANTIC STORMS

1992	1993	1994	1995	1996	1997
Andrew*	Arlene	Alberto	Allison	Arthur	Ana
Bonnie	Bret	Beryl	Barry	Bertha	Bill
Charley	Cindy	Chris	Chantal	Cesar	Claudette
Danielle	Dennis	Debby	Dean	Dolly	Danny
Earl	Emily	Ernesto	Erin	Edouard	Erika
Frances	Floyd	Florence	Felix	Fran	Fabian
Georges	Gert	Gordon	Gabriello	Gustav	Grace
Hermine	Harvey	Helene	Humberto	Hortense	Henri
Ivan	Irene	Isaac	Iris	Isidore	Isabel
Jeanne	Jose	Joyce	Jerry	Josephine	Juan
Karl	Katrina	Keith	Karen	Klaus	Kate
Lisa	Lenny	Leslie	Luis	Lili	Larry
Mitch	Maria	Michael	Marilyn	Marco	Mindy
Nicole	Nate	Nadine	Noel	Nana	Nicholas
Otto	Ophelia	Oscar	Opal	Omar	Odette
Paula	Philippe	Patty	Pablo	Paloma	Peter
Richard	Rita	Rafael	Roxanne	Rene	Rose
Shary	Stan	Sandy	Sebastien	Sally	Sam
Tomas	Tammy	Tony	Tanya	Teddy	Teresa
Virginia	Vince	Valerie	Van	Vicky	Victor
Walter	Wilma	William	Wendy	Wilfred	Wanda

EASTERN PACIFIC STORMS

1992	1993	1994	1995	1996	1997
Adolph	Alma	Andres	Agatha	Adrian	Aletta
Barbara	Boris	Blanca	Blas	Beatriz	Bud
Cosme	Cristina	Carlos	Celia	Calvin	Carlotta
Dalilia	Douglas	Delores	Darby	Dora	Daniel
Erick	Elida	Enrique	Estelle	Eugene	Emilia
Flossie	Fausto	Fefa	Frank	Fernanda	Fabio
Gil	Genevieve	Guillermo	Georgette	Greg	Gilma
Henriette	Hernan	Hilda	Howard	Hilary	Hector
Ismael	Iselle	Ignacio	Isis	Irwin	Ileana
Juliette	Julio	Jimena	Javier	Jova	John
Kiko	Kenna	Kevin	Kay	Knut	Kristy
Lorena	Lowell	Linda	Lester	Lidia	Lane
Manuel	Marie	Marty	Madeline	Max	Miriam
Narda	Norbert	Nora	Newton	Norma	Norman
Octave	Odile	Olaf	Orlene	Otis	Olivia
Priscilla	Polo	Pauline	Paine	Pilar	Paul
Raymond	Rachel	Rick	Roslyn	Ramon	Rosa
Sonia	Simon	Sandra	Seymour	Selma	Sergio
Tico	Trudy	Terry	Tina	Todd	Tara

1992	1993	1994	1995	1996	1997
Velma	Vance	Vivian	Virgil	Veronica	Vincente
Winnie	Wallis	Waldo	Winifred	Wiley	Willa
Xina	Xavier	Xina	Xavier	Xina	Xavier
York	Yolanda	York	Yolanda	York	Yolanda
Zelda	Zeke	Zelda	Zeke	Zelda	Zeke

*Name is being retired

CENTRAL PACIFIC TROPICAL CYCLONES

List 1

Akoni	(Ah-koh'-nee)
Ema	(Eh'-mah)
Hana	(Hah'-nah)
Io	(Ee'-oo)
Keli	(Keh'-lee)
Lala	(Lah'-lah)
Moke	(Moh'-keh)
Nele	(Neh'-leh)
Oka	(Oh'-kah)
Peke	(Peh'-keh)
Uleki	(Oo-leh'-kee)
Wila	(Vee'-lah)

List 2

Aka	(Ah'-kah)
Ekeka	(Eh-keh'-kah)
Hali	(Hah'-lee)
Iniki*	(Ee-nee'-kee)
Keoni	(Keh-on'-nee)
Li	(Lee)
Mele	(Meh'-leh)
Nona	(Noh'-nah)
Oliwa	(Oh-lee'-vah)
Paka	(Pah'-kah)
Upana	(Oo-pah'-nah)
Wene	(Weh'-neh)

List 3

Alika	(Ah-lee'-kah)
Ele	(Eh'-leh)
Huko	(Hoo'-koh)
Ioke	(Ee-oh'-keh)
Kika	(Kee'-kah)
Lana	(Lah'-nah)
Maka	(Mah'-kah)
Neki	(Neh'-kee)
Oleka	(Oh-leh'-kah)
Peni	(Peh'-nee)
Ulia	(Oo-lee'-ah)
Wali	(Wah'-lee)

List 4

Ana	(Ah'-nah)
Ela	(Eh'-lah)
Halola	(Hah-loh'-lah)
Iune	(Ee-oo'-neh)
Kimo	(Kee'-moh)
Loke	(Loh'-keh)
Malia	(Mah-lee'-ah)
Niala	(Nee-ah'-lah)
Oko	(Oh'-koh)
Pali	(Pah'-lee)
Ulika	(Oo-lee'-kah)
Walaka	(Wah-lah'-kah)

NOTE: All letters in the Hawaiian language are pronounced, including even double or triple vowels.

*Name is being retired

Introduction to the Main Name List

Here's what our A-to-Z listing of names is all about: Each name, from the most ancient appellations to the most contemporary cognomens, is listed and then followed by its origin. We've classified the origins quite broadly, not distinguishing Low German from Middle German, or Middle Low German from Middle High German. To us, it's all German — just as English is English, not Old English or Anglo-Saxon.

After the name and origin, we offer each name's meaning. We found many names to have several meanings along with several origins. We've chosen to present the most positive meanings we could find, and listed them with the appropriate origins.

Although it's interesting to know the early meanings of names, we feel that *today's* association with names is more important. After years of interviews and observation, we think that, to a degree, people are influenced by what others expect of them because of their name's stereotypical image. For instance, you wouldn't expect to be saved by a lifeguard named Melvin or served by a flight attendant named Yetta. How many accountants are called Biff? How many bookkeepers Bambi? And when was the last time you watched a TV news anchor-woman named Bertha?

There are exceptions. We mustn't forget that there was a heroic military leader named *Norman* (Schwarzkopf) and a sexy, raunchy pop-culture superstar named *Madonna*.

So, we suggest you pay attention to the way your contemporaries react to a name, at least as much as — or more than — you are influenced by the name's original meaning.

In some cases, the name, its origin, and meaning are followed by a little more information about the name or about a person who has the name. Many of those entries tell you a celebrity's professional name and the name he or she was given at birth. We think it's intriguing to know a successful person's professional name — the name they *chose* — and what it was changed from. (If you too think it's intriguing, be sure to check out the chapter "Celebrities . . . Once Upon a Time.") Although most of the people we feature in the main list of names are in show business, we do have politicians, writers, artists, and others. We've chosen just a smattering of these names simply because if we went into detail with each and every name, you would need a derrick to lift the book — and much more than nine months to go through it!

Following the name, its origin, and meaning (and, in some cases, anecdotal information) are variations of the name, including shortened or lengthened versions, foreign versions, nicknames, and various spelling options.

Our goal is to help you find the perfect name for your perfect little baby. Our method: giving you the greatest choice of names. If we've succeeded, we'd love to hear from you. Please send us a birth announcement with the good news — and the good name.

Every good wish,

Joan Wilen and Lydia Wilen
P.O. Box 416
Ansonia Station
New York, NY 10023

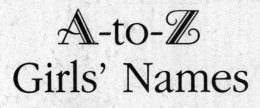

A-to-Z
Girls' Names

A

Aba — Ghanaian: Girl born on Thursday

Abbie — See: Abigail

Abena/Abina — African: A girl born on Tuesday

Abigail — Hebrew: Born of a joyous father
Abageal, Abbe, Abbey, Abbi, Abbie, Abigayle, Abby, Abbye

Abira — Hebrew: Strong

Abra — Hebrew: Earth Mother

Acacia — Greek: Naive
Cacia, Casee, Casey, Casi, Casia, Kaci, Kacia, Kacie

Acantha — Greek: Thorny

Ada — English: Prosperous, happy; German: Noble
Adda, Addie, Aida

Adah — Hebrew: Crown, ornament
Addia, Addy
This was a very popular name in the 1800s because of the famous actress/writer Adah Isaacs Mencken.

Adamma — Nigerian: Child of beauty

Adara — Greek: Beauty; Arabic: Virgin

Adelaide — German: Noble, kind; Place name: Capital of South Australia
Adala, Adalia, Adalie, Adaline, Adel, Adela, Adele, Adelia, Adelina, Adelind, Adelinda, Adeline, Adella, Adila, Dalina, Daline, Del, Delin, Delina, Della, Delly

Adeline — See: Adelaide

Adelle — See: Adelaide

Adelpha/Adelphe — Greek: Sisterly, beloved sister

Adena/Adina — Greek: Noble, delicate, gentle

Adolpha — German: Defender of honor
Adolfina, Adolphina, Adolphine, Dolfine, Dolphina

Adoncia — Spanish: Sweet

Adoree — Latin: To adore, worthy of divine worship
Adora, Adoria, Doree, Dori, Doria, Dorie, Dory

Adrienne — French: Dark one; Latin: From the Adriatic
Adria, Adrian, Adriana, Adriane, Adrianna

Agatha — Greek: Kind, good
Agathe, Agathia, Aggie, Aggy, Gatha

*...many bookshelves because of the famous
...a Christie.*
...person
..., Agnese, Agnesa, Annis, Ina, Nessa
...ed one

Aileen — Greek: Light
Ailene, Ailey, Alene, Aline, Allie, Eileen, Eleen, Eleena, Ileana, Ileane, Ileanna, Ilene, Iliana, Illeane, Illianna, Leana, Lena, Liana, Lina

Aiyana — Native American: Eternal bloom

Alanna — Celtic: Fair, beautiful; Hawaiian: Awakening
Alaine, Alana, Alane, Alayne, Allene, Allena, Allyn

Alarice/Allaryce — German: Ruler of all
Alar, Alarica, Alrica

Alba — See: Alberta

Alberta — English: Noble, brilliant
Alba, Albertina, Albertine, Ali, Allie, Ally, Berrie, Berry, Berta, Elberta, Elbertina, Elbertine

Alda — German: Rich

Alex/Alix — See: Alexandra

Alexandra — Greek: Defender of humankind
Alejandra, Alessandra, Alex, Alexa, Alexina, Alexine, Alexis, Ali, Alix, Alixe, Alyx, Lexi, Lexie, Lexy, Sandra, Sondra, Zandi, Zandra, Zandy
The first woman known to have this name was Queen Alexandra of Judea, who died in 69 B.C.

Alfonsine/Alphonsine — German: Noble family
Alfee, Alfi, Alfie, Alfy, Alonsa, Alphy, Fonsie

Alfreda/Alfrieda — German: Psychically in tune
Alfreta, Elfrida, Elfrieda

Ali/Allie/Ally — Nickname for names beginning with "Al"; *Ali* is also given as an Arabic name, "from Allah"

Alice — Greek: Truth
Aleta, Aletha, Alethea, Alicea, Alicia, Alisha, Alison, Allis, Allison, Allyce, Allys, Allyson, Alyce
It's a name used frequently in the arts, such as in Lewis Carroll's
Alice in Wonderland; *Booth Tarkington's* Alice Adams; *the films*
Alice Doesn't Live Here Anymore, *starring Ellen Burstyn, and*

Alice, *starring Mia Farrow; and, now in syndication, the TV series "Alice," starring Linda Lavin.*

Alida — Latin: Small winged one; Place name: An ancient city in Asia Minor noted for the manufacture of beautiful clothing.

Aleda, Aleta, Aletta, Alette, Alleda, Allida, Dela, Dila, Leda, Lida, Lita, Lyda, Lyta

Aliza — Hebrew: Joy

Aleeza, Alizah

Allegra — Italian: Joyous

Allison — See: Alice

Alma — Italian: Soul, spirit, warmhearted; Latin: Nourishing, bountiful

The ancient Romans called several goddesses Alma Mater (it meant nourishing or bounteous mother). Today, we call the school(s) we attended our alma mater.

Almira — Arabic: Princess, the exalted

Almera, Almyra, Elmira, Mera, Mira

Alpha — Greek: First one

Althea — Greek: Healthy, wholesome

Altheda, Althy, Thea

American tennis player Althea Gibson was the first black person to win a major tennis championship — she won the women's singles title at both the U.S. Open and at Wimbledon in 1957 and 1958.

Alva — Latin: White

Alvera — Latin: The all-truthful

Alvina — German: Noble friend

Alvinia, Elvena, Elvina, Vina

Alyssa — Greek: Logical

Alissa, Alyssum, Elissa, Ilyssa, Lissa, Lyssa

Amanda — Latin: Lovable

Amandee, Amandine, Amandis, Manda, Mandi, Mandie, Mandy, Mandye

In 1728, poet James Thomson wrote "Spring," which contained these two memorable lines:
"And thou, Amanda, come, pride of my song!
Formed by the Graces, loveliness itself."

Amarinda — Greek: Long lived

Amara, Mara, Rinda

Amaris — Hebrew: Whom God has promised

Amaryllis — Greek: Refreshing stream
Rilla, Ryllis

Amber — French: A deep-yellow jewel
Amberlie, Amby

Ambrosina — Greek: Immortal
Ambrosine, Brosina

Amelia — German: Industrious, stirring
Amalia, Amalie, Amelie, Amilia, Emelia, Emelie, Emelina, Mell, Millia
Amelia Earhart, the first female pilot to cross the Atlantic, certainly lived up to the meaning of this name.

Amelinda — Spanish: Beloved

Amethyst — Greek: An anti-intoxicant
This purple gemstone was and still is thought to have powers that can remedy drunkenness.

Amira — Arabic: Highborn girl
Amera, Amerah, Amirah, Amyra, Amyrah, Mera, Mira

Amity — Latin: Friendly

Amy — Latin: Beloved
Aimee, Amie, Amoret, Amoretta, Amorette, Amorita, Amye

Anastasia — Greek: Of the resurrection
Anastasie, Asia, Nastassia, Stacey, Stacie, Stacy, Stasia, Tacey, Tasia
This name belonged to the daughter of Russia's last czar, Nicholas II; her story has been popularized in books, plays, and films. After the Russian royal family was massacred in 1918, many theories about Anastasia's escape and survival emerged.

Andrea — Latin: Womanly
Andee, Andi, Andra, Andreana, Andria, Andriana, Andy

Anemone — Greek: Wind flower
In Greek legend, the nymph with this name was pursued by the wind and changed into a delicate flower.

Angel — See: Angela

Angela — Greek: Angel, messenger
Angel, Angele, Angelica, Angelika, Angelina, Angeline, Angelique, Angelot, Angey, Angie, Anjelica, Anjelika

Anica/Anika — Spanish: Graceful

Anita — See: Ann/Anne

Ann/Anne — Hebrew: Graceful
Ana, Anetta, Anina, Anisa, Anita, Anitra, Anna, Annette, Anney, Annick, Annie, Annina, Annisa, Anny, Anushka, Anya, Ayn

This name is known as "the name of queens," and for good reason: Anne, queen of Great Britain and Ireland; Anne of Austria; Anne of Brittany; Anne of Denmark; Anne Boleyn of England; Empress Anna of Russia; and, in modern times, Princess Anne of England.

Annabel — Hebrew: Beautiful, graceful
Annabella, Annabelle

Annamarie — Hebrew: Graceful, wished-for child (it's a combination of Ann and Mary)
Annemarie, Annamaria, Annemaria

Annette — See: Ann/Anne

Annora — Latin: Honor
Annorah, Anora, Anorah

Anthea — Greek: Flowerlike

Antoinette — See: Antonia

Antonia — Latin: Priceless
Antoinette, Antonetta, Antonette, Netta, Nettie, Netty, Tona, Toni, Tonia, Tonie, Tony, Tonya

Apollonia — Greek: Belonging to Apollo, the Greek god of sunlight, music, medicine, prophecy, and poetry

April — Latin: Open to the sun
Averel, Averil, Averyl, Avril

Arabella — Latin: Fair and beautiful altar
Ara, Arabela, Arabele, Arabelle

Ardelia — Latin: Zealous, ardent
Arda, Ardel, Ardella, Ardelle, Ardith, Ardra

Arden — Celtic: Lofty, eager
Arda, Ardena, Ardene

Ardis/Ardyce — Latin: Fervent, eager

Arela/Arella — Hebrew: Angel

Aretha — Greek: The best
Areta, Retha
Talk about the best and you'd have to talk about Aretha Franklin, the "Queen of Soul."

Ariana — Latin: Very holy, or pleasing one
Ari, Ariadna, Ariadne
Ariana was the mythological princess of ancient Crete.

Aricia — Greek: Princess of the royal blood of Athens
In Racine's version of Phaedra, *Aricia is Hippolytus's lover.*

Ariel — Hebrew: Lioness of God
Ariell, Ariella, Arielle

Arlen — See: Arlene

Arlene — Celtic: A pledge
Arla, Arlana, Arleana, Arleen, Arlen, Arlena, Arlette, Arlie, Arline, Arlise, Arliss, Arly, Arlyn, Arlyne, Arlynn, Arlyss

Armina — Latin: Of high degree
Armeda, Armida, Arminda, Armine, Armyn

Arnelle — Latin: The eagle rules
Arnella, Arnetta, Arnette

Artemis — Greek: Moon goddess
Artema, Artemisa, Artemise, Artie

Asha — Swahili: Life

Ashira — Hebrew: Wealthy

Ashley — English: From the ash-tree meadow
Ashlee, Ashleigh, Ashlie, Ashly

Asia — See: Anastasia

Astera — Greek: Star
Asta, Astra, Astre, Astrea, Astria

Astred/Astrid — Norse: Divine strength

Athena — Greek: Goddess of wisdom, reason, and purity

Aubrey — German: Elf-wise ruler
Aubrianna, Aubrianne, Aubrie, Aubry

Audrey — German: Noble
Audi, Audie, Audra, Audre, Audrea, Audreanna, Audree, Audrie, Audrielle, Audrina, Audrine, Audris, Audry

Augusta — Latin: High, revered
Auguste, Augustina, Augustine, Austina, Gus, Gussie, Gussy, Gusta, Gusti
Roman emperors took the title "Augustus" when they took the throne, while "Augusta" was the title of honor given to their female kin (mothers, wives, daughters, and sisters).

Aura — Greek: Breath of air
Aural, Aure

Aurelia — Latin: Golden
Aurea, Aurel, Aurelie, Aurie, Aurilla

Aurora — Latin: Goddess of the dawn
Aurore, Rora, Rori, Rorie, Rory

Autumn — Nature name: From the autumn/fall season

Ava — Latin: Bird

Avis — German: Refuge in war; Latin: Bird
This name is famous because of the car-rental company.

Aviva — Hebrew: Springtime, youthfulness, freshness
  Avivah, Viva
Ayla — Hebrew: Oak tree
  In Jean Auel's best seller, Clan of the Cave Bear, *the Cro-Magnon heroine is called Ayla.*
Azalea — Greek: Dry; English: Name of a flower
Aziza — Arabic: Beloved; Swahili: Very beautiful
Azura — French: Blue sky
  Azora, Azure, Azurine

B

Babette — See: Barbara
Bambalina — Italian: Little one
  Bambee, Bambi, Bambie
Bambi — See: Bambalina
Baptista — Latin: Baptizer
  Baptiste, Batista
Bara — Hebrew: To select
  Bari, Barra
Barbara — Greek: A stranger
  Bab, Babbie, Babette, Babita, Babs, Barb, Barbary, Barbe, Barbee, Barberi, Barbetta, Barbette, Barbey, Barbi, Barbie, Barbra, Barby, Barbye, Bobbee, Bobbi, Bobbie
  This is considered a power name for women: Barbra (née Barbara) Streisand, Barbara Walters, Barbara Bush. The name also enjoys favor with young girls because of the doll Barbie.
Barika — Swahili: Successful
Barrie — Irish: Spearlike
Basha — Polish: A stranger
Basilia — Greek: Regal
  Basile, Basilie, Basille
Bathilda/Bathilde — German: Commanding maiden of war
Bathsheba/Batsheva — Hebrew: Daughter of an oath, seventh daughter
Beatrice — Latin: She brings joy, bestower of blessings
  Bea, Beatrisa, Beatrix, Beatriz, Beattie, Beatty, Bebe, Trix, Trixi, Trixie, Trixy

How true when you think of the joy Beatrix Potter, author of Peter Rabbit *(among other tales), has brought to so many for so long.*

Becky — See: Rebecca

Bedelia — French: Strength

Belinda/Belynda — Spanish: Beautiful

Bella — Italian: Beautiful
Bel, Bela, Belah, Belia, Belita, Bell, Belle, Belva, Belvia

Bellanca — Greek: Stronghold; Italian: Blonde

Benedicta — Latin: Blessed; Spanish: Well spoken
Benedetta, Benedette, Benita, Bennie

Berdine — German: Shining from within

Bernadette — German: Courageous as a bear
Bernadene, Bernadetta, Bernadette, Bernadina, Bernadine, Bernadinia, Bernetta, Berni, Bernie, Bernita, Berny
The Song of Bernadette, *the book and film about the saintly visionary, popularized the name in the early 1940s.*

Bernice — Greek: Carrier of victory
Berènice, Berni, Bernie, Berny, Bernyce, Bernye, Berrie, Berry

Bertha — German: Glorious one
Berta, Berte, Berthe, Berti, Bertia, Bertie, Bertina, Bertine, Berty
This was a popular name in Victorian times, when it was also the name of a wide, ruffled — and concealing! — lace collar worn on low-cut dresses. A huge slot machine payoff in Las Vegas is known as a Big Bertha.

Beryl — Greek: Crystal clear
Berry, Beryle, Berylee, Berylla, Rylla

Bessie — See: Elizabeth

Beth — Hebrew: House of God
Bethel

Bethany/Bethani — Place name: A village near Jerusalem
Bethanie, Bethenee

Betsy — See: Elizabeth

Betty — See: Elizabeth

Beulah — Hebrew: Married woman
The biblical term for Israel is Land of Beulah.

Beverly — English: From the meadow of the beavers
Bev, Beverlee, Beverlie, Bevvy, Buffy

Bevin — Irish: Sweet singing maiden

Bianca — See: Blanche

Bibi — Arabic: Lady

Billie/Billy — German: Wise protector
  Billee, Billeena, Billi
Bina — Hebrew: Intelligence
Birdie — English: Little bird
  Bird, Birdella, Birdena, Birdene, Birdita
Blain/Blaine — Irish: Slender
  Blane, Blayne
Blair/Blaire — Celtic: Place; Scottish: Field of battle
Blaise — Latin: Stammers
  Blaize, Blayze, Blaze
Blake — English: Fair haired and pale
  Blakelee, Blakelie, Blakely
Blanche — French: Fair, pale
  Bianca, Blanca, Blancia, Blanka, Blinni, Blinnie, Blinny
  Playwright Tennessee Williams immortalized the name with the
  character Blanche DuBois in "A Streetcar Named Desire."
Blessing — English: A blessing
Bliss — English: Perfect joy
Blossom — English: Flower, bloom
Blythe — English: Cheerful one
  Blithe, Bly, Blyth
Bo — Chinese: Precious
  Thanks to actress Bo Derek, this name is thought of as "a ten."
Bobbie/Bobby — See: Barbara, Roberta
Bonita — Spanish: Pretty little one
Bonnie — Latin: Good one; Scottish: Charming, pretty
  Bona, Bonna, Bonnee, Bonni, Bonnibella, Bonnibelle, Bonny
Brandy/Brandi — Dutch: Fine wine
  Brandee, Brandice, Brandie, Brandyce, Brandyn
Brenda — German: Sword, fire stoker
Brenna — Celtic: Dark haired
Brett — Irish: From Britain
  Bret, Bretta, Brit, Britt, Britta, Brittany, Britte
Briana — Celtic: Strong
  Brea, Breanne, Bree, Bria, Brianna, Brianne, Brielle, Brina,
  Bryana, Bryanna
Bridget — Irish: Mighty, spirited
  Berget, Biddi, Biddie, Biddy, Birgitta, Bridgie, Bridie, Brigid,
  Brigida, Brigit, Brigitta, Brigitte, Brita
Brina/Bryna — Slavic: Protector
Bronwen/Bronwyn — Welsh: White bosomed

Brook/Brooke — English: To break out, bubbling stream
Model Brooke Shields has inspired many parents over the last decade to bestow this name upon their little girls.
Brunella — German: Wise, brown-haired woman
Brunetta, Brunilla
Bryna — Irish: Strength
Brynn — Irish: Heights
Bryn, Bryna, Brynna, Brynelle
Bunnie/Bunny — English: Small rabbit

C

Cadence — Latin: Melodious
Cadenza, Cadi, Cadie, Cady
Cai — Vietnamese: Female
Caitlin — See: Catherine
Calandra — Greek: Lark
Cal, Calandre, Calandria, Calla, Calli, Callie, Cally
Calantha/Calanthe — Greek: Lovely blossom
Caledonia — Latin: From Scotland
Caley — Gaelic: Slender
Caela, Caila, Cailley, Caleigh, Cayla, Cayley
Calida — Spanish: Loving, ardent
Caleda, Callida
Calista — Greek: Most beautiful
Callise, Callistra
Callan — German: Chatter
Calli, Callie, Cally
Camelia — Latin: A beautiful flower
Camille — Latin: Handmaiden
Cam, Camilia, Camilla, Cammi, Cammie, Cammila, Cammy
For a good cry, see the film classic Camille, *with Greta Garbo playing the title role.*
Candice — Greek: Pure, glowing white
Candace, Candee, Candi, Candida, Candide, Candie, Candis, Candra, Candy, Candyce, Kandace, Kandie, Kandy
The success of the sitcom "Murphy Brown," starring Candice Bergen, awakened an interest in the names Murphy and Candice.

Candida/Candide — See: Candice
Caprice — Italian: Whimsical, unpredictable
  Cappi, Cappy, Capri
Cara — Latin: Dear one
  Carah, Cari, Carita, Kara, Karah
Caress — French: Tender touch
  Caressa, Carress, Carressa, Charis
Carey — Welsh: Loving
  Caree, Cari, Carie, Carrey, Carri, Carrie, Carry, Cary
Carina — Spanish: Little darling
  Carena, Carin, Carine, Carinna
Carla — See: Carol/Carole
Carmel — Hebrew: God's vineyard; Place name: Mount Carmel, in Israel overlooking the Mediterranean
  Carmela, Carmella
Carmen — Spanish: Rosy red; Latin: Song
  Carmin, Carmina, Carmine, Charmaine
  There's not only a song for Carmen, but an entire opera by Bizet.
Carnation — Latin: Flesh colored; English: Name of a flower
Carnelian — Latin: A red gem
Carol/Carole — French: Song for rejoicing
  Carey, Cari, Carla, Carleen, Carlen, Carlene, Carlin, Carlina, Carline, Carlita, Carly, Carlyn, Carlynne, Caro, Carola, Carolin, Carolina, Caroline, Carolyn, Carolyne, Carri, Carrie, Carroll, Charyl, Cheryl, Cherylynne, Karla, Karole, Karolina, Karoly, Sheryl
Caroline — See: Carol/Carole
Caron — French: Pure
Carrie — See: Carol/Carole
Casey — See: Acacia
Cassandra — Greek: A prophetess for humankind
  Cass, Cassandre, Cassandry, Cassia, Cassie, Cassondra, Sanda, Sandee, Sandi, Sandie, Sandra, Sandy, Sondra
Cassidy — Irish: Curly haired
Casta — Latin: Modest, pure
  Castara, Casti, Casty
Catherine — Latin: Woman of purity (Also see: Katherine)
  Caitlin, Caitlyn, Caitrin, Caitrine, Carin, Caryn, Catarina, Catarine, Catharina, Cathee, Catherina, Cathi, Cathie, Cathleen, Cathlene, Cathryn, Cathrynne, Cathrynnia, Cathy, Catriona, Caty, Caye, Trina

Cathleen — See: Catherine

Cecania — German: Free

Cecelia — Latin: One who cannot see
Cacillia, Cacille, Ceci, Cecil, Cecile, Cecily, Ceil, Celee, Celia, Celie, Cicely, Cissi, Cissie, Cissy, Sisillia, Sisillya
Despite its meaning, this name has seen its share of fame: it's in poems by Pope and Dryden, in Chaucer's Canterbury Tales, *in paintings by Raphael and Rubens, in a hit song of the 1920s, and in a song sung by Simon & Garfunkel.*

Celandine — Greek: Swallow

Celeste — Latin: Heavenly
Cele, Celeka, Celena, Celene, Celesta, Celestee, Celestina, Celestine, Celestyn, Celestyna, Celina, Celinda, Celinka

Celia — See: Cecelia

Cella — Italian: Free one

Cerelia — Latin: Of the spring

Cerise — French: Cherry
Carise, Charise, Charrissee

Chandra — Hindi: Of the moon
Chandara, Chandria, Chandry

Chantal — French: Sing out loud
Chantalle, Chantel, Chantelle

Chara — Greek: Joy

Charissa — Greek: Graceful
Char, Chari, Charie, Charis, Charisse

Charity — Latin: Benevolent, loving
Charita, Charry
Thanks to Neil Simon's play and film, it's hard to hear this name without thinking of Charity Blackstock, better known as "Sweet Charity."

Charlotte — German: Strong but feminine
Carlota, Carlote, Carlotie, Carlotta, Carlotte, Char, Charla, Charleen, Charlene, Charlotta, Charmaine
If the film Hush, Hush, Sweet Charlotte *comes to mind, you can replace that thought with English novelist Currer Bell, the pen name used by Charlotte Brontë.*

Charmaine — See: Carmen, Charlotte

Charmian — Greek: Source of joy

Charo — Spanish: Nickname meaning "little Rosa"

Chastity — Latin: Purity
Sonny and Cher gave their daughter this name in 1969.

Chaya — Hebrew: Life

Chelsea — English: Port, landing place
Chelsee, Chelsey, Chelsie, Chelsy

Chenoa — Native American: White dove

Cher — French: Dear one
Chere, Cheri, Cherice, Cherie, Cherye, Sher, Shere, Sherri, Sherrie, Sherry

Cheryl — See: Carol/Carole

Chesna — Slavic: Peaceful
Ches, Chessa, Chessy, Chezna

Chiquita — Spanish: Little girl
Chickee, Chickie, Chicky
Anyone with this name is sure to be top banana!

Chloe — Greek: New grass
Chlo, Clo, Cloe, Cloey

Chloris/Cloris — Greek: Pale flower
Actress Cloris Leachman has brought attention to this name ever since she appeared on "The Mary Tyler Moore Show."

Cho — Japanese: Butterfly

Cholena — Native American (Delaware): Bird

Christabelle — Greek: Fair Christian
Christabel, Christabell, Christabella, Christobella, Christobelle

Christina/Christine — Greek: Christian one
Caristina, Caristine, Chris, Chrisa, Chrissi, Chrissie, Chrissy, Christa, Christiana, Christiane, Christie, Christy, Chryste, Cris, Crissi, Crissie, Crissy, Cristina, Cristine, Cristy, Kris, Kristina, Kristine, Tina

Chrysanthemum — Greek: A gold flower

Cicely — See: Cecilia

Cinderella — French: Little one of the ashes
Cindee, Cindie, Cindy
The children's classic fairy tale has made this name symbolize happy endings.

Cindy — See: Cinderella, Cynthia, Lucinda

Cipriana — Italian: From Cyprus
Cipriann, Cypriana, Cyprienne

Clair/Claire — See: Clara

Clara — Greek: Bright, clear
Clair, Claira, Claire, Clarabelle, Clare, Clareta, Claretta, Clarette, Clarice, Clarie, Clarinda, Clarissa, Clarita, Clary, Clarye, Klara

Claudia — Latin: Lame one
Claude, Claudetta, Claudette, Claudina, Claudine, Claudy
Despite its unfortunate meaning, this name is one of the oldest surviving names in Britain and became quite popular in France because of Queen Claude.

Cleantha/Cliantha — Greek: Glory flower

Clementine — Greek: Merciful one
Clem, Clemence, Clemency, Clementia, Clementina, Clemenza, Clemmie

Cleopatra/Cleo — Greek: Famed
The most famous woman to have this name was the queen of Egypt — that is, until Elizabeth Taylor!

Clio/Cleo — Greek: Proclaimer

Clorina — Persian: Renowned

Cloris — See: Chloris

Clothilda — German: Notable war maid
Clotilda, Clotilde, Tilda, Tildie, Tildy

Clover — English: Fragrant flower

Cody — English: Pillow
Codey, Codi, Codie

Colette — Latin: Victorious
Coletta, Collatte, Collie
Sidonie Gabrielle Colette (1873–1954) was the famous French novelist who used only her surname, Colette.

Colleen — Irish: Girl
Collene, Colline, Collyne

Columba — Latin: Dove
Columbia, Columbina, Columbine

Comfort — Latin: To strengthen

Conception — Latin: Beginning
Concepcion, Conceptiona

Concha — Greek: Shell
Conchetta, Conchette, Conchita

Connie — See: Constance

Constance — Latin: Firmness, steadfastness
Conni, Connie, Conny, Constancia, Constancy, Constantia, Constanza, Konstanza, Konstanze

Consuela — Spanish: Wonderful friend
Consolata, Consuelo

Cora — Greek: Maiden
Coretta, Corette, Corey, Cori, Corina, Corinna, Corinne, Corissa,

Corisse, Corrine, Corry, Corynna, Kora, Koran, Koren, Kori, Kory

Corabelle — Greek: Beautiful maiden
Corabell, Corabella

Coral — Latin: Coral from the sea
Coralie, Coralina, Coraline

Corazon — Spanish: Heart
Because of the dramatic events in the Philippines in 1986, which resulted in the presidency of Corazon Aquino, the name Corazon is now known worldwide and represents "courage" as well as "heart."

Cordelia — Welsh: Sea jewel; Celtic: Daughter of the sea
Corda, Cordella, Cordelle, Cordie, Cordy
According to old Welsh legend, Cordelia was the daughter of Ler, King of the Sea. Appropriately enough, Shakespeare named one of King Lear's daughters Cordelia.

Coretta — See: Cora

Corinna/Corinne — See: Cora

Corliss — English: Cheerful
Corlie

Cornelia — Latin: Womanly virtue
Cornela, Cornelie, Cornelle

Cosette — German: Pet lamb
Cossetta, Cozette

Cosima — Greek: Order, harmony

Courtney — English: Of the court
Courtlynn

Crescent — Latin: To increase, to create
Cres, Crescence, Crescencia, Cresentia, Cressie, Cressy

Crystal — Latin: Clear as ice
Chrystal, Cryssie, Crystie, Krystal

Cybela/Cybele — Greek: Divine Mother

Cybil — See: Sibyl

Cymbaline — Celtic: Lord of the sun

Cynara — Greek: Thistle plant

Cynthia — Greek: Moon
Cinda, Cindee, Cindi, Cindy, Cyndie, Cyndy, Cynthie

Cyrena — Greek: From Cyrene (ancient African capital)
Cyra, Cyri

Cyrilla — Latin: Lordly, proud
Cerella, Cira, Ciri, Cirilla, Cyri

D

Dacey — American English: Southern girl

Dacia — Place name: In ancient Rome, the region north of the Danube

Dagmar — Danish: Joy of the land
This was the name of a queen of Denmark.

Dahlia/Dalia — Norse: From the valley
This is also an exotic flower named for Dahl, a Swedish botanist.

Daisy — English: Name of a flower
Daisee, Daisie
The name became very popular in the 1890s when Henry Dacre wrote the song that starts: "Daisy, Daisy, give me your answer, do! I'm half crazy, all for the love of you." Picking off the petals of a daisy is said to determine whether "(s)he loves me" or "(s)he loves me not."

Dakota/Dakotah — Native American (Sioux): Friend

Dale — German: Valley dweller
Dael, Daile, Dalena, Dayle

Dalila — Swahili: Gentle

Dallas — German: Playful; Scottish: From the meadows of the valley

Dama — Latin: Gentle lady

Damaris — Greek: Gentle, trusting
Damara

Damiana — Greek: One who tames
Damiana is an herb that some believe has aphrodisiacal properties.

Damita — Spanish: Little noble lady

Dana — Celtic: Mother of the gods
Danae, Danella, Danelle, Danice

Danica — Slavic: Morning star

Daniela/Daniele — Hebrew: Judged by God
Danella, Danelle, Danetta, Danette, Dani, Dania, Danice, Danicee, Daniella, Danielle, Danita, Danna, Danni, Dannia, Dannie, Danny

Daphne — Greek: Laurel tree

Daffi, Daffie, Daffy, Daffye, Daphna, Daphnie, Daphney, Daphny
Novelist Daphne du Maurier helped popularize this name.

Dara — Hebrew: Heart of wisdom; English: Compassion
Daralice, Daralise, Dareen

Darby — Irish: Free person
Darbiana, Darbianne, Darbie, Darbra

Darcie — Celtic: Dark girl; French: Of the fortress
Darcee, Darcy, Darsey, Darsy

Dardanella — Greek: Feminine of Dardanos, a son of Zeus

Daria/Darya — Greek: Possessing wealth

Darlene — French: Little darling
Darell, Darelle, Darla, Darleen, Darline, Darly, Darryl, Darylle

Darryl — See: Darlene

Davida — Hebrew: Beloved one
Daveda, Davene, Davina, Davita, Devina, Veda, Vida

Dawn — English: Daybreak

Daya/Dayah — Hebrew: Bird

Deanna — See: Diana

Deborah — Hebrew: Bee, to speak kind words
Deb, Debbi, Debbie, Debby, Debi, Debora, Debra, Devora, Devore

Deirdre — Irish: Raging one; English: Young girl
Dede, Dee, Deidra, Deidre, Derdre, Didi, Didie, Dierdra, Dierdre

Delicia — Latin: Delightful one
Delica, Delice, Delight, Delize, Delizia

Delilah — Hebrew: Poor, heir; Arabic: Guide, leader
Dalila, Delila, Lila, Lilah

Della — Greek: Visible; German: Noble
Dehlia, Delea

Delma — Spanish: Of the sea; German: Noble protector

Delpha — Greek: Dolphin
Delphi, Delphine, Delphina, Delfine

Delta — Greek: The fourth
Delta Burke made a name for herself as one of the original four "Designing Women" on the popular sitcom.

Demetria — Greek: Of Demeter, Greek goddess of the harvest
Demeter, Demetra, Demetri, Demetrice, Demetris, Demi, Demmi, Dimitra

Demi — See: Demetria

Actress Demi Moore, born Demi Guynes, knows that an unusual first name worked for her. Maybe that's why she and husband Bruce Willis named their daughters Rumer Glenn and Scout LaRue.

Dena — English: From the valley

Denise — French: Follower of Dionysus, the Greek god of wine
Denni, Dennie, Denny, Dennye, Denyse

Desdemona — Greek: Ill-fated one
Desdemonda, Desmona

Desire/Desiree — French: Hoped for, long awaited
Desideria, Desirata

Deva — Hindi: Divine

Devona — English: Defender

Devora — See: Deborah

Diamanta — French: Like a diamond
Diamante, Diamond, Diamonique

Diana/Diane — Latin: Divine, bright one
Deana, Deandra, Deane, Deanna, Dede, Dee, Deena, Deenie, Dena, Di, Diahnn, Dian, Diandra, Dianna, Dianne, Didi, Dyan, Dyana, Dyane, Dyanna, Dyanne
Diana Spencer brought new appeal to the name when she married Great Britain's Prince Charles in 1981 and became Lady Diana, Princess of Wales.

Diantha/Dianthe — Greek: Divine flower

Dillian — Latin: Worshiped one
Dilli, Dilliana

Dilys — Welsh: Genuine

Dina — See: Dinah, Geraldina/Geraldine

Dinah — Hebrew: Judgment
Dina, Dinorah, Dyna, Dynah
The song says it all: "Dinah, is there anyone finer?"

Dionne — Greek: Daughter of heaven
Dion, Diona, Dione, Dionna, Dyon, Dyonne

Dita — Czech: Rich gift

Dixie — American English: Girl from the South; Norse: Active sprite

Dodie — Hebrew: Beloved
Doda, Dodi, Dody

Dollie/Dolly — See: Dorothy

Dolores — Spanish: Sorrowful one
Delores, Deloris, Dolorita, Doloritas

Dominique — French: Belonging to God
Dom, Domeniga, Domina, Domine, Dominga, Domini, Dominica, Dominiqua

Donata — Italian: Gift from God

Donna — Italian: Woman worthy of respect
Dona, Donee, Donella, Donia, Donie, Donni, Donny

Dora — Greek: Gift
Doral, Doralea, Doralyn, Doralynn, Dorelai, Dorella, Dorelle, Doretta, Dorette, Dori, Dorian, Dorita, Doro

Dorcas — Greek: Gazelle
Dorcia

Dorena/Dorene — French: Golden girl
Doreen, Doreena, Dorina, Dorine

Doria — Greek: From the sea

Dorinda — Greek: Beautiful one

Doris — Greek: From the sea
Dori, Dorice, Dorisa, Dorita, Dorri, Dorrie, Dorris, Dorry, Dory, Dorys, Dorysa

Dorothy — Greek: God's gift
Dolley, Dolli, Dollie, Dolly, Dorotea, Doroteya, Dorothea, Dorothee, Dortha, Dorthy, Dot, Dotti, Dotty
All forms of this name were popular in the United States in the early 1800s, thanks to trendsetting first lady Dorothea Payne Madison, better known as Dolley Madison.

Drew — Greek: Masculine
Actress Drew Barrymore drew our attention to this name when she played the little girl in the 1982 film E.T.

Drina — Spanish: Helper of humankind

Drusilla — Greek: Eyes of innocence
Dru, Druci, Drucie, Drucilla, Drucy, Drusie, Drusy

Dulcie — See: Dulcinea

Dulcinea — Spanish: Sweet
Delcina, Delcine, Dulce, Dulcea, Dulcet, Dulcia, Dulcie, Dulcine, Dulcy
The woman with this sweet name helped Don Quixote dream the impossible dream in "The Man of La Mancha."

Dyani — Native American: Deer

Dyna — Greek: Powerful

E

Earlene — English: A title of nobility

Eartha — English: Child of the earth
Erda, Erta
The exotic singer/actress Eartha Kitt made this name known in America.

Easter — English: Of the springtime

Ebony — English: Symbol of black beauty

Echo — Greek: Repeated sound
In mythology, Echo was a nymph whose love for Narcissus was unrequited. She pined away for his affection until only her voice remained . . . remained . . . remain . . . rema . . . .

Edana — Celtic: Fiery one

Edda — English: Rich, prosperous

Eden — Hebrew: Pleasure

Edina — English: Prospering, joyful

Edith — English: Wonderful gift
Eda, Ede, Edeva, Edi, Edie, Edita, Editha, Edithe, Ediva, Edy, Edyth, Edythe, Eydie
This name was held by two of our country's first ladies: Edith Kermit Carow (wife of Theodore Roosevelt) and Edith Bolling Galt (wife of Woodrow Wilson).

Edlyn — English: Of the nobility

Edmonda — English: Rich protector
Edmondia, Edmunda

Edna — Hebrew: Delightful, renewal
Eadie, Eadna, Eddi, Eddie
Edna Ferber, novelist (Giant) and playwright ("Show Boat"), is the most famous Edna in America — especially among cross-word-puzzle creators!

Edwina — English: Rich friend
Eadwina, Eadwyne, Edwinette, Win, Winnie

Efrona — Hebrew: Sweet-singing bird

Efia — Fante (African): Born on a Friday

Eileen — Irish: Glowing light; Also see: Aileen
Eilene, Ileen, Ilene

Elaine — Greek: A light

Elana, Elane, Elani, Elayna, Elayne, Laina, Laine, Lainie, Layna, Layne, Laynie

Eleanor — French: Brilliant light

Elanor, Elanora, Elanore, Eleanora, Eleanore, Elenora, Elenore, Elinor, Elinore, Elladine, Elle, Elna, Elnora, Elnore, Elora, Elore, Leanor, Lenore, Leonora, Leonore, Nora, Norah

Question: Can you name a first lady and a song that both have the initials E. R.? Answer: Eleanor Roosevelt and "Eleanor Rigby," respectively.

Electra/Elektra — Greek: Shining star

Eleora/Eliora — Hebrew: The Lord is my light

Elissa/Elyssa — See: Elizabeth

Elita — French: Special one

Eliza — See: Elizabeth

Elizabeth — Hebrew: Consecrated to God, oath of God

Babette, Belita, Bess, Besse, Bessie, Bessy, Betsey, Betsy, Betta, Bette, Betti, Bettina, Bettine, Betty, Betze, Elisabeth, Elisabetta, Elissa, Eliza, Elizabet, Helsa, Lisette, Lissie, Lizabet, Lizabeth, Lizzie, Lizzy

This regal name is associated with European royalty, but American royalty also favors the name. Do you know who Elizabeth Bloomer Warren Ford is? We knew her as Betty Ford when she was our first lady. President James Monroe was married to an Elizabeth — Elizabeth Kortright, whose nickname was Eliza. President Andrew Johnson's wife was born with the name Eliza — Eliza McCardle — and let's not forget Bess Wallace, wife of President Harry S. Truman.

Ella — English: Elfin

Eletta, Elette, Elli, Ellie, Elly, Ellye

Say "Ella" to anyone who loves jazz and they'll assume you're referring to the great Ella Fitzgerald, inducted into the Jazz Hall of Fame in 1985.

Ellen/Ellyn — Greek: Light

As you proceed through the "E" list of names, you'll see several first ladies mentioned, and there are two right here: Ellen Lewis Herndon, wife of Chester Arthur, and Ellen Louise Axson, first wife of Woodrow Wilson.

Elma — Greek: Pleasant

Eloisa/Eloise — See: Louisa/Louise

Elsa — German: Noble woman

Elsey, Elsie

Elvira — German: Elfin charm
Elva, Elve, Elvera, Elvina, Elvire, Elwire, Elwirea

Elysia — Latin: Blissful, rapturous
Elisa, Elise, Elyse, Ilise, Ilysa, Ilyse

Emalia/Emelia — Latin: Flatterer

Emerald/Emeraud — French: A green jewel

Emily — German: Industrious one
Amalea, Amalia, Amalie, Amelia, Amelie, Ameline, Amelita, Emelda, Emelina, Emeline, Emelita, Emera, Emilia, Emilie, Emiline, Emlyn, Emma, Emmaline, Emmalyn, Emmey, Emmy, Emmye
This is a name of some pretty industrious writers: Emily Dickinson, who wrote some eighteen hundred poems, and Emily Brontë, who is best known for her novel Wuthering Heights.

Emma — See: Emily

Emmanuella/Emmanuelle — Hebrew: God is among us

Endora — Hebrew: Fountain
If you don't personally know anyone with this name, yet it still seems familiar to you, it may be because you've watched "Bewitched," the TV sitcom in which Samantha's mother (Agnes Moorehead) was called Endora.

Enid — Celtic: Purity

Enola — French: Ennobled

Erica/Erika — Norse: Eternal ruler, the queenly
Ericha, Rica, Ricka, Ricki, Rickie, Ricky, Rikki
In keeping with the name's definition, Erica Kane, the leading character on "All My Children," seems to be the eternal queen of daytime TV. Susan Lucci has played that part for over twenty years . . . without winning an Emmy, despite countless nominations!

Erin — Irish: Peace
Erinn, Erinna, Erinne, Eryn

Erma — See: Irma

Ernestine — German: Earnest one
Erna, Ernesta, Ernestina, Tina

Esmerelda/Ezmerelda — Greek: Precious jewel
Esmie, Ezmie

Esperanza — Spanish: Hope

Estelle — Latin: Star
Estel, Estele, Estell, Estella, Estrelita, Estrelite, Estrella, Stella, Stellita

Esther — Hebrew: Star
  Essie, Essy, Essye, Ester, Etti, Ettie, Etty
Ethel — German: Noble
  Ethelda, Ethelin, Etheline, Ethyl
Etta — German: Little, tiny
Eudora — Greek: Priceless gift
Eugenia — Greek: Wellborn
  Eugenie, Geena, Gena, Gene, Genia, Genie, Gennie
Eulalia — Greek: Articulate, well spoken
  Eula, Eulalie, Eulaylia, Lallie, Lally
Eunice — Greek: Happy victory
  Unice, Younice
Euphemia/Euphemie — Greek: Of great fame
  Effie, Effy, Ephemia, Ephie, Euphemy
Eurydice — Greek: Broad separation
Eustacia — Latin: Fruitful
  Stacey, Staci, Stacie, Stacy, Tacia, Tacie
Evangeline — Greek: Proclaimer of good news
  Angel, Angie, Evan, Evangelina
Eve — Hebrew: Life giving
  Eba, Eva, Evaleen, Evalene, Evelina, Eveline, Evelyn, Evey, Evie, Evita, Evonne, Evy
  Here we could discuss Eve, the first woman, or the films The Three Faces of Eve *and* All About Eve. *But since a lot of pregnant women will be reading this, we've chosen a thought-provoking theory called the Eve Principle. It's the idea that all fetuses initially are female, until a biological process occurs in the womb, making about half of them male.*
Evelyn — See: Eve
Ezrela — Hebrew: Reaffirmation of belief in God

F

Fabia — Latin: Bean grower
Faith/Fayth — Latin: The believing, the faithful
Fallon — Irish: In charge
Fancie/Fancy — Greek: Imagination
Fannie/Fanny — See: Frances

Farrah — English: Lovely, attractive; Arabic: Happy
Farrah Fawcett-Majors burst on the scene in 1976 to star in "Charlie's Angels." And if you meet a Farrah today, chances are good that she was born at the end of the seventies.

Fatima — Muslim: Descendant of the wife of the prophet Mohammed

Faun/Fawn — Latin: Young deer

Fay/Faye — French: Fairy, magical creature
Fayette, Fayine, Fayne
Fay Wray was the leading lady in the original film version of King Kong.

Fayme — French: Held in high esteem

Fedora — See: Theodora

Felda — German: From the field

Felicia — Latin: Happy
Felice, Felicie, Felicity, Felidad, Felita, Feliza, Felizia

Fenella/Finella — Celtic: White shouldered
Fionulla, Fynola

Fern — English: Wing, feather, fern plant

Fernanda — Spanish: World traveler, adventurer
Ferdinanda, Ferdinande, Fernandetta, Fernandette, Fernandia, Fernandina

Fidela — Latin: Faithful one
Fidelia, Fidelita, Fidelity

Fifi — See: Josephine

Filomena/Philomena — Greek: Loving, harmony

Fiona/Fionna — Irish: Ivory skinned

Fira — English: Fiery

Flavia — Latin: Blonde one

Flora — Latin: Flower
Fleur, Flo, Flor, Flore, Florella, Floria, Florie, Floris, Florrie, Florry

Florence — Latin: Flowering, successful
Floran, Florance, Florancia, Florentia, Flori, Florida, Florina, Florinda, Florine, Flossi, Flossie, Flossy
On July 4, 1820, Florence Nightingale was born and named for the city of her birth — Florence, Italy. She became the first and most famous of war nurses.

Flower — French: Blossom

Fortune — Latin: Destiny, chance
Fortuna, Fortunata

Frances — Latin: Free

Fan, Fanchetta, Fanchette, Fanchon, Fania, Fanni, Fannie, Fanny, Fanya, Fran, Francesca, Franci, Francie, Francine, Francisca, Francoise, Franki, Frankie, Frannie, Franny, Frannye

First lady Frances Folsom was the wife of President Grover Cleveland.

Francesca — See: Frances

Francine — See: Frances

Franki/Frankie — See: Frances

Frayda/Frayde — Yiddish: Joy

Freda/Freida/Frieda — See: Frederica

Frederica — German: Peaceful ruler

Federa, Federe, Federicka, Freda, Fredda, Freddie, Freddy, Frederique, Freida, Frida, Frieda, Fryda, Ricki, Rickie, Ricky, Rikki

This name was created by the followers of Frederick the Great, the eighteenth-century king of Prussia, who wanted to honor their king by naming their newborn daughters after him.

Freya — Norse: Highborn lady

In Norse mythology Freya is the goddess of love and beauty.

Fritzi/Fritzie — German: Benevolent ruler

Frodina/Frodine — German: Learned friend

Fulvia — Latin: Golden haired

G

Gabrielle — Hebrew: Woman of God

Gabey, Gabella, Gabi, Gabie, Gabriela, Gabriele, Gabriella, Gabrilla, Gaby, Gavra, Gavrale, Gavrell, Gavrella

Gaia — Greek: The earth

Gail — English: Lively

Gael, Gaela, Gale, Galey, Galie, Gayla, Gayle, Gayleen, Gaylene, Gaylia

Gala — Spanish: From Gaul

Galatea — Greek: Milky white

Galina/Galinka — Russian: White light

Galya/Galye — Hebrew: God has redeemed

Gana — Hebrew: Garden
Gania, Ganya
Ganesa — Hindi: Good luck
Gardenia — Early American English: Beautiful scented flower
The flower is named after the American botanist Dr. Alexander Garden (1730–91).
Garland — French: Wreath of flowers
Garnet — German: A dark-red jewel
Garnetta, Garnette, Garnettia
Gavrilla — Hebrew: Heroine
Gay/Gaye — French: Merry
Gayora — Hebrew: Valley of light
Gelasia — Greek: Inclined to laughter
Gela, Gelacey, Gelasie, Lacey, Lacie, Lacy, Lasia
Gemina — Greek: Twin
Gemie, Gemini, Geminie, Mina
Gemma — Italian: Jewel
Gena — See: Eugenia, Gina
Gene — See: Eugenia
Genevieve — See: Guinevere
Georgia — Latin: Earth lover
Georgeanna, Georgeanne, Georgena, Georgene, Georgette, Georgey, Georgianna, Georgianne, Georgie, Georgina, Georgine, Georgy, Jorja, Jorji, Jorjie, Jorjy
Artist Georgia O'Keeffe was born in Wisconsin but named for the southern state.
Geraldine — German: Mighty with a spear
Deena, Deenie, Deeny, Dina, Geralda, Geraldina, Gerarda, Gerarde, Gerardetta, Gerardette, Geri, Gerri, Gerrie, Gerry, Giralda, Giralde, Giraldina, Giraldine, Jeri, Jerrie, Jerry
Geraldine (Gerry) Ferraro, the first woman to run for the vice-presidency, was named for her brother, Gerald, who had died in an accident two years before she was born.
Geranium — Greek: Crane (the bird, not the machinery!)
Gerda — German: Protected one
Germaine — French: From Germany
Germa, Germain, Germana, Germane, Germayne, Jermaine, Jermayne
Gertrude — German: Spear maiden
Gerta, Gerti, Gertie, Gertrud, Gertruda, Gerty, Truda, Trude, Trudel, Trudi, Trudie, Trudy, Trudye

Who'd have thought that Gertie, the most familiar form of this old-fashioned name, would be the name of Elliot's kid sister (played by Drew Barrymore) in the film E.T.?

Geva — Hebrew: Hill

Ghislaine — German: Sweet pledge

Gianina — Italian: God is gracious
Gia, Gianetta, Giannina, Ginetta, Ginette, Giovana, Giovanna, Giovanne

Gigi — See: Gilberta

Gilana — Hebrew: Joy
Geela, Gila, Gilada, Gilah, Gilia, Gillie, Gilly

Gilberta — German: Brilliant
Gigi, Gilberte, Gilbertina, Gilbertine

Gilda — English: Covered with gold

Gillian — Latin: Young child
Gillee, Gilli, Gillie, Gilly, Gillye

Gina — Japanese: Silvery
Geena, Gena

Ginat — Hebrew: Garden

Ginger — Latin: The ginger spice
It's the nickname of Virginia Rogers, best known for her dance routines with Fred Astaire.

Giselle — German: Pledge
Gisela, Gisele, Giselia, Gizel, Gizela, Gizelle, Sella, Zella, Zelly

Gita — Slavic: Pearl

Gladys — Latin: Sword
Glad, Gladey, Gladie, Gladsy, Gleda, Gledy

Glenda — Irish: From the valley
Glendan, Glendane, Glendeen, Glendene, Gleni, Glenina, Glenine, Glenna, Glennis, Glyn, Glyna, Glynis, Glynisa, Glynnis, Glynnisa, Glynny

Gloria — Latin: Glory
Glorey, Glori, Glorian, Gloriann, Glorianna, Glorianne, Glorien, Glory, Glorya

Glynis/Glynnis — See: Glenda

Godiva — English: Gift of God

Golda — English: Gold
Goldan, Goldey, Goldi, Goldie, Goldina, Goldy
Golda Meir became prime minister of Israel in 1969.

Grace — Latin: Graceful one, favor, blessing

Gracella, Gracia, Gracie, Gracielle, Grata, Gratia, Gratiana, Gratiane, Grayce, Graycey, Graycia, Gracy
Actress Grace Kelly did a lot to inspire parents to name their daughters Grace, and even more so when she became Princess Grace of Monaco.

Greer — Scottish: Watchwoman

Gregoria — Greek: The awakened

Greta/Gretta — Greek: Pearl
Grata, Gretal, Gretchen, Gretel, Gretyl

Gretchen — See: Greta/Gretta

Griselda — German: War heroine
Griseldies, Grishilda, Grizel, Grizelda, Grizella, Selda, Zelda

Guenevere/Guinevere — Welsh: White wave
Genevieva, Genevieve, Genevra, Genna, Genni, Gennie, Gennifer, Genny, Ginevra, Ginevre, Guenevera, Guenn, Guinn, Guinna, Guinnavere, Zenavere, Zenevera, Zenevieve

Gulla — Norse: Divine sea

Gunda — Scandinavian: Battle maiden

Gwendolyn — Welsh: White browed, fair
Gwen, Gwendolen, Gwendolin, Gwenna, Gwenni, Gwenny, Gwennye, Gwyna, Gwyndolin, Gwyned, Gwyneth, Gwynne

Gypsy — English: Wanderer
Ask your parents about Gypsy Rose Lee, a wonderful character and the inspiration for the award-winning musical play and film Gypsy.

Gytha — English: Gift

H

Habiba — Arabic: Lover

Hadara — Hebrew: Bedecked in beauty

Hadassa/Hadassah — Hebrew: Flowering myrtle
Dassa, Dassi
Hadassah is best known as a Jewish women's philanthropic organization.

Haidee — Greek: Honored, well behaved

Hailey — Scottish: Hero; English: Field of hay
Hailee, Haili, Haleigh, Hali, Haylee, Hayley, Haylie

Halfrida — German: Peaceful heroine
Hallie — Greek: Thinking of the sea
Hallee, Halli, Halley
Hana/Hanae — Japanese: Blossom
Hanele/Hannele — Hebrew: Merciful
Hannah — Hebrew: Graceful
Hana, Hanna, Hanni, Hannie, Hanny, Hannye
Happi/Happy — English: Delighted
Harlene — English: Meadow of the hares
Harlee, Harleen, Harley, Harlie
Harmony — Latin: Unity, in tune
Harriet — French: Ruler of the home
Harra, Harre, Harri, Harrie, Harrietta, Harriette, Harriot, Hatti, Hattie, Hatty
Hattie — See: Harriet
Hazel — English: Forceful authority
Heather — English: Shrub with violet flowers
Hedda — German: Strife
Heda, Hedara, Hedarina, Hedde, Heddi, Heddie, Heddy, Hedvig, Hedwig, Hedy
Heidi — German: Noble, kind
Helaine/Helayne — See: Helen
Helen — Greek: Shining light
Helaine, Helayne, Helena, Helene, Helenka, Helli, Jelena, Jelene, Lainie
This was one of the most popular names in Greece and in Troy. It's also been popular in America for a long time. President William Howard Taft's first lady was Helen Herron. The first lady of the Broadway stage is Helen Hayes. The first lady to make "I Am Woman" a hit song was Helen Reddy.
Helga — German: Religious
Helica/Helice — Greek: Spiral
Heloise — German: Glory, battle; French: Renowned fighter
The columnist Heloise has made her name synonymous with helpful household hints.
Helsa — English: Swan
Henrietta — German: Ruler of private property
Enrica, Enrice, Enrichetta, Enricia, Etta, Ettie, Etty, Hendrika, Henki, Henny, Henrie, Henrieta, Henriette, Henryetta, Hetty, Yetta
Hepzibah — Hebrew: Filled with joy

Hera — Latin: Queen

Hermione — Greek: Noble woman
  Hermanie, Hermia, Hermina, Hermy

Hermosa — Latin: Lovely

Herta/Hertha — German: Mother Earth

Hesper — Greek: Evening star

Hester/Hesther — Greek and Hebrew: Star
  Hettie, Hetty

Hilary/Hillary — Greek: Pleasant, cheerful

Hilda — German: Battle maiden
  Hilde, Hildie, Hildy, Ilda, Ildie, Ildy

Hildegarde — German: Stronghold
  Hildegarde is a famous chanteuse whose theme song is "Darling Je Vous Aime Beaucoup."

Hilma — German: Protection

Hinda — Hebrew: Deer

Hisa — Japanese: Long lasting
  Hisae, Hisako, Hisayo

Hollace — English: From the holly tree
  Hollis, Holly

Honey — English: Sweet one, sweet liquid from a bee

Honora — Latin: With honor
  Honia, Honor, Honore, Honoria, Honorine, Nora, Norah

Hope — English: Optimistic expectation
  This name was popular among the Puritans and was the name of the character played by Mel Harris on the TV series "Thirtysomething."

Hortense — Latin: Gardener
  Hortencia, Hortensia, Hortie, Ortense

Huberta — German: Brilliant mind

Hulda — German: Loved one
  Huldie, Huldy

Hyacinth — Greek: A sweet-smelling flower; Also see: Jacinta
  Hyacindy, Hyacintha, Hyacinthia, Jacinta

I

Ida — English: Prosperous; German: Youthful; Norse: Diligent
Idalina, Idaline, Idella, Idelle, Idetta, Idette, Idona, Idonia
Ida Saxton was married to President William McKinley.

Idelia — German: Noble

Idola — Greek: Idolized

Ignacia — Latin: Ardent
Ignatia, Ignea, Ignia, Nacia, Nacy

Ila — English: Insulated

Ilana — Hebrew: Tree
Ileana, Ileane, Ileanna

Ilka — Slavic: Industrious
Elka, Elke, Elky, Ilke, Ilkie, Ilky

Ilona — Hungarian: Beautiful
Ilonka, Lona, Lonka

Ima — Japanese: Now, the present

Imelda — Spanish: Powerful fighter

Imogene — Latin: Image, blameless, innocent
Emogen, Emogene, Emojean, Imogena
*In the early days of television, Imogene Coca was Sid Caesar's
brilliantly funny co-star on "Your Show of Shows."*

Ina — See: Agnes

Ines/Inez — Greek: Chaste, pure

Inga/Inge — See: Ingrid

Ingrid — Norse: Hero's daughter
Inga, Ingaberg, Inge, Ingeberg, Inger
*When Swedish actress Ingrid Bergman made a name for herself
in America, her very "foreign" name became a very familiar
name to Americans.*

Iola — Greek: Violet colored

Iolana — Hawaiian: To soar like a hawk

Iona/Ione — Greek: Violet-colored stone

Irene — Greek: Peace
Erena, Erene, Irena, Irenie, Ireny, Irina, Irine, Iriny

Iris/Irisa — Greek: Rainbow; English: Name of a flower

Irma/Erma — Latin: Noble; German: Power
Ermina, Ermine, Irme, Irmina, Irminie

Erma Bombeck, best-selling author and humor columnist, is syndicated in over one thousand newspapers and read by thirty million people throughout the world.

Irvette — English: Friend from the sea

Isabel — Spanish: Consecrated to God
Isa, Isabeau, Isabelita, Isabella, Isabelle, Isobel, Isobela, Isobella, Isobelle, Issi, Issie, Issy, Izabel, Ysabel, Ysobel
Isabella I, the queen of Castile and Aragon, and wife of Ferdinand II, financed Christopher Columbus's voyage to the New World.

Isadora/Isidora — Latin: Gift of Isis (the Egyptian moon goddess)
Sadora, Sadore, Zadora, Zohra
Isadora Duncan was one of the world's most innovative dancers — and performed barefoot most of the time.

Isolda/Isolde — Welsh: Fair lady
Isolte, Yseult, Yseulta, Ysolda, Ysolde

Ivah — Hebrew: God's gracious gift

Ivana — Hebrew: God is gracious
Ivania, Ivanka, Ivanna, Ivannia
Czechoslovakian-born Ivana Trump named her daughter Ivanka, which, in Czechoslavakian, is an affectionate way of saying "little Ivana."

Ivy — English: Clinging vines, a symbol of faithfulness
Ivee, Ivi, Ivie, Ivye

J

Jacinta — Greek: Beautiful; Spanish: Hyacinth
Jacanta, Jacenta, Jacente, Jacinda, Jacinte, Jacintha, Jacinthe, Jacinthia, Jacynthe, Jacynthy

Jackie — See: Jacqueline

Jacoba — Hebrew: Supplanter
Jaci, Jacobina, Jacobine, Jacy, Jake, Jakee, Jakoba

Jacqueline — Hebrew: Supplanter
Jacki, Jackie, Jacklyn, Jackuelin, Jacky, Jaclyn, Jacque, Jacquetta, Jacquette, Jacqui, Jacquie, Jacquita, Jaquelina, Jaqueline, Jaquite, Jaquith, Jaquithe

This became a popular name for newborns in the 1960s after Jacqueline Bouvier Kennedy became our first lady.

Jada — Hebrew: Wise

Jade — Spanish: A jade gem
Jadee, Jaeda, Jaida, Jaide, Jayde

Jael — Hebrew: Mountain goat, to ascend

Jaffa — Hebrew: Beautiful
Jafit, Yaffa, Yaffit

Jaime — French: I love

Jamie — Hebrew: Supplanter

Jamila — Arabic: Beautiful
Jameela, Jameelah, Jami, Jamilah, Jamilia, Jamille

Jan — See: Jane

Jane — Hebrew: God's gracious gift
Jan, Jana, Janel, Janelle, Janet, Janetta, Janette, Jania, Janice, Janie, Janina, Janine, Janis, Janith, Janithe, Janithia, Janka, Janna, Jannel, Jannelle, Janot, Jayne, Jaynee
The expression "plain Jane" has no meaning in today's world, what with the likes of women like Jane Pauley, Jane Curtin, and Jane Fonda.

Janet/Janice/Janis — See: Jane

Jardena — Hebrew: Flowing downward

Jarvinia — German: Keen intelligence

Jasmine — Persian: A fragrant flower
Jasmina, Jasse, Jassey, Jassi, Jassie, Jassy, Yasmine

Jean — French: God is gracious
Gene, Genia, Jeanee, Jeanette, Jeanie, Jeanne, Jeannetta, Jeannette

Jelena — Russian: Shining light

Jemima — Hebrew: Little dove
Jamima, Jamime, Jamyma, Jemma, Jemmie, Jemmy, Mima, Yemima

Jenica — Hebrew: God is gracious
Jenice, Jenicee, Jenicy

Jennifer — Welsh: White, fair
Genna, Gennifer, Gennifera, Genny, Jen, Jena, Jenafer, Jenifer, Jenna, Jennee, Jenney, Jenny
We think this name's unequaled popularity started more than twenty years ago, with the phenomenal success of Erich Segal's book Love Story *(and the film of the same title), in which the female lead is named Jenny Cavilleri.*

Jenny — See: Jennifer

Jeremia — Hebrew: Exalted of the Lord
   Jeremie, Jeremya, Jeremyea, Jerrey, Jerri, Jerry

Jessica — Hebrew: Wealthy
   Jess, Jessa, Jessaca, Jessalin, Jessalyn, Jessaman, Jessamine, Jessamyn, Jesse, Jessee, Jessie, Jessy

Jewel — French: Precious stone
   Jewela, Jewell, Jewelle, Jewelyn

Jezebel — Hebrew: Follower of idols

Jihan — Turkish: Universe

Jill — Greek: Youthful
   Jillee, Jilli, Jillian, Jillie, Jilly, Jillye, Jyll
   Jack and Jill went up the hill, to fetch a pail of water. . . .

Jo — See: Josephine

Joan — Hebrew: God's gracious gift
   Joanie, Joann, Joanna, Joanne, Jo-Annie, Joany, Johanna, Johnna, Johnelle, Johnetta, Johnette, Jonetta, Jonette, Jonetty, Joni, Jonie, Jony
   Joan is a female power name. Joan Crawford, Joan Collins, Joan Sutherland, Joan Baez, Joan Rivers, and Joan Lunden are all strong and powerful women.

Joann/Joanna/Joanne — See: Joan

Jobina — Hebrew: The persecuted
   Jobee, Jobie, Joby, Jobyna

Jocelyn — Latin: Happy, joyful
   Jocelen, Jocelin, Jocelina, Joceline, Joselin, Josselin, Josselyn

Jocosa — Latin: Playful
   Jodetta, Jodette, Jodi, Jodia, Jodie, Jody

Jodi/Jody — See: Jocosa

Joelle — Hebrew: The Lord is willing
   Jo-el, Joela, Joell, Joella, Joellen, Joellyn

Jolan — Hungarian: Violet blossom

Jolie — French: Pretty
   Jolena, Jolene, Joli, Jolie, Jolina, Joline, Joly

Jonina — Hebrew: Little dove

Jonita — Latin: Jovial

Jora — Hebrew: Autumn rain
   Jorah, Jori, Jory

Jordan — Hebrew: Flowing downward
   Jordaine, Jordana, Jordanne, Jordena, Jordyn, Joree, Jorey, Jori, Jorry, Jory

Josephine — Hebrew: She shall add
Fifi, Fifine, Jo, Joeta, Joey, Josefa, Josefina, Josepha, Josephina, Josephiney, Josee, Josey, Josi, Josie, Josy
Napoleon's wife was Empress Marie Josèphe Rose, but everyone called her Josephine.

Josie — See: Josephine

Joy — Latin: Joyfulness
Joi, Joia, Joya, Joyann, Joyelle

Joyce — Latin: Joyous
Joice, Joy, Joycee, Joycey, Joyci, Joycie, Joyous

Juanita — Spanish: God is gracious
Anita, Juana

Jubilee — Latin: Joyful time

Judith — Hebrew: Praised one
Judi, Judie, Judy, Judyth, Judythe

Judy — See: Judith

Julia — Latin: Youthful
Jule, Julea, Julee, Juley, Juli, Juliana, Juliane, Juliann, Julianna, Julianne, Julie, Juliet, Julietta, Juliette, Julina, Juline, Julita, Julitta

June — Latin: Month of June, youthful
Junella, Junetta, Junette, Junia, Junie, Juniet, Junieta, Junina

Juno — Latin: Queen of the heavens

Justine — Latin: Justice
Giustina, Giustine, Justeen, Justina
Actress Justine Bateman from the hit sitcom "Family Ties" inspired a new interest in this turn-of-the-century name.

K

Kali — Sanskrit: Energy

Kalika — Greek: Rosebud

Kalila — Arabic: Loved one

Kalinda — Sanskrit: Sun

Kama — Sanskrit: Love

Kamaria — African: Moonlike

Kamilia — Slavic: Sweet flower

Kara — See: Cara

Karen/Karin — Greek: Pure
  Karena, Karene, Karina, Karine
Karida — Arabic: Virginal
Karima — Arabic: Noble, generous
Karli — Turkish: Covered with snow
Kate — See: Katherine
Katherine — Greek: Pure (Also see: Catherine)
  Kass, Kassi, Kassia, Katalin, Kate, Katerina, Katerine, Katha, Katharine, Kathe, Kathee, Kathey, Kathie, Kathleen, Kathryn, Kathryna, Kathryne, Kati, Katie, Katina, Katine, Katinka, Katrinka, Katuscha, Katuska, Katy, Katya, Kay, Kaye, Ketti, Kettia, Kit, Kittie, Kitty
  This name is a classic throughout the Western world, and one of its most famous recipients is three-time Academy Award–winner Katharine Hepburn.
Kathleen — See: Katherine
Kay — See: Katherine
Keely — Irish: Beautiful one
Kefira — Hebrew: Young lioness
Keiko — Japanese: Adored one
Kelda — Scandinavian: Clear mountain spring
Kelila — Hebrew: Crown of laurel
  Kaile, Kayle, Kelula
Kelli/Kelly — Irish: Warrior woman
  Kellee, Kelley, Kellie, Kellina
Kelsey — Norse: From the ship's island
  Kelcee, Kelci, Kelcie, Kelsee, Kelsy
Kendra — English: Knowledge
Kerani — Indian: Sacred bells
Keren — Hebrew: Ray, beam
Kerensa — Cornish: Love
  Karensa, Karenza, Kerenza
Kerry — Irish: Dark haired
  Keri, Kerree, Kerrey, Kerri, Kerrie
Kezia — Hebrew: From Cassia
  Kazia, Kessi, Kessie, Kessy, Kezzi, Kezzie, Kezzy, Kizzie, Kizzy
  Cassia is the name of a group of trees and shrubs, one of which has cinnamonlike bark.
Kichi — Japanese: Fortunate
Kiki — Egyptian: Castor plant
Kimberley — English: From the meadow

Kim, Kimberlee, Kimberlie, Kimberly, Kimbie, Kimbra, Kimmee, Kimmi, Kimmie, Kimmy

Kimberly is the diamond-mining center in South Africa. The name also comes from kimberlite, a rock formation often containing diamonds.

Kineta — Greek: Active one

Kira/Kyra — Persian: Sun

Kirsten — Danish: Christian follower
   Kirstan, Kirstane, Kirsti, Kirstie, Kirstin, Kirstina, Kirsty, Kirstyn

Kisa — Russian: Pussycat

Kitty — See: Katherine

Kizzy — Nickname for Kezia: (Also see: Kezia)
   Kizzy was the name of one of the leading characters in the miniseries "Roots," which first aired on TV in 1977. Leslie Uggams played the part. Soon after the show's first airing, the name started appearing on birth certificates across the country.

Koko — Japanese: Stork (an Oriental symbol of longevity)

Kolina — Swedish: Maiden

Kora — See: Cora

Kristen — Norse: Christian follower
   Krista, Kristel, Kristela, Kristella, Kristelle, Kristee, Kristi, Kristin, Kristina, Kristine, Krysta, Krystyn, Krystyna

Kumi — Japanese: Braid
   Kumiko

Kyla/Kyle — Irish: Lovely

Kyna — Irish: Wise

Kyoko — Japanese: Mirror

L

Lacey/Lacie/Lacy — See: Gelasia

Laila — Arabic: Dark haired, night
   Laili, Lailie, Lelia, Leyla

Lainie — See: Elaine, Helen

Lakeisha — Swahili: Favorite one
   Lakecia, Lakeesha, Lakicia, Lekeesha, Lekeisha

Lala — Slavic: Tulip

Lalita — Sanskrit: Pleasing, charming

Lana — Latin: Woolly
Lanata, Lanetta, Lanette, Lanna, Lannata, Lanneta, Lanni, Lannie, Lanny
This name was popular in the 1940s and '50s when actress Lana Turner starred on the silver screen.

Lane — English: From the narrow road
Laney, Lani, Lanie, Layne, Laynie

Lara — Latin: Shining
This popular Russian name got the attention of expectant parents in America when the film Dr. Zhivago *was released in 1965. The part of Lara was played by Julie Christie, and the song "Lara's Theme" inspired many namings.*

Laraine — Latin: Sea bird
Larana, Larane, Larayne

Larissa — Greek: Cheerful, lighthearted
Laryssa, Larysse, Laryssia, Lissa, Lyssa

Lark — English: A songbird

Latoya — Spanish: Victorious one
This name is now a familiar one, thanks to singer LaToya Jackson.

Latricia — Latin: Of noble descent
Latrecia, Latreece, Latreshia, Latrice, Letrice, Letricia

Laura — Latin: Laurel wreath or crown
Laure, Laurette, Lauri, Laurice, Laurie, Lora, Loretta, Lorette, Lori, Lorita, Lorra, Lorray, Lorree, Lorrey, Lorrie
The Romans used the laurel wreath as a symbol of victory. They also believed that a laurel crown could protect them from lightning.

Laurel — Latin: Laurel tree
Laural, Laurall, Laurell

Lauren — Latin: Laurel wreath or crown
Laureen, Laureena, Laurena, Laurene, Loreen, Loren, Lorena, Lorene, Lorenza, Lorinda
This name became popular when actress Lauren Bacall became a star in the 1940s, when Lauren Tewes was on the TV series "The Love Boat" from 1977 to 1984, and when eighties supermodel and actress Lauren Hutton was splashed across the pages of magazines. Of course, fashion designer Ralph Lauren (born Ralph Lefkowitz) has helped keep the name quite prominent.

Laurie — See: Laura

Laveda — Latin: Innocent one

Laverne/LaVerne — Latin: Springlike
Laverna, Laverney, Lavernia, Lavernie, Laverny, Lavernya
Lavinia/Lavinie — Latin: Purified, women of Rome
Lavena, Lavenia, Lavina, Levina, Levinia, Livinia, Lovinia
Leah — Hebrew: Weary
Lea, Leigha, Lia
Leala — French: Loyal one
Leal, Lealia, Leanna, Lelah, Loyale, Loyola
Leda/Leta — Greek: Lady, joy, gladness
Lee — English: From the meadow in the pasture (Also, a nickname for names starting or ending with "Lee")
Leanna, Leeann, Leeanna, Leeanne, Leecynth, Leigh
Leeat — Hebrew: You are mine
Liat
Leeba/Liba — Yiddish: Beloved
Leila — Arabic: Born at night
Layla, Layle, Lela, Lelah, Leyla, Leylia
Leilani — Hawaiian: Heavenly flower
Lemuela — Hebrew: Consecrated to God
Lena/Lina — Latin: Temptress
Leni, Lenni, Lennie, Lenny
Lenore — See: Eleanor, Leonora
Leoda/Leota — German: Woman of the people
Leona — Latin: Lion
Leola, Leone, Leonelle, Leoney, Leonie, Leony, Leonya, Liona, Lionelle, Lionetta
The most famous owner of this name is real-estate/hotel magnate Leona Helmsley, who is currently serving time for tax evasion.
Leonora — Greek: Light
Leanor, Leanora, Leanore, Lenora, Lenore, Leonore
Leontine/Leontyne — Latin: Lionlike
Leontyn, Liontin, Liontine, Lyontin, Lyontine, Lyontyn, Lyontyne
In 1966, opera singer Leontyne Price was the first black person to open a New York Metropolitan Opera season.
Leslie — Scotch: From the gray fortress
Les, Lesley, Lesli, Lesly, Lezlee, Lezley, Lezlie, Lezly
Letha — Greek: Forgetfulness
Leticia/Letitia — Latin: Joy
Leta, Lethia, Letisha, Letishia, Letti, Lettie, Letty, Tish, Tisha
In the early 1800s, there was a first lady named Letitia — the wife of President John Tyler.

Levana/Levona — Latin: Rising sun
Levania, Levanna
Lewanna — Hebrew: Beaming white one, the moon
Lian/Liann — Chinese: Graceful willow
Liana/Liane — French: Binding
Libby — Hebrew: Oath of God
Lib, Libbee, Libbey, Libbie
Lida — Slavic: Beloved of the people
Lien — Chinese: Lotus
Lila/Lilah — See: Delilah
Lilac — Persian: Lilac flower
Lili/Lily — See: Lillian
Lilith — Hebrew: Spirit of the night; Assyrian: Storm goddess
Lilis, Lillis, Lillys, Lillyth, Lyllis, Lyllith
Lillian — Latin: Lily flower
Lil, Lili, Lillia, Lilian, Liliann, Lilli, Lillie, Lilly, Lillyan
Linda — Spanish: Pretty
Lin, Lindy, Lyn, Lynda, Lyndey, Lyndi, Lyndie, Lyndy
In the mid-1940s and throughout the 1950s, Linda was one of the most popular names in the U.S. Born during that time were Lynda Carter, Linda Evans, Linda Ellerbee, Linda Gray, and Linda Ronstadt.
Lindsay/Lindsey — English: From the isle of linden trees
This was originally a boy's name, but it caught on as a girl's name at the end of the 1970s. TV's "Bionic Woman," Lindsay Wagner, may have had an influence on this trend.
Linetta/Linette — Celtic: Graceful
Lanet, Linet, Lineta, Linnet, Lyneta, Lynetta, Lynette
Linnea/Lynnea — Swedish: The national flower
Liron — Hebrew: The song is mine
Lisa — Hebrew: Dedicated to God
Leesa, Leeza, Lisetta, Lisette, Lissa, Liza, Lizetta, Lizette, Lyssa
Livana — Hebrew: White
Livia — See: Olive
Livona — Hebrew: Spice
Livonia, Livonna, Livonne
Liza — See: Lisa
Lois — Greek: Battle maiden, renowned in battle
Lola — Spanish: Sorrowful one; English: Strong one
Lolita

Lolita — Spanish: Sorrows
Vladmir Nabokov's 1958 novel of the above name, about a twelve-year-old seductress, and the subsequent film version (1962) made Lolita a well-known name. It's now a way of describing a sexy young girl: "She's a regular Lolita!"

Lorelei — German: Alluring
Loralee, Loralei, Lorelee, Lorilee, Lorilei, Lura, Luralee, Luraleen, Luralene, Luraline, Luralyne

Loretta — See: Laura

Lorice — Latin: Slender vine

Lorna/Lorne — English: Lost love
This name was created by R. D. Blackmore in the 1860s for his novel Lorna Doone.

Lorraine — German: Famous in battle; Place name: Former province of eastern France, then Germany (1871), and France again (1919)
Laraine, Laurraine, Lorain, Loraine, Lorayne, Lorrayn, Lorrayne
This province was the hometown of Joan of Arc. The saint is also referred to as "Joan of Lorraine."

Lottie/Lotty — See: Charlotte

Lotus — Greek: Dreamlike, lotus flower

Louella/Louelle — English: Elf, sprite
Loella, Loelle, Lou, Lu, Luella, Luelle, Lula, Lulu

Louisa/Louise — German: Noted woman of war
Eloisa, Eloise, Loisa, Loise, Louisetta, Louisette

Luana/Luane — German: Graceful woman of battle
Louanna, Louanne, Luanna, Luanne

Luba — Slavic: Lover

Lucille — See: Lucy

Lucinda — Latin: Bringer of light
Cinda, Cindee, Cindey, Cindi, Cindie, Cindy, Lucindee, Lucindia, Lucindy

Lucretia — Latin: Riches, treasure
There was a first lady named Lucretia, and she was married to President James Garfield.

Lucy — Latin: Light bearer
Lucee, Lucia, Lucie, Lucilla, Lucille, Lucine
"I Love Lucy"! Who doesn't? It is said that every minute of every day an "I Love Lucy" episode airs somewhere in the world.

Ludmilla — Slavic: Loved by the people

Lulu — See: Louella

Luna — Latin: Moon
  Lunet, Lunetta, Lunette

Lurleen/Lurlene — German: Alluring
  Lurel, Luretta, Lurette, Lurleena, Lurline, Lurlyna

Lydia — Greek: Cultured, voluptuous; Place name: A country in Asia Minor
  Lidia, Lidya, Lyd, Lyddi, Lyddie, Lydie
  The country of Lydia was the first place to have had a system of coinage.

Lynn/Lynne — English: Waterfall
  Linn, Linnelle, Lynelle, Lynette

Lyris — Greek: Lyrical
  Lyra

Lysandra — Greek: Liberator of men

M

Mabel/Mable — Latin: Lovable
  Mab, Mabe, Mabela, Mabella, Mabelle, Maybel, Maybella, Maybelle

Madelina/Madeline — Greek: Tower of strength
  Mada, Madalena, Madalyn, Maddi, Maddie, Maddy, Madelaine, Madeleine, Madelena, Madelene, Madella, Madelle, Madelon, Madelyn, Magda, Magdalena, Magdalene, Maud, Maude

Madge — See: Margaret

Madonna — Latin: My lady
  Once it was a name spoken with reverence, but now people have a whole new attitude toward the name, due to the overwhelming success of the superstar born Madonna Louise Ciccone.

Maeve — Celtic: Joy; Gaelic: Delicate, fragile

Magda — See: Madelina/Madeline

Maggie — See: Margaret

Magnolia — French: A tree with large pink blossoms
  The tree was named for French botanist Pierre Magnol.

Mahalia — Hebrew: Tenderness
  Mahala, Mehala, Mehalia

Maida — German: Maiden
  Mady, Maidel, Maidena, Maidene, Maidie, Mayda
Maisie — See: Margaret
Majesta — Latin: Majestic
Mala — See: Marlene
Malka — Hebrew: Queen
  Malkeh, Malki, Malkit
Mallory — French: Wild duck, "mailed one" (referring to a suit of mail worn by knights); Latin: To beat with a hammer
  In most older name books, this name is listed for boys. It became a popular girls' name in the 1980s, probably because of Justine Bateman's character, Mallory Keaton, on "Family Ties."
Malu — Hawaiian: Peacefulness
Mame — See: Mary
Manda/Mandy — See: Amanda
Mangena — Hebrew: Melody
Manuela — Spanish: God is with us
  Manuelia, Manuelle, Manuely
Mara — See: Mary
Maranda/Miranda — Latin: Admirable
Marcella — Latin: Fierce, warlike
  Marcela, Marcelle, Marcellina, Marcelline, Marchita, Marcia, Marcie, Marcy, Marcyann, Marcyanna, Markie, Markita, Marquita, Marsha, Martia
Marcia/Marsha — See: Marcella
Margaret — Greek: Pearl
  Madge, Magee, Maggie, Maggy, Maisie, Margalo, Margarita, Marge, Margery, Margey, Margie, Margit, Margita, Margitta, Margitte, Margo, Margot, Margrit, Margritta, Margritte, Marguerita, Marguerite, Margy, Marji, Marjie, Marjo, Marjorie, Marjory, Marketa, Meg, Megan, Meggie, Meghan, Meta, Peg, Pegeen, Peggie, Peggy
  Margaret Mitchell, author of the best-seller Gone with the Wind, *influenced the naming of babies not only with her story's characters but with her own, more conservative name.*
Margery — See: Margaret
Margo — See: Margaret
Marguerite — See: Margaret
Maria/Marie — See: Mary
Marian/Marianne — See: Mary
Maribel/Maribelle — Hebrew: Beautiful but bitter

Marice — German: Marsh flower
Marigold — English: Orange and yellow flower
Marilyn — See: Mary
In theatrical circles, often this name is paired with last names that begin with the same letter; e.g., Marilyn Miller, Marilyn Maxwell, Marilyn Monroe, and Marilyn Michaels.
Marina — Latin: Sea maiden
Maris — Latin: From the sea
Marisa, Marissa, Marisse, Marrisa, Marris, Marysa, Merisa, Merissa, Merys
Marjorie — See: Margaret
Markie — See: Marcella
Marla/Marlo — See: Mary
Marlo Thomas as "That Girl" (1966–71) was responsible for bringing attention to this name.
Marlene — Hebrew: The exalted
Mala, Malena, Malina, Marlee, Marleen, Marlena, Marlina, Marline, Marlyne
Marlene Dietrich was born Maria Magdalene Dietrich. She combined the first part of her first name (Mar) and the last part of her middle name (lene) and came up with a name (Marlene) that proved very lucky for her.
Marmara — Greek: Radiant
Marnina — Hebrew: Cause of joy
Marni
Marsha — See: Marcella
Martha — Aramaic: Lady, mistress
Marta, Martela, Martele, Marthe, Martie, Martita, Marty
We all know that Martha Dandridge Custis married George Washington and became the first first lady of the United States. But did you know that a Martha — Martha Wayles Skelton — was America's third first lady? This Martha was married to Thomas Jefferson.
Martina — Latin: Warrior of Mars
Considering the meaning of this name, it's no wonder that Martina Navratilova is a tennis player who's out of this world.
Marva — Hebrew: Sage (the fragrant herb)
Marvel — Latin: Full of wonder
Marvella, Marvelle
Mary — Hebrew: Wished-for child, star of the sea
Maire, Mairi, Mame, Mamie, Manon, Manya, Mara, Maralin,

Maraline, Mari, Maria, Mariam, Marian, Marianna, Marica, Marice, Marie, Mariel, Mariella, Marielle, Marietta, Mariette, Marilla, Marilyn, Marion, Mariska, Marite, Marla, Marlie, Marlin, Marlo, Marya, Maryann, Maryanna, Maryanne, Marye, Marylyn, Mayme, Miriam, Mitzi, Mollie, Molly

With the number of famous songs and poems featuring the name, we agree with George M. Cohan: "Mary's a Grand Old Name"!

Maryann/Maryanna/Maryanne — See: Mary

Mathilda/Mathilde — German: Powerful one
Matilda, Matilde, Matti, Mattie, Matty, Tilda, Tildie

Maud/Maude — See: Madelina/Madeline

Maureen — French: Dark skinned
Maura, Maure, Maurene, Maurine, Maurise, Maurita, Mauritzia, Moreen, Morena, Moryne

Mavis — French: Songbird

Maxine — Latin: Greatest one
Max, Maxi, Maxie, Maxy

May — Latin: Great
Mae, Mai, Maia, Maya, Maye

Meda — Latin: Healer
Medea, Medora

Meg — See: Margaret

Megan/Meghan — See: Margaret

Melanie/Melany — Greek: Dressed in dark clothes
Lani, Lanie, Lannie, Lanny, Mel, Mela, Malania, Melli, Mellie, Melly

Melanie Hamilton, a character in Gone with the Wind, *made the name popular both in 1934, when the novel was published, and in 1939, when the film was released. Olivia De Havilland played the part of Melanie.*

Melantha — Greek: Dark flower

Melba — Celtic: From the mill stream

Melina — Greek: Canary yellow

Melinda — Greek: Gentle
Malinda, Malynda, Melynda, Melyndy, Mindee, Mindi, Mindie, Mindy

Melissa — Greek: Honeybee
Malissa, Melecent, Melessa

Singer Melissa Manchester, and Melissa Gilbert, the star of "Little House On The Prairie," have made this an appealing name.

Melodie/Melody — Greek: Song
Melosa — Spanish: Sweet, gentle
Mercedes — Spanish: Merciful
  Merci, Mercie, Mercy
Meredith/Meredyth — Welsh: Protector from the sea
  Meridyth, Merridith, Merridyth, Merritha
Merla/Merle — French: Blackbird
  Merl, Merlie, Merly, Meryl, Meryle, Myrla, Myrlena, Myrlene
Merry — English: Amiable, festive, pleasant, jolly
  Meri, Merrey, Merrie, Merrielle, Merrilee, Merrill
Meryl — See: Merla/Merle, Merry
  Two-time Academy Award-winner Meryl Streep is largely responsible for the popularity of this name in the past decade.
Meta — Latin: Ambition
Mia — Italian: Belonging to me
Michaela — Hebrew: Who is like the Lord?
  Micaela, Micaele, Michael, Michaele, Michaelina, Michaeline, Michalah, Michel, Michelina, Micheline, Michelle, Micki, Mickie, Micky, Midge, Miguela, Miguelina, Migueline, Miguelita, Mikaela, Mikaele, Mike, Mikie
Michelle — See: Michaela
Mignon — French: Dainty, graceful, delicate
  Mignona, Mignone, Mignonetta, Mignonette
Mila — Czechoslovakian: Loved by the people
Mildred — English: Kind counselor
  Mil, Mildreda, Mildrid, Milley, Milli, Millie, Milly
Milena — German: Mild
Millicent — German: Strength
  Melicent, Melisanda, Melisande, Milicenta, Milicente
Mimi — Italian: My, my! (Also, a pet name for Miriam, Marie, and other "M" names)
  Opera lovers know that Mimi is the heroine of Puccini's masterpiece, La Bohème.
Mina — See: Gemina
Mindy — See: Melinda
Minerva — Greek: Wisdom
  Min, Minetta, Minette, Minnie, Minny
Minna — German: Tender affection
Minnie — See: Minerva
Mira — Latin: Wonderful
  Mirella, Mirelle, Myra, Myril, Myrilla

Mirabella/Mirabelle — Latin: Of spectacular beauty
Mirabel, Mirabela
Miriam — See: Mary
Misty — English: Clouded vision
Mitzi — See: Mary
Miyoko — Japanese: Generation's beautiful child
Modesty — Latin: Humble, modest
Modesta, Modestia, Modestina, Modestine, Modestyna, Modestyne
Moira — Irish: Great woman
Moirae, Mora, Moyra
Mollie/Molly — See: Mary
Mona — Greek: Solitary
Monica — Latin: Advice giver
Moniqua, Monique
Morgan — Welsh: Woman of the sea
Moriah — Hebrew: God is my teacher
Mariah, Moria
Muriel/Murielle — Greek: Fragrant one
Murphy — Celtic: Sea warrior
Ever since the TV sitcom "Murphy Brown" caught on, girls have taken over this once mostly male name.
Musetta — Latin: A little music
Musette
Myra — French: Quiet song; Latin: Scented oil
Myrna — Irish: Polite, tender, beloved
Merna, Mirna, Morna
Myrtle — Greek: Victorious crown; Latin: Name of a flower
Myrta, Myrtell, Myrti, Myrtice, Myrtie, Myrtis

N

Nadia — Slavic: Hope
Nada, Nadeen, Nadie, Nadine, Nady, Nadya
Romanian gymnast Nadia Comaneci put this name on the map when she won our hearts in the 1976 Olympics.
Naiad/Naida — Greek: Water nymph
Nayad, Nyad

TV commentator Diana Nyad made a name for herself as a world-class swimmer. Last names too can be portents of things to come.

Nalani — Hawaiian: Calmness of the skies

Nancy — Hebrew: Grace
Nan, Nana, Nance, Nancee, Nanci, Nancie, Nanette, Nani, Nanica, Nanine, Nanna, Nannie, Nanny

Nanette — See: Nancy

Naomi — Hebrew: Pleasant, charming

Nara — Japanese: Oak (symbol of stability)

Natalie — Latin: Child of Christmas
Nat, Nata, Natala, Natalia, Natalina, Natalita, Natasha, Nathalia, Nathalie, Natty, Talie, Tasha

Natasha — See: Natalie

Nathania — Hebrew: Gift of God
Natania, Nataniela, Natanielle, Nathaniella

Navit — Hebrew: Beautiful

Naysa — Hebrew: Miracle of God

Nealy/Neely — Irish: Champion

Neda/Nedda — Slavic: Born on Sunday

Nelda — English: Of the elder tree

Nell — Greek: Light
Nellee, Nelli, Nellie, Nelly

Neoma — Greek: New moon

Nerine — Greek: Nymph of the sea
Nerice, Nerissa, Nerita

Nessa — See: Agnes, Vanessa

Netta/Nettie/Netty — See: Antonia

Neva — Spanish: Snowy

Nicola/Nicole — Greek: The people's victory
Cola, Nicaela, Nichola, Nichole, Nickie, Nicol, Nicolette, Nicolina, Nike, Nikee, Nikki, Nikola, Nikole, Nikoleen, Nikolene

Nina — Spanish: Girl
Nena, Ninetta, Ninette, Ninon
The Niña was one of Christopher Columbus's three ships; ships are almost always "female."

Nissa — Danish/Swedish: Friendly elf
Nisan, Nisse, Nissen, Nissie, Nissy, Nyssa

Nita — Native American (Choctaw): Bear

Noel — French: To be born
Noella, Noelle, Noellyn

Noelani — Hawaiian: Beautiful girl from heaven
Noga — Hebrew: Morning light
  Nolcha
Nola — Latin: Noble woman; Gaelic: White shoulder
Nona — Latin: The ninth
  Nonie, Nonna
  Originally reserved for the ninth child of the family, no wonder
  this name is not a very common one!
Nora/Norah — See: Eleanor, Honora
Noreen — See: Norma
Nori — Japanese: Doctrine
Norma — Latin: As a rule, pattern
  Noreen, Noreena, Norena, Norene, Norine
  Speaking of patterns, fashion designer Norma Kamali has her
  name and her career all sewed up!
Numa — Arabic: Beautiful
Nydia — Latin: Safe refuge
  Neda, Nedda
Nysa — Greek: Beginning

O

Obelia — Greek: Pillar of strength
Octavia/Octavie — Latin: The eighth
  Octava, Octavine, Tavia, Tavie, Tavy
  In ancient Roman families, if the eighth child was a girl, she
  most likely would have been given this name.
Odelia/Odelie — Hebrew: I will praise God
  Odela, Odele, Odelet, Odelette, Odelinda, Odella, Odelle,
  Odile, Odillia, Othelia
Odessa — Greek: Long journey
Odetta/Odette — French: Love of one's home; German: Wealth
  In the ballet Swan Lake, *Odette is the good swan and Odile is the*
  evil swan. Both parts are often danced by the same ballerina.
Okalani — Hawaiian: From heaven
Olathe — Native American: Beautiful
Oleander — American English: An evergreen with red or white
blossoms
  Oliana

Olga — Russian: Holy
Olia, Olienka

Olive — Latin: Olive tree
Livia, Livie, Livvie, Livvy, Livy, Olivette, Olivia, Ollie, Olva
*Olive trees have been known to live up to two thousand years.
The olive branch — as in "The dove returned to the ark with an
olive branch in its beak" (Gen. 8:11) — has long been a symbol
of peace.*

Olivia — See: Olive

Olympia/Olympie — Greek: Heavenly, of Olympus (the mountain home of the gods)
Olympia Dukakis, the Moonstruck *mother of Cher, won an
Oscar for her performance.*

Ona — Lithuanian: Graceful one
Oona, Una

Ondine — Latin: Of the water
Ondina, Undine

Oona — See: Ona

Opal — Hindi: Jewel
Opalina, Opaline
*The opal, which is said to have a magic rainbow within its
depths, is thought to be created from water and crystalline rock
formations.*

Ophelia — Greek: Immortality, wisdom, to help
Ofelia, Ofellia, Offie, Ofilia, Orphellia, Orphie, Orphillia,
Phelia

Ora — Hebrew: Light
Orah, Oralee, Orit, Orlee, Orlice, Orly

Orabel — French: Of golden beauty
Orabella, Orabelle, Oribel

Oralia/Oralie — Latin: Eloquent speaker

Oriana — Celtic: Of white skin, fair
Oriane, Oriel, Oriella, Orielle

Oriole — Latin: Fair haired

Orlena/Orlene — Latin: Golden

Orna — Latin: Decorate

Orpah — Hebrew: Fawn; German: Fatherland
Ophrah, Oprah
*It is said that TV star Oprah Winfrey's name was supposed to be
Orpah, but her mother misspelled it. Oprah's name spelled back-
ward, Harpo, is the name of Oprah's production company.*

Otillia — Greek: Fortunate maid of battle
  Otilla, Otillie, Otilly, Tilla, Tillie, Tilly

P

Padmani — Sri Lankan: Flower
Page/Paige — English: Young; Greek: Child
  Paget, Pagette, Payge
Paka — Swahili: Pussycat
Palma — Latin: Palm tree
  The leaves of this tree resemble the palm of one's hand.
Paloma — Spanish: Dove
  Palometa, Palomita
  Jewelry designer Paloma Picasso has a perfume named Paloma.
Pamela — Greek: Loving, kind
  Pam, Pamelia, Pamelina, Pamella, Pammi, Pammie, Pammy
Pandora — Greek: All-gifted
  Pan, Pandi, Pandie, Pandy
Pansy — French: A velvety, somewhat unusual-looking flower
Patience — French: Enduring
Patricia — Latin: Of the nobility, wellborn, patrician
  Pat, Patria, Patrica, Patrice, Patrizia, Patsy, Patti, Pattie, Patty,
  Tricia, Trish, Trisha, Trishia
Patsy/Patti/Patty — See: Patricia
Paula — Latin: Small
  Paola, Paoleta, Paolina, Paoline, Paule, Pauletta, Paulette, Pau-
  ley, Pauli, Paulie, Paulina, Pauline, Paulita, Pauly, Pavla, Polly,
  Pollyanna
Pauletta/Paulette — See: Paula
Pauline/Pauline — See: Paula
Pazia — Hebrew: Golden girl
  Paz, Paza, Pazice
Pearl — Latin: Ham (for the hamlike shape of the sea mussel)
  Pearla, Pearle, Pearlie, Pearlina, Pearline, Pearly, Perla, Perle,
  Perlie, Perly
  *Pulitzer Prize–winning, American-born author Pearl S. Buck
  spent her early years in China, and her books reflect her first-
  hand knowledge of that country.*

Peg/Peggy — See: Margaret

Penda — Swahili: Love

Penelope — Greek: Weaver
Penni, Pennie, Penny
In Homer's Odyssey, *Penelope was the wealthy wife of Ulysses who put off her suitors by promising to marry one of them only after she finished weaving her tapestry. To prevent that from happening, she would weave all day and, at night, unravel the work she had completed. Ten years later, it paid off when her husband, previously believed dead, returned from his wanderings.*

Penina/Peninah — Hebrew: Pearl

Penny — See: Penelope

Peony — Greek: Giver of praise; English: Name of a flower

Perdita — Latin: Lost
This is the name of the young heroine in Shakespeare's Winter's Tale.

Persephone — Greek: Prosperous
Peri, Perri, Perrie, Perry

Petra — Latin: Rock
Peta, Petrea, Petrina, Petrine, Petrissa, Petronia, Petronie, Pier, Pierette

Petula — Latin: Seeker, saucy
Petulia, Petulie, Tula

Petunia — Native American (Tupi — a South American tribe): Sweet flower

Phaedra — Greek: Shining one
Phaedre, Phaidra, Phaidre, Phedra, Phedre

Phebe/Phoebe — Greek: Bright, shining

Philana — Greek: Friend of humankind

Phillippa — Greek: Lover of horses
Felipa, Felipe, Felippa, Felippe, Philippina, Philippine, Philli, Phillipe, Philly, Pippa, Pippi

Philomena — Greek: Loving harmony
Filomena, Filomene, Philomene, Philomine

Phyllis — Greek: Green bough
Phil, Philicia, Philis, Phillida, Phillis, Philly, Phylicia, Phyllys

Pia — Italian: Devout

Pier/Pierette — See: Petra

Pilar — Spanish: Supportive, responsible

Pippa — See: Phillippa

Pocahontas — Native American: Playful
Pocahontas was a nickname given to Indian Princess Matoaka. When she married John Rolfe and moved to England, she became Rebecca Rolfe.

Polly — See: Paula

Pollyanna — See: Paula

Pomona — Latin: Fruitful, fertile

Poppy — Latin: A bright-red flower

Portia — Latin: Offering
Portia was the bright young heroine in Shakespeare's Merchant of Venice *who outwits Shylock and saves her husband's life by disguising herself as a lawyer.*

Prima — Latin: Firstborn

Primrose — Latin: First rose

Priscilla — Latin: From ancient times
Cilla, Pris, Prissie, Prissy

Providence — Latin: Divine direction
Dancer Nicole Fosse's middle name is Providence, because that's the way her parents, Gwen Verdon and Bob Fosse, felt about their little "miracle child."

Prudence — Latin: Discretion
Pru, Prudi, Prudie, Prudy, Prue

Prunella — French: Plum colored

Pythia — Greek: Prophet
Thia

Q

Queen — English: Royalty
Queenee, Queenie, Queeny

Quella — English: Pacify

Quenby — Swedish: Womanly

Querida — Spanish: Beloved

Quintina — Latin: Fifth child

Quiric — Greek: Sunday's child

Quirita — Latin: Citizen

R

Rachel — Hebrew: Ewe, female sheep
Rachele, Rachelle, Rachie, Rae, Rahel, Rahil, Raitch, Rakel, Raquel, Raquelle, Ray, Rochel, Rochelle
First lady Rachel Donelson Robards was married to Andrew Jackson, America's first Democratic president.

Radmilla — Slavic: Worker for the people

Rae/Ray — See: Rachel

Raina/Rayna — See: Regina

Raissa — French: Thinker

Raizel — Yiddish: Rose

Ramona — Spanish: Protectress
Ramonda, Ramunda, Raymona
This name has enjoyed success as a song, a film, a series of children's books, and more.

Randi — English: Invincible
Randa, Randee, Randie, Randy

Rani — Hindi: Queen
Rana, Ranee, Rania

Ranita — Hebrew: Joy
Ranice, Ranit

Raphaela — Hebrew: Healed by God
Rafaela, Rafaella, Raphaella, Raphaelle

Raquel — See: Rachel

Rasheda/Rashida — Swahili: Righteous

Raven — English: Blackbird

Rayna/Reyna — Hebrew: Pure, clean

Razilee/Razili — Hebrew: My secret

Reba — See: Rebecca

Rebecca — Hebrew: To bind
Becca, Becka, Becki, Beckie, Becky, Reba, Rebeca, Rebeka, Rebekah
"To bind" is an appropriate meaning when you consider how many books use this name for their heroines: Sir Walter Scott's Ivanhoe, Rebecca of Sunnybrook Farm, *and Daphne du Maurier's* Rebecca, *to name just a few. When the latter was made into a film in Spain, Joan Fontaine, who starred as Re-*

becca, wore a cardigan in some scenes. The Spaniards picked up on that and began calling a cardigan a "Rebecca."

Regan — See: Regina

Regina — Latin: Queen
Raina, Rayna, Reagan, Rega, Regan, Reggi, Reggie, Reggy, Reina, Reine
Regina was the leading character in Lillian Hellman's play, "The Little Foxes." In the first film version of it, Bette Davis turned in a memorable performance as the ruthless Regina.

Reiko — Japanese: Gratitude

Remy — French: From Rheims (or Reims)
Although Rheims is a town in central France that's known for its champagne, Rémy Martin is a cognac made in Cognac, which is in eastern France.

Rena/Rina — Hebrew: Song
Renni, Rennie, Renny

Renata — Latin: Reborn
Reanae, Rene, Renee, Renie

Rene/Renee — See: Renata

Reva — Latin: Renewed strength

Rhea — Greek: Stream

Rhoda — Greek: A rose
Rho, Rhode, Rhodia, Rhodocella, Rhodocelle, Rhodora, Rhody
This name became well known because of Valerie Harper's character, Rhoda Morgenstern, on "The Mary Tyler Moore Show."

Rhonda/Ronda — Welsh: Grand, strong river
Can you hear this name without singing: "Help me, Rhonda. Help, help me, Rhonda"?

Ricarda — English: Powerful ruler
Rica, Ricki, Rickie, Ricky, Rikki

Ricki/Rickie/Ricky/Rikki — See: Erica, Frederica, Ricarda

Rima — Spanish: Rhyme, poetry
Rima is the name of the nature-child heroine in Green Man-sions. As a memorial to its author, W. H. Hudson, a statue of Rima was erected in London's Kensington Gardens.

Risa/Rise — Latin: Laughter

Rita — See: Margaret

Riva — French: Shore
Reeva, Rivalee, Rivi, Rivkah, Rivy

Roberta — English: Bright fame

Robbi, Robbie, Robby, Roberti, Robertie, Roberty, Robin, Robina, Robyn, Ruperta

Robin/Robyn — See: Roberta

Rochelle — See: Rachel

Rohana — Hindi: Sandalwood

Rolanda — German: Famous, notable
Rolli, Rollie, Rolly

Romelda — Latin: Glorious battle maiden
Milda, Romi, Romilda, Romy

Rona — Hebrew: My joy, my song; Place name: Island in the Hebrides off Scotland.
Ronena, Roni, Ronit

Ronni/Ronnie/Ronny — See: Rowena, Veronica/Veronika

Rori/Rorie/Rory — See: Aurora

Rosalee/Rosalia/Rosalie — Latin: Feast of roses

Rosalind — Spanish: Lovely rose
Ros, Rosalin, Rosalina, Rosalinda, Rosaline, Rosallyn, Rosalyn, Rosalynd, Rosalynda, Rosa Lynn, Roslyn, Roz, Rozalin, Rozalind, Rozallyn, Rozzy

Rosamond — Greek: Noted guardian
Rosamund, Rosamunda, Rosemond, Rosemonda, Rosemund, Rosemunda

Rosanna/Rosanne — Hebrew: Graceful rose
Ranna, Roanna, Roanne, Roseann, Roseanna, Roseanne
This name is enjoying popularity now with the help of actress/comedienne Roseanne Arnold, singer Roseanne Cash, and actress Rosanna Arquette.

Rose — Greek: Rose
Rosa, Rosetta, Rosette, Rosie, Rosita, Rosy, Roze, Rozelle, Rozina

Rosemary — Latin: Fragrant herb, dew of the sea
Rosamaria, Rosamarie, Rosemaria, Rosemarie

Rowena — English: Well-known friend
Rena, Ronni, Ronnie, Ronny, Ro, Row, Rowe

Roxane — Persian: Brilliant one
Roxana, Roxanna, Roxanne, Roxene, Roxi, Roxie, Roxy
If you want to hear "Roxane" pronounced with the passion of a poet and the heart of a romantic, rent the video of the 1950 film Cyrano de Bergerac, *starring Jose Ferrer.*

Roz — See: Rosalind

Ruby — French: A deep-red gem
Rubetta, Rubi, Rubia, Rubie, Rubina

Rudella/Rudelle — German: Famous one
Rue — German: Famous; English: Aromatic plant that was once called herb-of-grace
> *The "famous" meaning is appropriate for namesake Rue McClanahan, one of the stars of the hit TV sitcom "Golden Girls."*

Rula — Latin: Ruler
Rumer — English: Gypsy
Ruri — Japanese: Emerald
  Ruriko
Ruth — Hebrew: Beauty, compassion
  Rue, Ruthia, Ruthie, Ruthy
Ryba — Czechoslovakian: Fish

S

Sabina — Latin: Of the Sabines (an ancient Italian tribe)
  Sabea, Sabena, Sabia, Sabine, Savina, Savine
Sabra — Hebrew: Thorny cactus, to rest
Sabrina — Latin: From the border
  Sabreena, Sabrinna, Sabryna, Zabrina
> *If you like this name, see the wonderfully romantic 1954 film* Sabrina, *starring Audrey Hepburn. You'll end up loving the name.*

Sacha/Sasha — Russian: Helper and defender of humankind
Sachiko — Japanese: Joy
  Sachi
Sadie — Hebrew: Princess
  Sada, Sadella, Sadelle, Sadye, Syd, Sydel, Sydelle
Sakara — Native American: Sweet
Salena/Salina — Latin: Salt
Sally — See: Sara/Sarah
Salome — Hebrew: Woman of perfection, peace
Samantha — Aramaic: She who listens
  Sam, Sammi, Sammie, Sammy
> *From 1967 to 1972, and now in syndication, Samantha, played by Elizabeth Montgomery, practiced witchcraft with a twitch of her nose on the sitcom "Bewitched."*

Samara — Hebrew: Ruled by God

Sandra — See: Alexandra, Cassandra

Sara/Sarah — Hebrew: Princess
Sal, Sallie, Sally, Sarena, Sari, Sarice, Sarika, Sarina, Sarine, Sarit, Sarita, Sarra, Sarrah, Shara, Zara, Zarah

Saxon — Latin: Large stone
Saxi, Saxie, Sasunn

Scarlett — English: A rich red color
Scarlett O'Hara from Gone with the Wind *is probably the most famous name in contemporary American literature. And yet, we don't know anyone named Scarlett. Do you?*

Sean — Hebrew: The Lord is favored
Shawn, Shawna

Season — Latin: Time of sowing
Not only are the seasons — autumn, winter, spring, and summer — used as names, but so is the category. Soap opera fans may know of Season Hubley, who plays Angelique on "All My Children."

Seema — Greek: Symbol

Seena — German: Of the senate

Selena — Greek: Moon
Selene, Selina, Selyna, Selyne

Selma/Zelma — Norse: Divinely protected

Seraphina — Hebrew: Ardent one, angel
Sera, Serafina, Serafine, Seraphine

Serena/Serene — Latin: Calm, tranquil
Serenity

Shaine — Hebrew: Beautiful
Shaina, Shane, Shanie, Shayna, Shayne, Shifra

Shannon — Celtic: Slow waters; Gaelic: Old, ancient
Shana, Shandy, Shani, Shanna, Shanon

Shari — See: Sharon

Sharman — English: Receiving or giving a fair share

Sharon — Hebrew: Princess
Shara, Sharae, Sharai, Shari, Sharine, Sharona, Sharron, Shary, Sherri, Sherrie, Sherry

Shawn — See: Sean

Sheba — Hebrew: From Sheba (a southern Arabian region)

Sheena — Hebrew: God's gracious gift
Sheenah, Sheina, Shena, Shiona

Sheila — Celtic: Musical

Seela, Sela, Selia, Sheela, Sheelagh, Sheelah, Sheilagh, Shela, Shelagh

Shelby — English: Sheltered town

Shelley/Shelly — English: Island of shells

Sherri/Sherry — See: Cher, Sharon

Shira — Hebrew: Song
Shirah, Shiri

Shirley — English: From the bright meadow
Sherl, Sherleen, Sherlene, Sherline, Shirl, Shirlee, Shirleen, Shirlene, Shirline

Shirley Temple was a precocious child actress in the 1930s and became, as Shirley Temple Black, a U.S. ambassador in the 1970s. Throughout the thirties and into the forties, the whole country went crazy about this curly-haired kid and the name Shirley quickly became a popular one.

Shoshana — Hebrew: Flowering lily
Shoshan, Shoshi

Sibyl/Sybil — Greek: Prophetess
Cybil, Cybill, Cybilla, Sebila, Sevilla, Sibbie, Sibby, Sibel, Sibelle, Sibilla, Sybila, Sybille, Sybyl, Sybylla, Sybylle

Sidonia — Phoenician: Enchantress
Sid, Sidney, Sidonie, Syd, Sydney, Sydonia, Sydonie

Sigourney — French: Daring king

Sigrid — Norse: Beautiful victory

Silver — English: A precious metal

Sima — Aramaic: Treasure

Simone — Hebrew: One who hears
Simona, Simonetta, Simonette

Siobhan — Irish: The Lord is gracious
Shavon, Shavonne, Shivaughn

Sirena — Greek: Seductive singer

Skyler — Norse: Projectile; Dutch: Scholar
Schuyler, Schyler, Sky, Skye, Skylar

Solana — Spanish: Sunshine

Solange — French: Sun angel

Solita — Latin: Alone, solitary

Sondra — See: Alexandra, Cassandra

Sonia — Greek: Wisdom
Sonja, Sonni, Sonnie, Sonny, Sonya, Sunni, Sunnie, Sunny, Sunya

Sophia/Sophie — Greek: Wisdom

Sofia, Sofie, Sophronia, Sophy, Zofia, Zofie, Zosia
Sophie Tucker was from the old school of singers with heart. Her real name was Sophia; her nickname, "the Last of the Red-Hot Mamas." Some would say the nickname also fits actress Sophia Loren.

Sparkle — English: Glisten

Spring — Nature name: From the springtime

Stacy — See: Anastasia, Eustacia

Star — English: Celestial body
Starette, Starla, Starr, Starry

Stella — See: Estelle

Stephanie — Greek: Crowned
Stefa, Steffi, Steffia, Steffie, Steffy, Stepha, Stephana, Stephani, Stephania, Stephi, Stephie, Stevana, Stevena, Stevie

Stockard — English: From the yard of tree stumps

Sue — See: Susan

Suki — Japanese: Beloved

Sumi — Japanese: Clear, refined

Summer — Nature name: From the summertime

Sunny — See: Sonia

Susan — Hebrew: Lily flower
Sana, Sanna, Sonel, Sue, Sukey, Sukie, Susana, Susanna, Susannah, Susanne, Susette, Susi, Susie, Susu, Susy, Suzanna, Suzanne, Suzetta, Suzette, Suzi, Suzie, Suzy, Zsa Zsa
Susan B. Anthony, leader of the women's suffrage movement, and also known as "America's First Libber," has feminists naming their children in her honor. (In case you're wondering, her middle initial stands for Brownell.)

Susanna/Susanne — See: Susan

Suzu — Japanese: Little bell, long lived, round

Svetla — Czechoslovakian: Light
Svetlana

Sydelle — See: Sadie

Sydney — See: Sidonia

Sylvia — Latin: From the forest
Silva, Silvi, Silvia, Silvie, Silvy, Sylvie

Syna — Greek: Together

T

Tabitha — Aramaic: Gazelle
Tab, Tabba, Tabbi, Tabbie, Tabby
Tabitha is the third generation nose-twitcher on the hit TV series "Bewitched."

Tacita — Latin: Silent
Tace, Taci, Tacye

Taffy — Welsh: Beloved

Tai/Thai — American English: A person from Thailand
U.S. Olympic figure skater Tai Babilonia broke the ice by introducing this name to the world.

Talia — Hebrew: Heaven's dew, lamb
Tal, Tali, Talli, Thalia

Talitha — Aramaic: Maiden; Hebrew: Child
Taletha, Talla, Talli, Tallie, Tally

Tallulah — Native American (Choctaw): Running water
Lula, Tal, Tallou, Talloulah, Talula

Tamah — Hebrew: Innocent, honest
Tama, Tammi, Tammie, Tammy, Thamah

Tamara — Hebrew: Palm tree
Tama, Tamar, Tamarah, Tammi, Tammie, Tammy

Tammy — See: Tamah, Tamara
In the late 1950s and the early 1960s, the name was associated with a series of "Tammy" movies in which the title character was a wholesome and irresistible country girl. But then, in the 1980s, the name became associated with Tammy Faye Bakker, the wife of televangelist Jim Bakker.

Tani — Japanese: Valley

Tania/Tanya — Russian: Fairy queen

Tansy — Greek: Immortality
Tandie, Tansee, Tansey, Tansie, Tanzey

Tara — Irish: Tower
Tarah, Taryn

Tasha — See: Natalie

Tate — English: Cheerful
Tatiana, Tattie, Tatty, Tatum

Tatiana — See: Tate, Titania

Tatum — See: Tate
Actress Tatum O'Neal brought this name to the attention of the American moviegoing public.

Taylor — English: Tailor
Famous novelist Taylor Caldwell would probably like to know that this is becoming a name of the nineties: Garth Brooks named his daughter Taylor, and it's also the name of a spunky and sophisticated young woman on "All My Children." (Well, isn't that where many name trends start?)

Temperance — Latin: Moderation

Tempest — French: Storm
Tempest Bledsoe is one of the young actresses on "The Cosby Show."

Teresa — See: Theresa

Terri/Terry — See: Theresa

Tess/Tessa — See: Theresa
Writers seem to favor this name: Tess McGill, portrayed by Melanie Griffith, is the main character in Working Girl; *Tess of the D'Urbervilles by Thomas Hardy was made into a film called* Tess, *which starred Nastassja Kinski; Dick Tracy's girlfriend in Chester Gould's comic strip is Tess Trueheart; and the list goes on. . . .*

Thalassa — Greek: Sea

Thea — Greek: Goddess
Theasa

Thelma — Greek: Nursling, will
Telma
Thelma & Louise — *need we say more?*

Theodora — Greek: God's gift
Fedora, Tedda, Teddi, Teddie, Teddy, Tedra, Teodora, Theda, Theo, Theodosia

Theora — Greek: Thinker

Thera — Greek: Untamed

Theresa — Greek: Reaper
Tera, Teresa, Terese, Teresina, Teresine, Teresita, Teri, Terie, Terri, Terrie, Terry, Tess, Tessa, Tessi, Tessie, Tessy, Therese, Tresa, Tressa

Thirza — Hebrew: Pleasant
Thyrza, Tirza

Thomasina — Greek: Small twin

Sina, Thomasa, Thomasin, Thomasine, Tomasa, Tomasina, Tomasine, Tommi, Tommie, Tommy, Tommyna

Thora — Norse: Thunder
Thordia, Thordis

Thyra — Greek: Shield bearer

Tiffany — Latin: Appearance of the Divine
Tiffanee, Tiffi, Tiffiani, Tiffie, Tiffy, Tyfany, Tyffany
In the Middle Ages, this was a popular name, especially for children born on January 6, the Epiphany (the day the Christ child was first seen by the Magi). The name seemed to disappear for many years, then flourished as the name of an exclusive jewelry store on Fifth Avenue in New York City. In the 1970s, Tiffany resurfaced as a popular name for baby girls.

Tillie/Tilly — See: Otillia

Timothea — Greek: Honor to God
Timma, Timmi, Timmie, Timmy, Timo

Tina — See: Christina/Christine, Ernestine, Valentine

Titania — Greek: Great one
Tatiana
This is the name of the fairy queen in Shakespeare's Midsummer Night's Dream.

Tivona — Hebrew: Lover of nature

Toby — Hebrew: God is good
Toba, Tobey, Tobi, Tobie, Tova, Tovah, Tovey

Toni/Tonia/Tonie/Tony/Tonya — See: Antonia

Topaz — Greek: A gemstone

Tora — Japanese: Tiger

Tori — Japanese: Bird
Torey, Tory

Tosia — Polish: Priceless

Tova/Tovah — See: Toby

Tracy — Latin: Brave one
Trace, Tracee, Tracey, Traci, Tracie, Tracye, Trasy

Treva — Celtic: Prudent

Tricia — See: Patricia

Trilby — Italian: Sings with trills

Trina — See: Catherine

Trisha — See: Patricia

Trista — Latin: Melancholy

Trixie — See: Beatrice

Trudy — See: Gertrude

Tuesday — English: Born on Tuesday
Actress Susan Ker Weld changed her name to Tuesday, even though she was born on a Friday.

Tulia — Latin: Of the family; Place name: Town in Texas
Tuli, Tulia, Tulie, Tulley, Tulli, Tullia, Tully

Twila/Twyla — English: A method of weaving
Instead of using wool, famed choreographer Twyla Tharp uses dancers to weave her living tapestries.

U

Udele — German: Prosperous, rich
Uda

Ula — Celtic: Sea jewel

Ulani — Hawaiian: Lighthearted

Ulema/Ulima — Arabic: Wise

Ulrica — German: Ruler of all
Rica, Rikki, Rikky, Ulrika

Ultima — Latin: The greatest, the end, final
This is the name of a successful line of cosmetics.

Uma — Hebrew: Nation

Umeko — Japanese: Plum-blossom child

Una — See: Ona

Undina/Undine — Latin: A wave

Unity — English: Oneness

Urania — Greek: Heaven

Urbana — Latin: Courteous, belonging to the city

Uriana — Greek: The unknown

Ursula — Latin: Female bear
Ulla, Ursa, Ursala, Ursela, Ursola, Ursule, Ursulina

Uta — German: Fortunate maid of battle
As both an actress and an acting teacher, Uta Hagen is one of the most prestigious figures in New York theater circles.

V

Vala — German: Chosen one
Valda — German: Battle heroine
Valentine — Latin: Strong, healthy, valorous
Tina, Val, Vale, Valeda, Valencia, Valentia, Valentina, Valli, Vallie, Vally, Valora, Valore
Name your daughter for this saint and she'll always be your Valentine. (Also, think of the great selection of greeting cards you can choose from!)
Valerie — French: Strong
Valera, Valeree, Valeri, Valeria, Valery, Valory
Valeska — Slavic: Glorious ruler
Vana/Vanna — English: High (Also see: Vanessa)
Vanda — Slavic: Wanderer
Vanessa — Greek: Butterfly
Nessa, Nessi, Nessie, Nessy, Phanessa, Van, Vana, Vanna, Vanni, Vannie, Vanny
Vania/Vanya — Hebrew: God's gift
Vanora/Vanore — Celtic: White wave
Vardis — Hebrew: Rose
Varda, Vardia, Vardice, Vardina, Vardyce
Varina/Varine — Slavic: Stranger
Veda — Hindi: Sacred knowledge
Veerani — Sri Lankan: Perseverance
Vegena — Hawaiian: Maidenly
Velda — German: Wisdom
Veleda
Velika — Slavic: Great one
Velma — German: Resolute guardian
Velvet — Latin: A smooth, luxurious fabric
Venus — Latin: Goddess of love
Venda, Veneta, Venetia, Venita
Vera — Latin: True, faithful
Veradis, Veral, Vere, Verena, Verene, Verina, Verine, Verity, Verla
Verbena — Latin: Sacred plant
Verda — Latin: Young, fresh

Verna/Verne — Latin: Springlike
Vernette, Vernice, Vernine, Vernis, Vernita, Vernona

Veronica — Latin: True likeness
Ronnee, Ronni, Ronnie, Ronny, Veronike, Veronique, Veronka, Vonnee, Vonni, Vonnie, Vonny
Actress Veronica Lake was known in the 1940s for a hairdo that covered one eye, thus earning her the nickname "the Peekaboo Girl."

Vesta — Latin: Guardian of the sacred fire

Vevila — Irish: Melodious voice

Vicki/Vicky — See: Victoria

Victoria — Latin: Victorious one
Tori, Toria, Torri, Torrie, Torry, Vic, Vicki, Vickie, Vicky, Victorine, Vikki, Vitoria, Vittoria
Queen Victoria's sixty-four-year reign is the longest in English history. Because she was so loved by her people, many parents named their offspring in her honor.

Vida — See: Davida

Vilma — Russian: Protector
Valma

Vincentia — Latin: Conqueror
Vincenta, Vincenza, Vincie

Vinna — Spanish: From the vine
Vinni, Vinnia, Vinnie, Vinny

Violet — Latin: A violet flower
Vi, Viola, Violaine, Violanie, Violenta, Violeta, Violetta, Violette, Vyolet, Vyolette

Virginia — Latin: Maidenly, pure
Ginni, Ginnie, Ginny, Girgi, Girgie, Girgy, Jinnia, Vergi, Vergie, Vergy
Virginia Dare was the first child of English parents to be born in the U.S. It happened in 1587 on Roanoke Island. This first natural-born citizen was named both for the state of Virginia and in honor of Elizabeth, "the Virgin Queen."

Vita — Latin: Life

Viveca — Scandinavian: Alive, lively
Viva, Viveka

Vivian — Latin: Vital, full of life
Viv, Viviana, Vivianne, Vivie, Vivien, Vivienne, Vivy, Vivyan, Vivyanne

Voleta — Greek: Veiled one
Vrida — Spanish: Green

W

Walda — German: Ruler
Wallis — English: From Wales
Wallace, Walli, Wallie, Wally
This name was made famous by Wallis Warfield Simpson, the twice-divorced American whose friendship with England's King Edward VIII led to his abdication and their marriage.
Wanda — German: Wanderer
Wandi, Wandie, Wandis, Wandy
Waneta/Wanetta — Native American: Charger
Wendy — English: Fair
Wendee, Wendi, Wendie
This name's fame goes back to 1904 when J. M. Barrie's Peter Pan was published. Today, we associate the name with a frying pan and burgers!
Whitney — English: From clear water
Whitnee, Whitni, Whitnie, Whitny
This name has been at the top of the charts for young girls since singer Whitney Houston first appeared on the music charts.
Wilda — English: Untamed
Wilhelmina — German: Resolute guardian
Vilhemina, Vilhemine, Vilma, Wilameena, Wileen, Wilhelmine, Willa, Willee, Willella, Willetta, Willette, Willi, Willie, Willy, Wilma, Wilmena, Wilmett, Wilona, Wilone, Wylma
Willa — See: Wilhelmina, Willabelle
Willabelle — German: Chosen one
Willa, Willabel, Willabella, Willee, Willi, Willie, Willy
Wilma — See: Wilhelmina
Winda — Swahili: Hunter
Winema — Native American: Woman chief
Winifred — German: Friend of peace; Welsh: White wave
Freddi, Freddie, Freddy, Fredi, Win, Winni, Winnie, Winny, Wynn

Winona — Native American (Sioux): Firstborn daughter; Place name: Town in Minnesota
Wenona, Wenonah, Winnie, Winonah, Wynnona, Wynona
Actress Winona Ryder (née Winona Laura Horowitz) was born in Winona, Minnesota.
Winter — Nature name: From the wintertime
Wyanet — Native American: Beautiful
Wynne — Celtic: Fair
Wyn, Wyna, Wynetta, Wynette

X

Xanthe — Greek: Golden haired
Xantah
Xaviera — Arabic: Brilliant
Xaverie
Xena — Greek: The welcomed
Xene, Xenia, Ximena, Zena, Zenia
Ximena — Hebrew: He heard
Xylia — Greek: Wood dweller

Y

Yaffa/Yaffah — Hebrew: Lovely
Yamuna — Hindi: Sacred river
Yarmilla — Slavic: Merchant
Yasmine — See: Jasmine
Yedda — English: Singer
Yetta — German: To give (Also see: Henrietta)
Ynez — See: Agnes
Yoko — Japanese: Positive child, good
Yoko Ono, widow of Beatle John Lennon, has made this name known worldwide.

Yolanda — French: Violet flower
  Iolanda, Iolande, Iolantha, Iolanthe, Yolande, Yolane, Yolantha, Yolanthe
Yonina — Hebrew: Dove
  Yona, Yonah, Yoni, Yonina, Yoninah, Yonit, Yonita
Yorki — Japanese: Trustworthy
Yovela — Hebrew: Rejoicing
Yvette — See: Yvonne
Yvonne — French: Archer; Greek: Yew wood
  Evette, Evonna, Evonne, Ivonne, Vonni, Vonnie, Vonny, Yevette, Yvette

Z

Zabrina — See: Sabrina
Zada/Zaida — Arabic: Lucky one
Zahara — Swahili: Flower
Zahra — Arabic: White
Zandra — See: Alexandra
Zara/Zarah — See: Sara/Sarah
Zaza — Arabic: Flowery; Hebrew: Movement
Zehava — Hebrew: Golden
  Zehavi, Zehavit
Zelda — See: Griselda
Zelenka — Czechoslovakian: Little innocent one
Zelia — Greek: Zealous
Zella/Zelly — See: Giselle
Zelma — See: Selma
Zena — See: Xena/Xene, Zenobia
Zenevera/Zenavere/Zenevieve — See: Guenevere/Guinevere
Zenobia — Greek: Given life by Zeus
  Zena, Zenaida, Zenaide, Zenda, Zendia, Zizi
Zephyra — Greek: West wind
  Zepha, Zephra, Zephrys, Zyra
Zeva — Greek: Sword; Hebrew: Wolf
Zevida — Hebrew: Gift
  Zevuda

Zia — Hebrew: To tremble; Place name: Town in New Mexico

Zila — Hebrew: Shadow
Zilla, Zillah

Zinia/Zinnia — English: A brilliant flower
The flower zinnia was named for German botanist Johann Gottfried Zinn.

Zippora — Hebrew: Little bird, sparrow
Zippi, Zippie, Zipporah, Zippy

Zita — Spanish: Little rose

Ziva — Hebrew: Brilliance, brightness

Zizi — Hungarian: Dedicated to God

Zoe — Greek: Life
Zoa, Zoela, Zoeta, Zoia, Zolida, Zolita

Zofia/Zofie — See: Sophia/Sophie

Zohra — See: Isadora/Isidora

Zora — Slavic: Dawn
Zorah, Zorana, Zorane, Zorina, Zorine, Zyra

Zsa Zsa — See: Susan
Colorful show-business personality Zsa Zsa Gabor is best known for her many marriages, her run-in with the Los Angeles Police, and her unusual first name.

Zulema — Arabic: Peace
Sulema

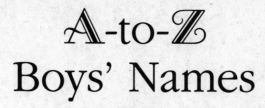

A-to-Z
Boys' Names

A

Aaron — Hebrew: Enlightened one, to sing, to shine, mountain
Aaran, Aaren, Aeron, Aharon, Aron, Haroun

Abbot/Abbott — Aramaic: Father
Ab, Abad, Abba, Abbe, Abbey, Abbie, Abby, Abott

Abdul/Abdullah — Arabic: Servant of the Lord, generous and powerful son of Allah

Abe — See: Abraham

Abelard — German: Highborn; English: Keeper of the abbey's larder
Abby, Abel, Abell, Able, Aleard

Abner — Hebrew: Father of light
Abner Doubleday was nicknamed "the Father of Baseball" because he invented the game. NOT! Baseball was actually created in England and originally called "rounders." In fact, Jane Austen refers to baseball in a novel written at the end of the 1700s.

Abraham — Hebrew: Father of the multitudes
Abe, Abie, Abira, Abrahan, Abram, Abramo, Abramus, Aram, Avram, Avrom, Bram, Ibaheem, Ibrahim
Abraham Lincoln, sixteenth president of the U.S., had many nicknames. The first that comes to mind is "Honest Abe," which some historians say Lincoln earned as a judge and referee at cockfights.

Ace — Latin: Unity, topnotch, first-rate
There are lots of positive associations with this name: It's the top card in a deck of cards; in racket games, a serve that one's opponent cannot return; a person who is an expert in his/her field; and, in the phrase "an ace in the hole," a hidden advantage.

Achilles — Greek: Without lips
Achill, Achille, Achilleus
The hero of Homer's Iliad *had a small but mortal weakness. He was invulnerable in all places except in the heel of his foot.*

Acim — Hebrew: The Lord will judge
Achim, Akim

Adam — Hebrew: Man, human being, son of the red earth

Adamo, Adams, Adan, Adao, Addam, Addams, Addis, Addison, Addy, Ade, Adham, Edam

According to biblical lore, Adam was, of course, the first man. And in case you've always wondered how the Adam's apple got its name, one theory says that it's a vestige of Adam's first sin — a piece of the forbidden fruit which lodged in his throat.

Addison — See: Adam

Adlai/Adley — Hebrew: Refuge of God; Arabic: To act justly

Adlai Ewing Stevenson was Grover Cleveland's vice president. Adlai Ewing Stevenson II was a statesman, diplomat, ambassador, and presidential candidate who was nicknamed "Egghead" because of his great intellect. And Adlai Ewing Stevenson III was a U.S. senator.

Adler — German: Eagle

Adley — Hebrew: The just

Adolph — German: Noble wolf

Adolf, Adolphus, Dolf, Dolph, Dolphus

Adonis — Greek: Masculine beauty

Adrian — Latin: Dark one

Adriance, Adriano, Adrien, Hadrian, Hadrien

Aherne — Celtic: Lord of the horses

Ahearn, Ahearne, Ahern, Hearn, Hearne

Ahmad/Ahmed — Arabic: Most praised

Aidan — Gaelic: Fire

Actor Aidan Quinn has brought this name to the attention of TV viewers and film fans.

Ainsley — Gaelic: He himself; English: My meadow or land

Ain, Ainslie, Ayn

Akira — Japanese: Bright boy

Al — Nickname for names starting with "Al"

Aladdin — Arabic: Height of religion

Laddie, Laddy

Alan/Allan — Celtic: Handsome

Ailin, Alain, Alano, Alen, Allen, Alleyn, Allyn

Alaric — German: Ruler of all

Alar, Alarick, Aleric, Alric, Alrick, Aric, Arick

Alastair — Greek: Avenging one

Alasdair, Alaster, Alastor, Alistair

Albert — German: Nobly bright

Adalbert, Adelbert, Ailbert, Alber, Alberto, Albie, Alby, Athelbert, Edelbert, Elbert

Alden — English: Old learned friend
Aldin, Aldwin, Aldwyn, Alwin, Elden, Eldin, Eldwin, Eldwyn

Aldous — English: From the old house
Aldis, Aldo, Aldus, Eldis, Eldous
Author Aldous Leonard Huxley, who gained fame for his satirical novels and short stories, is best known for Brave New World.

Aldrich — English: Wise ruler
Aldric, Aldridge, Allric, Alrick, Eldrich, Eldridge

Alec/Alex — See: Alexander
Sir Alec Guinness, a fine actor, is not the only talented thespian with this first name. Alec Baldwin is also right up there on the marquee, with his name above the title.

Alexander — Greek: Protector of humankind
Alec, Alejandro, Alejo, Aleksander, Alessandro, Alex, Alexandre, Alexio, Alexis, Alexius, Alic, Alisander, Alister, Alix, Alsandair

Alfie — See: Alfred

Alfred — English: Good counselor and judge
Aelfred, Ailfred, Alf, Alfie, Alfredo, Alfy
English poet laureate Alfred Lord Tennyson was the spokesperson for the Victorian age. Alfred E. Neuman is the mascot for Mad *magazine.*

Alger — German: Noble spearman

Algernon — French: With a mustache

Ali — Arabic: The greatest, a form of Allah (the title of the supreme being in the Muslim faith)

Allard — English: Determined, noble

Allen — See: Alan/Allan

Alonso/Alonzo — See: Alphonse/Alphonso

Aloysius — See: Lewis

Alphonse/Alphonso — German: Ready for battle
Alfons, Alon, Alonso, Alonzo, Alphie, Fons, Fonsie, Fonz, Fonzie, Lon, Lonnie, Lonny

Alva/Alvah — Hebrew: Exalted one
American inventor Thomas Alva Edison is one of a few noted Americans whose middle name is well known.

Alvin — German: Old friend
Alban, Albin, Aloin, Aluin, Aluino, Alvan, Alvie, Alvy, Alwin, Alwyn

Alvis — Norse: All-wise
Country-and-western singer Buck Owens was born Alvis Edgar Owens.

Amadeus — Latin: Love of God
Amadea, Amadeo, Amadis, Amado, Amias
The film Amadeus, *about the* wunderkind *composer Wolfgang Amadeus Mozart, taught us not only about his life, but how to pronounce his middle name.*

Amandus — Latin: Worthy of love
Amand, Amando

Ambros/Ambrose — Greek: Divine, immortal
Ambie, Ambrogio, Ambroise, Ambrosio, Ambrosius, Ambrotos, Ambrozio, Amby, Brose

Amiel — Hebrew: Lord of my people

Amin — Hindi: Faithful, loyal
Amen, Ammon, Amnon, Amon

Amos — Hebrew: Borne by God

Anatol/Anatole — Greek: Rising sun
Anatolio, Toli, Tolio

Andre — See: Andrew
Andre Agassi, the 1992 winner at Wimbledon, is sure to influence the name choice of expectant tennis fans.

Andrew — Greek: Strong, manly
Anders, Andie, Andre, Andrea, Andreas, Andres, Andrie, Andry, Andy
Seventh U.S. president Andrew Jackson was called "Old Hickory" by his soldiers in the War of 1812 because he was said to be as tough as hickory.

Andy — See: Andrew

Angelo — Greek: Angel
Ange, Angel, Angell, Angelos, Angie, Angy, Engel
Angel (Thomas) Cordero, Jr., won the Kentucky Derby twice and is one of the highest-earning jockeys of all time.

Angus — Celtic: Chosen one, unique strength

Anselm/Anselme — German: With divine protection
Anse, Ansel, Anselmi, Anselmo, Ansthelm, Elmo

Anson — English: Son of a nobleman
Anse, Hanson
Fans of "Happy Days" know Anson Williams as Warren "Potsie" Weber.

Anthony — Latin: Priceless, inestimable beyond praise
Antoin, Antoine, Anton, Antone, Antoni, Antonin, Antonio, Antonius, Antony, Toni, Tonio, Tony

Actor Anthony Hopkins won an Academy Award for his memorable performance in The Silence of the Lambs.

Anwar — Arabic: Shafts of light
Anwar Sadat was the Egyptian leader noted for promoting peace with Israel.

Apollo — Greek: Powerful

Archer — See: Archibald

Archibald — English: Very bold
Arch, Archer, Archibaldo, Archibold, Archie, Archy

Arden — French: Fiery, flashing
Ardie, Ardin, Ardy

Argus — Greek: Vigilant

Argyle — Celtic: From the land of the Irish

Ari — See: Aries, Aristotle

Aric — See: Alaric

Aries — Latin: Ram, first sign of the zodiac

Aristotle — Greek: Best of thinkers
Ari, Aristo
Aristotle (384–322 B.C.) is known as "the Pope of Philosophy." Aristotle Socrates Onassis (1906–75) is known as Jacqueline Kennedy's second husband and as "the Golden Greek" who parlayed his hourly earnings of twenty-five cents into millions before he was thirty.

Arlo — See: Harlow

Armand — German: Army man
Arman, Armando, Armin

Arnold — German: Strong as an eagle
Arn, Arnaldo, Arnaud, Arne, Arney, Arnie, Arno, Arnoldo, Arno, Arnot, Arny
As a bodybuilder, Arnold Schwarzenegger sure lived up to the meaning of this name. He was three-time winner of the Mr. Universe title and seven-time winner of the Mr. Olympia title.

Arthur — Welsh: Noble, high
Art, Artair, Arte, Arth, Artie, Artur, Arturo, Artus, Arty, Aurthur

Arvad/Arvid — English: Friend
Arv, Arvin, Arvy

Asa — Hebrew: Healer, physician

Asher — Hebrew: Happy one

Ashley — English: From the ash-tree meadow
Ashlin, Ashly

Americans know this name from the Gone with the Wind *character Ashley Wilkes, played in the film by English actor Leslie Howard. Recently Ashley has been enjoying great popularity as both a boy's and a girl's name.*

Aubrey — German: Powerful, elf ruler
Alberik, Auberon, Aubry, Aulberich, Avery

August/Auguste — Latin: The exalted, the sacred
Agosto, Aguistin, Agustin, Augie, Augustin, Augustine, Augusto, Augustus, Augy, Austen, Austin

Austen/Austin — See: August/Auguste

Averell — English: Born in April
Ave, Averil, Averill

Avery — See: Aubrey

Avi — Hebrew: My Father (implying God)

Axel — German: Divine reward
Aksel, Ax, Axe, Axtel, Axtell
Axel Foley is the Beverly Hills Cop *portrayed by Eddie Murphy.*

Azrael — Hebrew: The Lord is my help
Azar, Azrail, Azreel, Azriel

B

Bailey — Latin: Trusted public servant
Bailie, Baillie, Bailly, Baily, Bayley

Baldwin — German: Bold friend
Baldovino, Balduin, Baudoin, Baudouin

Balin — Hindi: Mighty soldier

Ballard — German: Bold, strong

Bancroft — English: From the bean field
Bannie, Banny

Barclay — English: From the birch-tree meadow
Barc, Berk, Berkeley, Berkie, Berkley, Berky

Barnabas — Hebrew: Son of prophecy
Barna, Barnaba, Barnabe, Barnaby, Barnebas, Barney, Barnie, Barny
The name and its derivatives lend themselves to popular TV characters: Barnabas (played by Jonathan Frid), the sympathetic vampire in the soap opera "Dark Shadows"; Barnaby

Jones (played by Buddy Ebsen), the private investigator in the series of the same name; Barney Miller (played by Hal Linden), a police captain in a sitcom of the same name; Barney Rubble (Mel Blanc's voice), Fred's neighbor in "The Flintstones"; and Barney Fife (played by Don Knotts), an inept deputy sheriff on "The Andy Griffith Show."

Barnett — English: Nobleman
Barnet, Barney, Barnie, Barny

Barney — See: Barnabas, Barnett

Barret/Barrett — German: Bearlike strength

Barry — Celtic: Pointed, spearlike

Bart — See: Bartholomew, Barton
Bart Simpson. If we need to explain who he is, chances are you won't want to know.

Bartholomew — Hebrew: Son of a farmer
Bart, Bartel, Barth, Barthel, Barthelemy, Barthol, Bartholomeus, Bartlet, Bartlett, Bartley, Bartol, Bartolome, Bartolomeo, Bartolos, Bat, Bortolo

Barton — English: From the barley farm
Bart

Baruch — Hebrew: Blessed

Basil — Greek: Royal
Bas, Basile, Basilio, Basilius, Vasilis, Vassily

Baxter — English: Baker

Bayard — English: With reddish brown hair

Beau — See: Beaumont, Beauregard

Beaumont — French: From a beautiful mountain
Beau, Bo

Beauregard — French: Beautiful view
Beau

Beck — English: A brook

Ben — Hebrew: Son (Also: Nickname for names starting with "Ben")

Benedict — Latin: Blessed
Bendix, Benedetto, Benedick, Benedicto, Benedike, Benedikt, Benedix, Benet, Benito, Bennet, Bennett, Benoit, Bento, Benzel

Benjamin — Hebrew: Favorite son
Benjie, Benjy, Bennie, Benny, Binyamin
Benjamin Franklin was a revolutionary, statesman, author, publisher, scientist, inventor, philanthropist, and philosopher. Yet even with Franklin's many talents, it took a young guy

named Benjamin Braddock (played by Dustin Hoffman), who was fresh out of college in the 1967 film The Graduate, *to make the name popular.*

Bennet/Bennett — See: Benedict

Benson — Hebrew: Son of Benjamin
Robert Guillaume played Benson DuBois, the governor's butler, in the TV sitcom "Benson."

Bentley — English: From the meadows

Benton — English: Moor-dweller
Most of the boys' names listed here were family names that are now being used as first names. Benton, as in Thomas Hart Benton, is a perfect example. Benton served as senator from Missouri for thirty years. He initiated the issuance of gold coins. In fact, he was so identified with gold coins that they were referred to as "Benton's Mint Drops."

Berkeley/Berkley — See: Barclay

Bernard — German: Brave as a bear
Barnard, Bearnard, Bern, Bernaldo, Bernardo, Bernarr, Bernhard, Bernie, Berny

Bert/Burt — English: Bright; See Burton (Also, a nickname for names starting or ending with "Bert")
Burt Reynolds was born Burton Leon Reynolds, Jr. When he and Bert Convy formed a company together, they called it Burt & Bert Productions.

Berthold — German: Brilliant ruler
Berthoud, Bertie, Bertold, Bertolde, Bertoldi, Berty

Bertram — English: Bright raven
Bartram, Bartrand, Bertran, Bertrand, Bertrando, Burtrand
Bertrand Russell was a British philosopher, essayist, mathematician, and active opponent of the arms race.

Bevan — Celtic: Young archer
Bev, Beven, Bevin

Bill/Billy — See: William
Nicknames such as these are big in show biz and used by Bill Cosby, Bill Bixby, Bill Murray, Billy Dee Williams, Billy Crystal, Billy Joel, and Billy Ray Cyrus, to name just a few.

Bingham — German: From the stone hamlet
Bing, Bingam

Birch — English: At the birch tree

Birney — English: Dweller on the brook island
Birn, Burney, Burny

Bjorn — Swedish and Norse: Bearlike
Swedish-born Bjorn Borg, a five-time winner at Wimbledon, is responsible for introducing this name to Americans.

Blaine — Gaelic: Thin one
Blainey, Blane, Blayn, Blayne

Blair — Gaelic: From the field

Blake — English: Fair haired, fair complected
Blake Edwards, director, producer, screenwriter, actor, and husband of Julie Andrews, was born William Blake McEdwards.

Blaze — German: Torch, firebrand
Biagio, Blaise, Blas, Blase, Blasien, Blasius, Blayze

Bo — See: Beaumont, Bogart

Boaz — Hebrew: Swift, strong

Bob/Bobbie/Bobby — See: Robert
If you thought Bill and Billy were popular show-biz nicknames, take a look at this: Bob Newhart, Bob Barker, Bob Saget, Buffalo Bob Smith, Bob Vila, Bob Hope, Bob Eubanks, Bob Denver, Bob Einstein, Bob Keeshan, Bob Costas, Bob Goulet, Bob Dylan, Bobby Vinton. This could take up the rest of the book, so we'd better cut the list short. Bobby Short.

Bogart — Danish: Archer
Bo, Bogie, Bogy

Bolton — English: Of the manor farm
Bolt

Bond — English: One who tills the soil

Boone — French: A blessing

Booth/Boothe — English: Hut

Borden — English: From the boar's valley

Boris — Slavic: Warrior
Actor Boris Karloff, the star of the 1931 film Frankenstein, *was born William Henry Pratt.*

Boyd — Irish: Fair haired
Bow, Bowen, Bowie, Boyde, Boyden

Brad — Nickname for names starting with "Brad"

Braden — English: From the wide valley
Brade, Bradie

Bradford — English: From the wide river-crossing

Bradley — English: From the broad meadow
Brad, Bradleigh, Bradly, Bradney

Brady — Irish: Spirited one

Bram — See: Abraham

Brandon — English: Swordlike
  Bran, Brand, Brandt, Brant, Branton
Brendan — Irish: Little raven
  Bren, Brend, Brenden, Brendin, Brendon, Brennan, Brennen,
  Brennon
Brent — English: Tall, erect
Bret/Brett — Celtic: Native of Brittany
  Brit, Britt
  *Bret Harte, teacher, gold seeker, and journalist, wrote novels and
  humorous poems of the early West.*
Brewster — German: Brewer
Brian — Irish: Strong, formidable
  Briano, Briant, Brien, Brion, Bryan, Bryant, Bryon
Brice/Bryce — Celtic: Swift moving, ambitious
Brigham — English: Dweller at the bridge
  *Mormon leader Brigham Young encouraged and practiced po-
  lygamy. Nicknamed "the Lion of the Lord," he is said to have had
  twenty-seven wives and forty-seven children. Now he is one who
  could have used this book!*
Brock — English: A badger
  *Brock Peters, one of the leading black film actors of the sixties
  and seventies, was born Brock Fisher.*
Broderick — English: From the broad ridge
Brodie/Brody — Irish: Ditch
Bronson — English: Son of the dark-skinned one
  Bron, Bronnie, Bronny, Bruns
Brooke — English: Dweller at the brook
  Brook, Brooks
Bruce — French: From the brushwood
  Broose, Brucie, Brucy
  *With the popularity of Bruce Willis and "the Boss," Bruce
  Springsteen, this name has taken on a more macho association
  than it had during the Johnny Carson "Tonight Show" era.*
Bruno — Italian: Brown-haired one
Bryan/Bryant — See: Brian
Buck — English: Male deer
  Buckie, Bucky
  *Buck Owens, country and western singer and host of "Hee
  Haw," was born Alvis Edgar Owens.*
Bud — German: To puff up
  Budd, Buddie, Buddy

Burgess — German: Townsman; English: Citizen

Burke — French: From the fortress
Berk, Berke, Bourke, Burk, Burkett

Burl — English: Wine servant
Byrl, Byrle
Actor and folk singer Burl Ives was born (believe it or not) Icle Ivanhoe.

Burr — Swedish: Youth

Burton — English: Bright fame
Burt

Byram — Aramaic: Celebration

Byrd — English: Birdlike

Byron — English: From the country estate

C

Caesar — Latin: Hirsute (hairy)
Casar, Cesar, Cesare, Cesario, Kaiser
Legend has it that Julius Caesar was born "from the incised womb of his mother" and named for the Latin words for the process (caesus — the past participle of caedere, to cut). That's why we now refer to that birth method as "Caesarean."

Cahil — Turkish: Young, innocent

Cain — Hebrew: Possession

Cal — Nickname for names starting with "Cal"

Caleb/Kaleb — Hebrew: Dog, impetuous and bold, faithful

Caley — Gaelic: Lithe
Cale, Calie, Cally

Calhoun — Celtic: Warrior

Calvin — Latin: Bald one
Calve, Calvert, Calvino, Calvy
The thirtieth president of the U.S. was born John Calvin Coolidge. He was nicknamed "Silent Cal" because he was a man of few words. Maybe that's why he dropped the "John." That way, when asked his name, it was one less word to say.

Camden — Gaelic: Dweller in the winding valley

Cameron — Celtic: Crooked nose

Campbell — French: From a bright field

Canute — Latin: White haired
  Cnut, Knut, Knute

Carey/Cary — Welsh: Dweller near the castle
  Archibald Alexander Leach changed his name to Cary Grant.

Carl — See: Charles (Also, a nickname for names starting with "Carl")

Carlin — Gaelic: Little champion

Carlisle/Carlyle — English: From the loyal stronghold

Carlos — See: Charles

Carlton — English: Farmer's settlement
  Carl, Carleton, Carlie, Carly, Charl, Charley, Charlie, Charlton

Carmine — Latin: Song

Carney/Carny — Gaelic: Victorious warrior, winner

Carol/Carroll — See: Charles
  Carroll O'Connor was the big-time bigot Archie Bunker in the ten-season hit sitcom "All in the Family."

Carr — Norse: From the marshland

Carson — Welsh: Son of a marsh-dweller

Carter — English: Cart driver, maker of carts

Carver — English: One who carves
  Carv, Carvey, Carvy

Casey — Irish: Watchful one

Casimir — Slavic: A command for peace
  Cas, Cass, Kashmir, Kasimir, Kazimir

Casper — Persian: Holder of treasure; Place name: A town in Wyoming
  Caspar, Gaspar, Gasper
  Caspar or Gaspar is one of the three wise men (magi) from the East (Magi) who journeyed to Bethlehem to present the baby Jesus with gifts.

Cassidy — Irish: Ingenious one

Cassius — Latin: Vain
  Cash, Cass, Cassie, Cassy, Caz
  The full name of J. C. Penney, founder of the national chain store of the same name, is James Cash Penney. How is that for parents' intuition!

Cato — Latin: Wise one
  Cate, Caton

Cavanaugh — Celtic: Handsome

Cecil/Cecile — Latin: Dim sighted
  Cece, Cecilio, Cecilius, Cecyl, Kilian

Cedric — English: Chieftain
  Cedric is the father of Rowena, the heroine in Sir Walter Scott's Ivanhoe.
Chad — Celtic: Defender; Place name: A landlocked country in north-central Africa.
  The country gets its name from Lake Chad, on the western border with Niger and Nigeria.
Chaim — Hebrew: Life
  Hy, Hyman, Hymie
Chandler — French: Candlemaker
Channing — Latin: Singer
Chapman — English: Tradesman
  Chap, Chappie, Chappy
Charles — German: Strong, manly
  Carel, Carl, Carlino, Carlo, Carlos, Carol, Carolo, Carrol, Carroll, Caryl, Charley, Charlie, Charly, Chas, Chaz, Chick, Chickie, Chuck, Chucky, Karel, Karl
  This is a name for all mediums: songs ("Charlie, My Boy," "Clap Hands, Here Comes Charlie"), TV series ("Charles in Charge," "Charlie's Angels"), plays (Charley's Aunt), comic-strip characters (Charlie Brown), and films (Charlie Chan, Charley Varrick). Plus, it's a name for a lot of superachievers — Dickens, Lindbergh, Chaplin, de Gaulle, Darwin, Revson — and for royalty — French Kings I–X; Hungarian Kings I–IV; Spanish Kings I–V; Swedish Kings IX–XII; Neapolitan Kings I–III; Portuguese King I; English, Scottish, and Irish Kings I–II; and England's current Prince of Wales, Charles Philip Arthur George Windsor.
Charlton — See: Carleton/Carlton
Chase — French: Hunter
Chauncey — English: Church official
  Chance, Chancellor, Chancey, Chaunce
Chen — Chinese: Vast, great
Chester — Latin: From the walled camp
  Ches, Cheston, Chet
  This was a popular politician's name in the middle 1800s. There was Chester Alan Arthur, who was our twenty-first president, and U.S. senator Chester Ashley, from Arkansas. By insisting that the name of his state be pronounced "Ar-kansas," not "Ar-kensaw," Ashley made a name for himself. He would only answer roll calls when addressed as "the senator from Ar-kansas."
Chico — See: Francis

Christian — Greek: Follower of Christ
Chris, Christen, Christiano, Christin, Cris, Cristiene, Kris, Kriss, Kristian, Kristos

Christopher — Greek: Christ bearer
Chris, Christo, Christoffer, Christoforo, Christoph, Christophe, Christophorus, Christovao, Cristoforo, Cristogal, Kit, Kristo, Kristofor, Kristoforo
Thanks to Cristoforo Colombo, American history proper began on October 12, 1492, when the Genoan sailor landed on the sandy shore of San Salvador.

Chuck — See: Charles

Cicero — Italian: Sightseeing guide; Latin: Chickpea
Ciceron, Ciro, Cyrano, Cyro

Clarence — Latin: Illustrious one
Clair, Clare

Clark/Clarke — English: Learned one
Clark Gable, born William Clark Gable, was known as "the King of Hollywood."

Claud/Claude — Latin: Lame one
Claudio, Claudius, Claus

Clayborn/Clayborne — English: Born of the earth
Claiborn, Clay

Clayton — English: From the clay town

Clement — Latin: Merciful, kind
Clem, Clemence, Clemens, Clemente, Clementius, Clemmi, Clemmie, Clemmons, Clemmy, Clim, Klemens
> *"T'was the night before Christmas,"*
> *And whether rich or poor,*
> *We all know this poem,*
> *Thanks to Clement Clarke Moore.*

Cleveland — English: Cliff land; Place name: A city in Ohio
Cleve

Clifford — English: Dweller at the ford near the cliff
Cliff, Cliffie, Cliffy

Clifton — English: Farm by the cliff

Clinton — English: Hill town
Clint
Clint Eastwood, born Clinton Eastwood, Jr., is an actor, director, and producer.

Clive/Clyve — English: From the cliff
Clive Davis, world-renowned music impresario, and president

and founder of Arista Records, is responsible for launching the careers of Barry Manilow, Lisa Stansfield, Aretha Franklin, Dionne Warwick, and Whitney Houston.

Clovis — German: Of holy fame

Clyde — Welsh: Heard from afar

Cody — Irish: Helpful; English: Pillow
Kathie Lee Gifford (co-star of "Live with Regis & Kathie Lee") and husband Frank Gifford have a son named Cody. Since she reports on his progress almost daily on national TV, Kathie Lee is responsible for the fast-growing popularity of this name.

Colbert — English: Outstanding seafarer
Calvert, Cole, Colvert, Culbert

Colby — English: From a coal town

Coleman/Colman — English: Charcoal burner
Cole, Colum, Columbo, Columbus

Colin — Gaelic: Child
Colan, Collin

Collier — English: Miner
Colier, Colis, Collie, Colly, Collyer, Colyer

Conan — Celtic: Intelligent
Conal, Conant, Conlan, Connal, Kynan
This name was associated with Sir Arthur Conan Doyle, the creator of Sherlock Holmes. But that has changed since the release of the sword-and-sorcery films Conan the Barbarian *(1982) and* Conan the Destroyer *(1984).*

Connor — Celtic: Wise aid
Connaire, Connie, Conny

Conrad — German: Wise counsellor
Conrade, Conrado, Cort, Curt, Konrad, Kort, Kurt
Conrad Hilton was the founder of the major international hotel chain.

Conroy — Irish: Wise man

Constantin/Constantine — Latin: Firm, constant
Constant, Constantino, Constantinus, Konstantin, Konstantine

Conway — Celtic: Wise way

Cooper — English: Barrel maker
Coop

Corbet/Corbett — French: Raven
Corbie, Corbin, Corby

Cordel/Cordell — French: Small rope
Cord, Cordie, Cordy

Core/Cory — English: Chosen one
Correy, Corry, Currey, Curry

Cornelius — Latin: Battle born
Cornel, Cornelio, Cornell, Cornellus

Cosmo — Greek: Order, harmony, universe
Cosimo, Cosmos, Kosmo, Kosmos

Courtland — English: Dweller in the court
Cort, Court, Courtenay, Courtnay, Courtney

Craig — Scottish: From the stony hill

Creighton — English: From the town near the creek, rocky spot
Crei, Creight, Crichton

Crispin — Latin: Curly haired
Crepin, Cres, Crespin, Crisp, Crispino, Crispo, Crispus

Crosby — English: Dweller near the town crossing
Crosbey, Crosbie

Cullen — Irish: Handsome one
Cull, Cullan, Cullie, Cullin, Cully

Curran — Irish: Champion, hero
Curr, Currey, Currie, Curry

Curtis — French: Courteous one
Curcio, Curt, Curtiss
Curtis Sliwa is the courageous founder of the Guardian Angels.

Cyrano — Greek: From Cyrene (Also see: Cicero)
Of course you know of Cyrano de Bergerac, the fictional character created by Edmond Rostand. But do you know there was a French author, playwright, soldier, and adventurer with the same name, who lived from 1619 to 1655? The one thing the two Cyranos had in common was a very long nose.

Cyril — Greek: Lord
Ciril, Cirille, Cirillo, Ciro, Cy, Cyr, Cyrill, Cyrille, Cyrillus, Cyro, Kyril, Kyrillos

Cyrus — Persian: Sun
Ciro, Cy, Cyro, Kyros

D

Dakota/Dakotah — Native American (Sioux): Friend
Dalbert — German: From a bright place
Dal

Dale — German: Valley dweller
The surname of Dale Carnegie, author of
How to Win Friends and Influence People, *a*
negey." He changed the spelling when he u
at — you guessed it — Carnegie Hall.

Dallas — Celtic: Skilled; Place name: A city in

Dalton — English: From the valley

Daly — English: Counsellor

Damon — Greek: Constant one
Damas, Damian, Damiano, Damien
Damon Runyon, who was born Alfred Damon Runyon, was a
journalist and short-story writer who gave us "Guys and Dolls."

Dan/Dannie/Danny — See: Daniel

Dana — Norse: From Denmark
Daen, Dain, Dane, Dayn, Dene

Daniel — Hebrew: God is my judge
Dan, Daniell, Dannel, Dannie, Danny
This popular name, in all its forms, has always been big in show
biz: Consider Danny DeVito, Dan Duryea, Dan Daily, Danny
Thomas, Danny Aiello, Danny Kaye, Daniel Day-Lewis, Dan
Rowan, and Daniel J. Travanti, for starters.

Dante — Latin: Enduring one
Darte, Duran, Durand, Durant, Durante

Darby — Celtic: Free man

Darcy/Darsy — Irish: Dark looking
Darcel, Darcey, Darsey

Darius — Greek: Wealthy
Dare, Darie, Dario
This was the name of some ancient Persian rulers.

Darnel/Darnell — French: From the hidden place

Darrel/Darryl — English: Beloved
Darrell, Darrilo, Darrol, Daryl, Derrell, Derryl, Deryl
As a boy's name, it's more popular than you might think. It was
popular even before the TV sitcom "Newhart," with brothers First
Darryl and Second Darryl. There were movie mogul Darryl F.
Zanuck, baseball player Darryl Strawberry, and singer/song-
writer Daryl Hall (John Oates's partner), all of whom were given
the name at birth.

Darren/Darrin — See: Dorian

Darwin — German: Daring friend; English: Dear friend
Darwyn, Darwynn, Derwin, Derwynn

Da___ — Hebrew: Beloved, adored

___ack, Dak, Dake, Dave, Davey, Davidde, Davide, Davie, Davy, Dawood, Dawson, Dawud, Devi, Devid, Tavid

This name must be very beloved, or else it wouldn't have appeared on the top-ten names list for boys in the U.S. for the past forty years.

Dean — Latin: Religious official; English: Valley

Dino

Two U.S. secretaries of state — Dean Acheson and Dean Rusk — had this first name.

Dedrick — English: Gifted ruler

Dedric, Diedrick, Dietrich

Delano — French: Healthy dark man, nighttime

Del, Delane, Delaney

Franklin Delano Roosevelt, our thirty-second president, weighed ten pounds at birth.

Delbert — English: Bright as day

Dell — See: Wendel/Wendell

Delmer — Latin: From the sea

Delmar, Delmore

Demetrius — Greek: Lover of the earth

Demeter, Demetre, Demetri, Demetris, Demmy, Dimitri, Dimitrios

Dempsey — Celtic: Proud one

Denby — Norse: From the Danish land

Danby, Danbey, Denbey

Denis/Dennis — Greek: Lover of fine wine

Dennet, Dennett, Dennie, Denny, Densil, Denzel, Denzil, Dion, Dione, Dionisio, Dionysus

One day in 1951, the wife of cartoonist Hank Ketcham said to her husband, "Our son Dennis is a menace." And that's how an idea came into being. That year, Hank Ketcham sold "Dennis the Menace" to the Post-Hall syndicate, and the rest is cartoon history.

Academy Award–winning actor Denzel Washington was in the film Mo' Better Blues, *in which he played trumpeter Bleek Gilliam.*

Derek — See: Derrick

Dermot/Dermott — Irish: Free from envy

Derrick — German: Ruler, leader

Darrick, Dereck, Derek, Derk, Derreck, Derrek, Dirk, Dirke, Dyrk, Dyrke

Derry — Irish: Reddish haired

Derwin — English: Beloved friend

Desmond — Celtic: Man of the world
Des, Dess, Desmund

Deverell — Welsh: From the riverbank

Devin/Devine — Celtic: Poet
Devon, Devyn

Devlin — Irish: Brave one
Devland, Devlen, Devlyn

Dewey — Welsh: Treasured one

DeWitt — Flemish: Fair, blond
Dewitt, Dwight, Witt
Dwight D. Eisenhower, our thirty-fourth president, was born David Dwight Eisenhower. His parents called him Dwight, so he changed his first two names around just before attending West Point.

Dexter — Latin: Right-handed one

Dick — See: Dickson, Richard

Dickson — English: Son of the powerful ruler
Dick, Dixon

Diego — See: James

Digby — Norse: By the dike water

Dirk — See: Derrick

Dolf/Dolph — See: Adolph, Rudolph

Dominic/Dominick — Latin: Of the Lord
Dom, Domenic, Domico, Domingo, Domingus, Nick

Don/Donnie/Donny — See: Donald

Donald — Irish: Prince of the universe
Don, Donal, Donalt, Donley, Donnally, Donnell, Donnie, Donny
Donald Trump is trying to live up to the meaning of this name!

Donato — Latin: Given

Donovan — Irish: Dark warrior
The singer Donovan brought attention to this name in the 1960s, when his "Mellow Yellow" topped the charts.

Dooley — Greek: Dark hero

Dorian — Greek: Gift

Dare, Darey, Darren, Darrin, Doran, Dore, Dorey, Dorie, Doron, Dory

Bandleader/musician Herb Alpert has a son named Dore. The name was created by the first two notes of the musical scale — "do" and "re."

Doron — Hebrew: Gift of the Lord
Dotson — English: Son of Dorothy
Douglas/Douglass — Scottish: From the dark stream
   Doogie, Doug, Dougie, Dougy, Dug, Dugald

Before the nineteenth century, Douglas was as much a girl's name as it was a boy's. But in 1915, when the swashbuckling silent-film star Douglas Fairbanks came upon the scene, he gave the name a macho identity, as did his son, Douglas Fairbanks, Jr. New attention is now being paid to the name — or the nickname — because of the teenage doctor in the hit sitcom "Doogie Howser, M.D."

Dov — Hebrew: Bear
Doyle — Irish: Dark stranger
Drake — German: Male swan
Drew — Welsh: Wise
Drury — German: Sweetheart
Dudley — English: From the meadow.
   Dudley did Moore for this name than anyone.
Dugan — English: To be worthy
Duke — Latin: Leader
Duncan — Gaelic: Dark-skinned warrior
Dunham — Celtic: Dark man
Dunstan — English: From the brown-stone fortress
Durward/Durwood — English: Gatekeeper
Dustin — English: Valiant one

Sources say that Dustin Hoffman's mother was a movie fan and named her son after Dustin Farnum, the silent-screen cowboy star. Now mothers are naming their sons after the Academy Award–winning movie star Dustin Hoffman!

Dwayne — Celtic: From the dunes
   Duane, Dwaine
Dwight — See: DeWitt
Dylan — Welsh: From the sea
   Dillon, Dyllan, Dyllon

Acclaimed poet Dylan Thomas sold his first poem at the age of

twelve. However, the way the story goes, Dylan didn't actually write the poem; he took it from a local newspaper.

Talk about taking . . . Superstar songwriter and performer Bob Dylan, born Robert Allen Zimmerman, took his stage name from his idol, Dylan Thomas.

Dylan is currently one of the most popular fictional TV characters. He's played by Luke Perry on "Beverly Hills 90210."

E

Earl — English: Nobleman
Earle, Earlie, Early, Erie, Erle, Erly, Errol, Erroll, Jarle
Every Perry Mason fan knows the Erle version of this name because of author Erle Stanley Gardner, as does every crossword-puzzle fan.

Earvin — See: Irvin

Ebenezer — Hebrew: Stone of help
Eban, Eben
This name makes one think of "A Christmas Carol," a dickens of a story with a lead character named Ebenezer Scrooge.

Ed/Eddie/Eddy — Nicknames for names starting with "Ed"

Edan — Celtic: Fire

Eden — Hebrew: Place of delight

Edgar — English: Protector of property, happy warrior
Eadgar, Edgard, Edgardo, Ned, Neddie, Neddy
Edgar Allan Poe, poet, critic, and short-story writer, is considered the father of the modern detective story. In his honor the Mystery Writers of America named their annual award "the Edgar."

Edison — English: Son of Edward
Eddison, Edson

Edmond/Edmund — English: Prosperous protector
Eamon, Edmondo, Edmont, Edmundo, Ned, Neddie, Neddy

Edric — English: Rich king

Edsel — English: From the rich man's estate

Edward — English: Prosperous protector
Edik, Edouard, Eduard, Eduardo, Edvard, Ned, Neddie, Neddy, Ted, Teddie, Teddy

During World War I, Edward V. Rickenbacker was America's leading fighter pilot, and Edward became a hero's name. During World War II Rickenbacker volunteered to carry out missions for the War Department. When his B-17 went down in the Pacific Ocean, the whole country prayed for his safe return. After twenty-three days on a raft, he and seven other men were rescued. Once again, the name Edward became popular.

Edwin — English: Prosperous friend
Edlin, Eduiono, Evino
Edwin "Buzz" Aldrin and Neil Armstrong, the first men to walk on the moon, left behind the plaque that stated: "Here men from the planet earth first set foot upon the moon July, 1969 A.D. We came in peace for all mankind."

Efrem — See: Ephraim/Ephriam

Egan/Egon — English: All-powerful

Egbert/Egberto — English: Bright as a sword

Egor — See: George

Eldon — English: From the holy hill
Elden, Eldin, Eldyn
Eldin, the housepainter/artist on the TV sitcom "Murphy Brown," is such a likable character that this "bet-you-never-knew-anyone-with-this-name-before" name is starting to catch on.

Eli/Ely — Hebrew: On high

Elias — See: Elijah

Elihu — See: Elijah
Elihu Yale, for whom Yale University is named, is thought to be the first American millionaire. He made his money in black pepper, which, obviously, is nothing to sneeze at.

Elijah — Hebrew: The Lord is my God
Eli, Elia, Elias, Elie, Eliel, Elihu, Eliot, Ellie, Elliot, Elliott, Ellis, Elly, Ely

Eliot — See: Elijah
Eliot Ness, a federal law officer, took nine federal agents after the Capone mob at the end of the 1920s to the early 1930s. Because the agents couldn't be bought, the underworld called them "the Untouchables."

Elisha — Hebrew: The Lord is salvation

Ellery — German: One who lives near the elder tree
Ellary, Ellerey

Ellery Queen, author of the famous detective novels and stories, was really two people — cousins, in fact: Frederic Dannay and Manfred B. Lee. When they started their collaboration, they chose Ellery because it was the name of a friend at school, and Queen simply because it sounded good with Ellery. The rest is literary history!

Elliot/Elliott — See: Elijah

Ellis — See: Elijah

Ellison — English: Son of Ellis

Elmer — English: Of famed dignity
Aylmar, Aylmer, Elmar, Ulmer

Elmo — Greek: Amiable

Elroy — Latin: Royal

Elton — English: From the old estate
Reginald Kenneth Dwight, a fan of saxophonist Elton Dean and singer John Baldry, changed his name to Elton John — and added Hercules as a middle name, to give him the strength to succeed. It worked!

Elvis — Norse: All-wise
The birth certificate says Elvis Aron Presley, but the tombstone at Graceland says Elvis Aaron Presley. Elvis Costello, the British rock singer, was born Declan Patrick McManus.

Elwin/Elwyn — English: Friend to the elves
Elvin

Emanuel/Emmanuel — Hebrew: God is always with us
Emmanuele, Immanuel, Immanuele, Mannie, Manny, Manuel

Emerson — German: Son of the industrious leader

Emery — German: Industrious leader
Almerick, Amerigo, Amory, Emeri, Emeric, Emmery, Emory

Emile — German: Industrious; Latin: Eager to please
Amal, Emelen, Emil, Emilian, Emilio, Emilius, Emlen, Emlyn

Emmett — English: Hard worker
Emmet, Emmit, Emmitt, Emmot, Emmott
Emmett Ashford was the first black baseball umpire in the majors. In April of 1966, he started for the American League, and he worked his first World Series in 1970.
Emmett Kelly, world-renowned clown, was named by his Irish immigrant father in honor of Irish patriot Robert Emmett.

Engelbert — German: Bright as an angel
Englebert, Ingelbert, Inglebert

The singer Engelbert Humperdinck, christened Arnold George Dorsey at birth, borrowed his professional name from the composer of the opera Hansel and Gretel.

Enoch — Hebrew: Dedicated

Enos — Hebrew: Mortal man

Ephraim/Ephriam — Hebrew: Very fruitful
　Effie, Effy, Efrem, Ephrem, Ephrim

Erasmus — Greek: Lovable
　Erasmios, Erasmo, Erastus, Rasmos, Rasmus

Eric/Erick — Norse: Eternal ruler
　Arek, Arick, Erich, Erik

Ernest — English: Earnest
　Ernesto, Ernestus, Ernie, Ernst, Erny
　Ernest Hemingway was the journalist, novelist, and short-story writer. Ernie Davis was the first black man to win football's coveted Heisman Trophy. At the time — in 1961 — he was a halfback playing for Syracuse University.

Erroll — See: Earl/Earle

Erskine — Scottish: From the high cliff

Ervin/Erwin — Czechoslovakian: Friend of the sea

Esmond/Esmund — English: Gracious protector

Este/Estes — Italian: From the east

Ethan — Hebrew: Strong, firm

Eugene — Greek: Noble, wellborn
　Eugenio, Eugenios, Eugenius, Gene
　Four-time Pulitzer Prize–winner Eugene O'Neill is considered one of America's greatest playwrights.

Eustace — Latin: Stable, tranquil
　Eustache, Eustasius, Eustazio, Eustis

Evan — Welsh: Wellborn one
　Bowen, Evin, Ewan, Ewen, Owain, Owen, Yvain, Ywaine
　*The best-selling novelist (*The Blackboard Jungle*), screenwriter, and TV writer who was born Salvatore Lombino changed his name to Evan Hunter right after graduating from New York City's Hunter College.*

Evelyn — Hebrew: Life
　This name is quite popular in England as a male name (for example, author Evelyn Waugh); in America, it's more popular as a female name.

Everett — English: Mighty as a boar

Eber, Everard, Evered, Everet, Everhard, Everit, Everitt, Evraud, Evre, Ewardo, Ewart, Rhett

Everett Dirksen, the late great senator from Illinois, was not given a middle name at birth. Almost a year after Everett's birth, when William McKinley was elected president, Dirksen's dad decided to give his son the middle name of McKinley.

Ewing — English: Legal friend

Ezekiel — Hebrew: Strength of God
Ezechiel, Ezequiel, Zeke

Ezra — Hebrew: Helper
Esdras, Esra, Ezrah

F

Fabian — Latin: Prosperous farmer, bean grower
Fabe, Faber, Fabiano, Fabien, Fabio, Fabius, Fabyan

Fabron — Latin: Mechanic
Fabra, Fabriano, Fabrizio, Fabroni

Farley — English: From the far meadow
Fairleigh, Farleigh, Farlie, Farly

Farrel/Farrell — Irish: Valorous, heroic
Ferrel, Ferrell

Fedor — Russian: Gift of God

Felix — Latin: Fortunate
Felice, Felicio, Felike, Felizio
As long as there are TV reruns, there will be Felix Unger, the "neat one" on "The Odd Couple."

Fenton — English: Marshland dweller

Ferdinand — German: Peacemaker
Ferd, Ferdie, Ferdinando, Ferdy, Fergus, Fernando, Hernan, Hernando

Fergus — Celtic: Very choice man

Ferris/Farris — Irish: Choice one
The name has been immortalized on film in Ferris Bueller's Day Off, *with Matthew Broderick in the title role.*

Fidel — Latin: Faithful
Fidele, Fidelio

Fielding — English: From the field
Field, Fielder

Filbert — English: Brilliant
Filberte, Filberti, Filberto, Philbert, Philberto

Finlay — Irish: Fair-haired fighter
Findlay, Findley, Finley, Finn, Finnie, Finnley, Finny

Fisk/Fiske — English: Fish

Fitzgerald — English: Son of the spear-mighty
Can we ever hear this name without thinking of JFK?

Fitzpatrick — English: Son of a nobleman

Flavian — Latin: Fair, blond

Fleming — English: Man from the lowlands

Fletcher — French: Arrow maker

Flint/Flynt — English: Stream

Florian — Latin: To flourish
Fiorello, Flo, Florence, Florents, Florentz, Florenz, Florian, Florrie, Florry

Floyd — See: Lloyd

Fonda — Latin: Deep one

Forbes — Irish: Wealthy owner of the fields

Ford — German: River crossing

Forest — German: One who lives in the woods
Forrest, Forrester, Forrie, Forry, Forster, Foss, Foster

Francis — Latin: Free man
Chico, Fran, France, Francesco, Franchot, Francisco, Franciskus, François, Frank, Frankie, Franky, Frannie, Franny, Frans, Franz, Franze
While this is not a popular name today, there are three famous Americans with the name who come to mind: Francis Scott Key, Francis Albert Sinatra, and Francis Ford Coppola.

Frank — See: Francis, Franklin
Frank Baum, born Lyman Frank Baum, is the wizard who created the classic "Oz" stories. He also wrote under the pen names Schuyler Stanton, Floyd Akers, and Dith Van Dyne.

Franklin — Latin: Freeholder (of land)
Francklin, Francklyn, Frank, Frankie, Franklyn, Franky

Fraser — English: Curly haired
Frase, Frasier, Fraze, Frazer, Frazier
The hit TV sitcom "Cheers" has actor Kelsey Grammer playing the part of Dr. Frasier Crane. Both Kelsey and Frasier are fast becoming popular names.

Frayne — English: Stranger
  Fray, Frey, Freyne
Fred — See: Alfred, Frederic
  Fred Austerlitz sounds like a name for a storm trooper, not a song-and-dance man. Fred thought so, too, and changed his name to Fred Astaire.
Frederic — German: Peace king
  Fred, Freddie, Freddy, Fredek, Frederich, Frederick, Frederico, Fredericus, Frederigo, Frederik, Fredi, Fredo, Fredric, Friedrich, Fritz
Fritz — See: Frederic
Fuller — English: Clothing presser
Fulton — English: People's estate; Scottish: Leafy town

G

Gabriel — Hebrew: Devoted to God
  Gab, Gabbie, Gabby, Gabe, Gabie, Gabrelli, Gabriele, Gabriello, Gaby, Gavril
Gadiel — Hebrew: God is my fortune
  Gad, Gadi, Gadman
Gage — French: A pledge
Galen — Gaelic: Bright one, intelligent one
  Gael, Gaelan, Gaelen, Gail, Gale, Galeno, Gayle
Gallagher — Celtic: Eager helper
Galton — English: One who lives on rented land
Galvin — Irish: Sparrow
  Galvan, Galven
Gamble — Norse: Old
Gannon — Irish: Fair complexioned
Gardener — English: One who tends the garden
  Gar, Gardie, Gardiner, Gardner, Gardy
Gareth — Welsh: Gentle
  Gar, Garth, Gerth
Garett/Garrett — English: Mighty spear
  Garrard, Garrott
Garfield — English: Triangular field
  Cartoonist Jim Davis catapulted his feline cartoon character, Garfield, to the top of many best-seller lists.

Garland/Garlande — English: From the battleground
  Garlen
Garner — English: To gather, to store
Garnet/Garnett — A dark-red jewel
  Garnyd
Garrick/Garrich — German: Mighty ruler with a spear
Garth — See: Gareth
  The current popularity of this name comes from the success of country singer Garth Brooks.
Garvey — German: Spear bearer
Garvin/Garwin — German: Friend in strife
Garwood — English: From the fir-tree forest
Gary — English: Spear holder
  Gare, Garey, Gari, Garry
  Cartoonist Garry Trudeau got the name of his "Doonesbury" comic strip by combining "Doone" — slang at Yale for "a good-natured fool" — and "sbury" — the second part of Pillsbury, his college roommate's last name.
Gaspar — Spanish: Master of treasure
  Caspar, Casper, Gaspard, Gaspardo, Gaspare, Gasper, Jaspar, Jasper
Gaston/Gascon — French: From the Gascony region of France, hospitable
Gavin — German: Battle hawk
  Gavan, Gaven, Gawain, Gawen
  Actor Gavin MacLeod, well known for his role as the captain on the "Love Boat," was born Allan George William See. He changed his name to Gavin simply because he liked it, and took the name MacLeod as a tribute to his college acting teacher.
Gavrie — Russian: Man of God
  Gabril, Ganya
Gaylord — English: Lively one
  Gaillard, Gallaird, Gaye, Gayelord, Gayler, Gaylor
Gaynor — Irish: Son of a fair-haired man
  Gainer, Gaines, Gainor, Gayne, Gayner, Gaynes
Gearey/Geary — English: Adaptable to change
Gene — See: Eugene
Geoffrey/Geoffry — See: Jeffrey
George — Greek: Farmer
  Egor, Georas, Geordie, Georg, Georges, Georgi, Georgios, Georgy, Giorgio, Goran, Jorg, Jorge

*When Nathan Birnbaum first started in vaudeville, his acts were
so bad (how bad were they?) that he had to keep changing his
name in order to be hired again. Some of the names he used
were Captain Betts, Jed Jackson, Buddy Links, Willie Delight,
Harry Pierce, Jimmy Malone, and Willy Williams. When he
finally got an act that he felt good about, he decided to stick with
the name George Burns.*

Gerald — German: Mighty spearman

Garald, Garalt, Garcia, Garold, Gearalt, Gearard, Geralde,
Geraldo, Gerold, Gerrie, Gerry, Girald, Giralt, Giraud, Jerald,
Jerold, Jerrald, Jerry

*Gerald Ford's name at birth was Leslie Lynch King, Jr. His
mother got divorced and remarried Gerald Rudolff Ford, whose
name the future president adopted (changing Rudolff to Rudolph).*

Gerard — English: Brave with a spear

Garrard, Garrat, Garrett, Gerrard

Gershom — Hebrew: Exiled

Gersh, Gersham

Gibor — Hebrew: Strong

Gideon — Hebrew: Great warrior

Gifford — German: Magnificent gift

Giff, Gifferd

Gil — Nickname for names starting with "Gil"

Gilbert — German: Bright pledge

Gibbie, Gibby, Gil, Gilberto, Gilburt, Gilibeirt, Gill, Gillie, Gilly,
Gilpin, Guilbert, Wilbert, Wilbur, Wilburt

Gilchrist — Irish: Servant of Christ

Giles — Greek: Shield bearer

Egide, Egidio, Egidius, Gide, Gidi, Gilles, Gyles, Gylles, Jilly

Gilroy — Irish: King's servant

Glen/Glenn — Irish: From the valley

Glennie, Glenny, Glyn, Glynn, Glyynie, Glynny

Godard/Goddard — German: Firm nature

Godart, Goddart, Gotthard, Gotthart

Godfrey — See: Jeffrey

Godwin — English: Friend of God

Godewyn, Godine, Goodwin

Goliath — Hebrew: Giant

Gordon — English: From the cornered hill

Gordan, Gorden, Gordie, Gordy

Gore — English: Spear

Best-selling author Gore Vidal was named for his grandfather, Senator Thomas Pryor Gore of Oklahoma.

Gower — Welsh: Pure man of virtue

Grady — Irish: Illustrious, noble

Graham — German: From the gray home

Graeham, Graeme, Grahame

Genius inventor Alexander Graham Bell was one of the founders of National Geographic. *He once wrote an article for the magazine under the pen name of* H. A. Largelamb, *an anagram of A. Graham Bell.*

Granger — English: Farmer

Grange

Grant — Latin: Great

Noted artist Grant Wood, famous for his painting American Gothic, *said that all of his good ideas came to him while he was milking a cow.*

Granvill/Granville — French: From the big town

Grayson — English: Son of a judge

Gregory — Greek: Vigilant

Greg, Gregg, Greggie, Greggy, Gregoire, Gregoor, Gregor, Gregorio, Gregorius, Grischa

Tony Award–winner Gregory Hines was born on St. Valentine's Day. He certainly can act and dance his way into anyone's heart!

Gresham — English: From the grazing land

Griffin — Latin: Half eagle and half lion

Griff, Griffe, Griffie, Griffith, Griffy, Gryphon

Griffin Dunne, actor and producer, is bringing attention to a name that has been (until now) more common as a surname than a first name.

Griswold — German: From the gray forest

Grover — English: From a grove of trees

This may come as a surprise, but President Grover Cleveland's real name was Stephen Grover Cleveland, after Stephen Grover, a minister in his family's church.

Gunther — German: Bold one

Gun, Gunnar, Gunner, Gunter, Gunthar

Gurion — Hebrew: Great strength

Gustav — Swedish: Noble staff bearer

Gus, Gussie, Gussy, Gustaf, Gustave, Gustavius, Gustavo

Guthrie — German: Army warrior
Guy — French: Guide
  Guido, Guyon
Gwynn — Welsh: Fair, blond one
  Guin, Gwin, Gwinn, Gwyn

H

Hackett — German: Little woodsman
  Hacket, Hackit, Hackitt
Haddan — English: From the heather-filled land
  Hadan, Haden, Hadon, Hadden, Haddon, Hadleigh, Hadley
Hadrian — Latin: From Adria (an Italian city in the north)
  Hadrian was a Roman emperor who had the famous Hadrian
  Wall built in Britain in about 121 A.D. It's one of the largest
  Roman remains preserved by the British government.
Hakeem — Arabic: Wise
  Hakim
Hale — English: Hero, from the hall
  Haele, Haley
Halil — Turkish: Intimate friend
Hall — English: From the manor
Halsey — English: Greeting, salutation
  Halstead, Halsted
Hamal — Arabic: Gentle lamb
Hamilton — English: Fortified castle
  Hamel, Hamelton, Hamil
Hamish — See: Jacob
Hamlet — German: Little home
  The best-known Hamlet is Shakespeare's Prince of Denmark,
  who is thought to be (or not to be) English literature's first truly
  modern character.
Hamlin/Hamlyn — French: Little home-lover
Hank — See: Henry
  Hank Aaron, the Baseball Hall of Famer, broke Babe Ruth's
  home-run record in 1974, when he hit his 715th home run while
  playing for the Atlanta Braves.
Hanley — English: From the high meadow
  Hanly, Henley, Henly

Hans — See: John

It's a good thing that Hans Christian Andersen was a great children's storyteller. As he was dyslexic, it was difficult for him to read.

Hanson — Scandinavian: Son of Hans

Hansen, Hanssen, Hansson

Haram — Hebrew: Mountaineer

Harden — English: To make bold

Harde, Hardie, Harding, Hardy

Harel — Hebrew: God's mountain

Harlan — English: From the battle land

Harland, Harlen, Harley, Harlin, Harlyn

Harlow — English: From the battle hill

Arle, Arlo

Harold — Norse: Army commander

Hal, Haldon, Harald, Haraldo, Harral, Harry, Herald, Herold, Herrick, Herry

Harold Washington made history on April 12, 1983, when he was sworn in as the first black mayor of Chicago.

Harper — English: Harp player

Harp, Harpo

Harrison — Son of Harry

Harris

Actor Harrison Ford made a big name for himself as Han Solo in Star Wars *and became a major international star after playing the title role in the "Indiana Jones" films.*

Harry — See: Harold

As a young boy, magician Ehrich Weiss changed his name to Harry Houdini. The first name came either from his nickname, "Ehrie," or from Harry Kellar, America's most popular magician at the time. After reading about Jean Eugene Robert-Houdin, France's greatest magician, the young boy added an "i" to the second half of the last name and took the name Houdini.

Hartley — English: From the deer pasture

Hart, Harte, Hartleigh, Hartly, Hartman

Harvey — German: Warrior; Celtic: Eager for battle

Harv, Hervé, Hervey

Hasan/Hassan — Arabic: Handsome

Haskel/Haskell — Hebrew: Understanding

Haslet/Haslett — English: From the land of hazel trees

Haz, Hazlet, Hazlett

Hasting — German: Swift one
  Hastings, Hasty
Havelock/Havelocke — Norse: Contest at sea
Haven — English: Place of refuge
  Hagan, Hagen, Hazen
Hawley — English: From the hedged meadow
Hayes — English: From the hedged place
  Hayden, Haydon, Hayward, Haywood, Heywood
Heathcliff — English: From the heath by the cliff
  Cliff, Heath, Heathcliffe
  Heathcliff is the passionate hero of Emily Brontë's Wuthering Heights. *But who, in this day and age, would use the name? Well, the lead character on the hit TV series "The Cosby Show" (1984–92) was Dr. Heathcliff Huxtable, played by Bill Cosby.*
Hector — Greek: Steadfast
  Ettore
  In the Iliad, *Hector is the oldest son of Priam and Hecuba, and he possesses these human virtues: compassion, affection, loyalty, piety, and devotion to his parents.*
Helmut — French: Warrior
Henry — German: Ruler of an estate
  Enrico, Enrique, Enzio, Hank, Heindrick, Heinie, Heinrich, Heinrik, Heintz, Hendrick, Hendrik, Henny, Henri, Henrik
  Producer, director, and actor Henry Winkler created one of the most charismatic characters in the history of television: Arthur "the Fonz" Fonzarelli on "Happy Days."
Herbert — German: Brilliant soldier
  Erberto, Harbert, Hebert, Heberto, Herb, Herberte, Herbie, Herby, Hilbert
  President Herbert Hoover's wife, Lou Henry, called her husband Bert. When you think about it, it makes sense, because he was "her Bert" (Herbert).
Hercules — Greek: Gift of glory
  Ercole, Heracles, Herc, Hercule
  Agatha Christie's fictional detective is Hercule Poirot.
Herman — German: Noble warrior
  Armand, Armando, Armin, Arminio, Armond, Armyn, Ermanno, Ermin, Harman, Harmon, Herm, Hermann, Hermie, Hermon, Hermy
Hermes — Greek: Lordly

This son of Zeus is known as Mercury to the Romans and is noted for his inventiveness.

Hernando — See: Ferdinand

Herrick — See: Harold

Herschel — Hebrew: Deer
Hersch, Hersh, Hershel, Hirsch, Hirschel
Herschel Walker is the first football player to turn pro before his college eligibility expired.

Hewett/Hewitt — French: Small and intelligent one

Hilary/Hillary — Latin: Merry, cheerful
Alair, Hilar, Hilare, Hilario, Hilarius, Hilery, Hill, Hillery, Hillie, Hilly

Hillel — Hebrew: Greatly praised

Hilton — English: From the hill estate

Hiram — Hebrew: Most noble one
Hi, Hirah, Hy, Hyram

Hobson — English: Goodly, beautiful

Hogan — Irish: Youth

Holden — English: From the hollow in the valley
Holbrook, Holbrooke
As popular as J. D. Salinger's classic novel Catcher in the Rye *was, and continues to be, the name of the book's hero, Holden Caulfield, has not caught on.*

Hollis — English: From the holly-tree grove

Holt — English: From the forest

Homer — Greek: A pledge
Homere, Homero, Homerus, Omero
Homer is the author of the classic epics the Iliad *and the* Odyssey.

Horace — Latin: Timekeeper
Horacio, Horatio, Horatius, Orazio

Horatio — See: Horace

Horten/Horton — English: From the gray estate

Hosea — Hebrew: Salvation

Houghton — German: From the manor on high

Houston — English: Hill town; Place name: A city in Texas that was named for soldier and statesman Sam Houston

Howard — English: Guardian
Hovard, Howe, Howey, Howie
Knock, knock. Who's there? Howard. Howard who?

Howard you like to have the money earned by "the Bashful Billionaire," industrialist and recluse Howard Hughes?

Howland — English: From the hill
Howell

Hubert — German: Alert, chipper
Eubie, Hobard, Hobart, Hube, Hubey, Hubie
Hubert H. Humphrey, former U.S. senator and vice-president, was nicknamed "Pinky" in high school because his skin sunburned easily.

Hudson — English: Son of the hooded one

Hugh — English: Intelligent
Hew, Hewe, Huey, Huggin, Hughes, Hughie, Hugo, Hugues, Hutch, Hutchin, Ugo
TV personality Hugh (Malcolm) Downs lives up to the meaning of his first name. This all-around sportsman is an airplane pilot, the author of more than a half dozen books and an orchestral suite, and a science and astronomy buff.

Hume — German: Home lover

Humphrey — German: Peace-loving protector
Humfrey, Humfrid, Humfried, Humfry, Humph, Humphrie, Humphry, Hunfredo, Onfredo, Onfroi
Who can hear this name without thinking of Humphrey Bogart, the actor with the tough-guy screen image?

Hunter — English: Hunter
Hunt, Huntington, Huntly

Hurd — English: Strong minded, hard

Hussein — Arabic: Small and handsome one
Husain, Husein, Hussain

Huxley — English: Huckster

Hyatt — English: From the high gate

Hyman — See: Chaim

I

Iago — See: Jacob

Ian — See: John
Ian (Lancaster) Fleming was a journalist and the author of thirteen thrillers, in which the hero is James Bond (Agent 007).

Ibsen — German: Archer's son

Ichabod — Hebrew: Glory has departed
Ichabod Crane is the naive and shy schoolmaster in Washington Irving's "Legend of Sleepy Hollow."

Ignatius — Latin: Fiery, determined
Iggie, Iggy, Ignace, Ingnacio, Ignacius, Ignats, Ignaz, Ignazio, Inigo

Igor — Norse: Hero

Ingamar — Norse: Famous son
Ingar, Ingemar, Inger, Ingmar

Innis — Irish: From the island
Inis, Innes, Inness, Inniss

Ira — Hebrew: Watchful, vigilant

Irving — English: Friend of the sea
Earvin, Erv, Ervin, Erwin, Irv, Irvin, Irvine, Irwin
Jewish songwriter Irving Berlin (born Israel Baline) wrote "White Christmas" and "Easter Parade," songs celebrating two of the most important Christian holidays. Earvin "Magic" Johnson performed his magic on the basketball court for the L.A. Lakers and was part of the U.S. "Dream Team" in the 1992 Olympics. Irvin C. Mollison was the first black federal judge in the U.S.

Irwin — See: Irving

Isaac — Hebrew: Laughter
Ike, Ikey, Ikie, Isaak, Isacco, Itzaak, Itzak, Izaak, Yitzaak, Yitzak
Writer Isaac Asimov was known for variety (writing in areas as diverse as science fiction and limericks) and volume (creating more than four hundred books). Because of his clear and articulate writing style, he was called "the Great Explainer."

Isaiah — Hebrew: God is my helper

Ishmael — Hebrew: The Lord will hear
The famous first line in Herman Melville's Moby Dick *is "Call me Ishmael." The name in this fictional story was inspired by the biblical Ishmael, "the dweller in the wilderness."*

Isidor/Isidore — Greek: Gift
Esidor, Isadore, Isidoro, Isodoro, Izzie, Izzy

Israel — Hebrew: The Lord's warrior
Israelos, Srully, Yisrael, Ysrael
Playwright Israel Horowitz once had four Off-Broadway hits in four months. He's written more than thirty-five plays, which have been translated into more than twenty languages, and on

any given night more than twenty of these plays are performed
throughout the world.

Itzak — See: Isaac, Yitzhak
Itzak Perlman has been hailed as one of the world's greatest
classical violinists. The violin he plays is a Stradivarius from the
year 1714.

Ivan — See: John
Ivan Lendl, world tennis champion from Czechoslovakia, pro-
nounces his name E-vahn'.

Ivar — Norse: Archer
Ifor, Ive, Iver, Ives, Ivon, Ivor, Yves, Yvor, Yvors

J

Jack — See: Jacob, John
Born John Uhler Lemmon III, actor Jack Lemmon once used a
stage name at Harvard, billing himself as Timothy Orange (obvi-
ously he likes citrus names).

Jackson — See: Jacob, John

Jacob — Hebrew: Supplanter
Cob, Cobie, Coby, Giacobo, Giacomo, Giacopo, Hamish,
Iacovo, Iago, Jack, Jackie, Jackson, Jacky, Jacobo, Jacques, Jac-
quet, Jaime, Jake, Jakie, Jakob, Jakov, Jakub, James, Jamesie,
Jamesy, Jamey, Jamie, Jasch, Jay, Jayme, Jamie, Jim, Jimmie,
Jimmy, Jimson, Jock, Seamus, Shamus

Jael — Hebrew: Mountain goat, symbol of the Zodiac sign Capri-
corn

Jake — See: Jacob

James — See: Jacob
Five U.S. presidents were named James: Buchanan, Garfield,
Madison, Polk, and Carter.

The world-famous fictional Secret Agent 007 was named by
his creator Ian Fleming after the author of a book that always
graced Fleming's coffee table: Birds of the West Indies *by orni-*
thologist James Bond.

Jamil — Arabic: Handsome

Jan — See: John

Japhet — Hebrew: Enlargement
Japheth, Yaphet, Yaphett

Jared — See: Jordan

Jarl — Norse: Nobleman
Jarley

Jaron — Hebrew: To sing

Jarrett — English: Spear-brave
Jaret, Jarrot, Jarrott

Jarvis — English: Driver; German: Sharp as a spear
Jarvey, Jervey, Jervis

Jason — Greek: Healer
Mention Jason Priestly of "Beverly Hills 90210" to most young teenage girls today, and watch their reaction.

Jaspar/Jasper — See: Gaspar/Gasper

Jay — See: Jacob

Jean — See: John

Jedediah/Jedidiah — Hebrew: Beloved by the Lord
Jed, Jedah, Jedd, Jeddie, Jeddy

Jedrek — Polish: Strong, manly

Jefferson — English: Son of Jeffrey
Jeff, Jeffer, Jefferies, Jeffers, Jeffie, Jeffy

Jeffrey — French: Divinely peaceful
Geoff, Geoffrey, Geoffry, Godrey, Goffredo, Gottfried, Jeff, Jeffery, Jeffie, Jeffy
Two contemporary leading men in films use the short form of this name: Jeff Bridges and Jeff Goldblum.

Jeremiah — Hebrew: Exalted of the Lord
Geremia, Jer, Jereme, Jeremias, Jeremy, Jerrie

Jeremy — See: Jeremiah
Jeremy Irons, born in England, is the Academy Award–winning actor known for playing haunted, upper-class types.

Jermaine — German: From Germany

Jermyn — Hebrew: One from Germany
Germaine, Germano, Jarman, Jermaine, Jerman

Jerome — Latin: Sacred name
Gerome, Geronimo, Gerrie, Gerry, Hierom, Hieronymus, Jere, Jereme, Jeromo, Jeronimo, Jerrome
Reclusive writer J. D. Salinger, author of Catcher in the Rye, *was born Jerome David Salinger.*

Jerrell — English: Strong, open minded
  Jerel, Jerrel, Jerryl, Jeryl
Jerry — See: Gerald (Also, a nickname for names starting with "Ger" and "Jer")
Jerzy — Polish: Farmer
Jesse — Hebrew: Preeminence
  Jess, Jessie, Jessy
  Olympic superstar Jesse Owens got his name because of a simple misunderstanding. He was born James Cleveland Owens and had always been called J. C. But when he went to a Cleveland, Ohio, grammar school and told the teacher his nickname, she thought he said Jesse. That's what she wrote down, that's what he was soon called, and that's how the world knows this great athlete.
Jethro — Hebrew: Wealth, abundance
Jilly — See: Giles
Jim/Jimmie/Jimmy — See: Jacob
  Jim Palmer, the only American League pitcher to win the Cy Young Award three times, was elected to the Baseball Hall of Fame in his first year of eligibility (1990). And he looks good in Jockey underwear, too!
Joab — Hebrew: Praise the Lord
Joachim — Hebrew: The Lord will judge
  Achim, Akim, Joaquin, Joaquino, Kim
Job — Hebrew: Afflicted one
Jody — Latin: Playful
  Jody Powell, President Carter's press secretary, was born Joseph Lester Powell, Jr. He was nicknamed Jody after the young boy in the book The Yearling, *by Marjorie Kinnan.*
Joe — See: Joseph
Joel — Hebrew: The Lord is God
  Ioel, Yoel
Johann/Johannes — See: John
  Johann Sebastian Bach produced many musical compositions — and almost as many children: seven with his first wife and thirteen with wife number two.
John — Hebrew: God is gracious
  Eoin, Gian, Gianni, Giannini, Giovanni, Hanan, Hans, Hansel, Hanson, Iain, Ian, Ioannes, Ivan, Jack, Jackie, Jackson, Jacky, Jan, Janos, Jean, Jehan, Jen, Jens, Jock, Jocko, Johan, Johann, Johannes, Johnnie, Johnny, Johnson, Jon, Jonnie, Jonny, Jon-

son, Juan, Juanito, Sean, Seann, Shamus, Shane, Shawn, Yvan, Zane

This name is one of America's classic names for boys. There have been four presidents with the name: John Quincy Adams, John Adams, John Tyler, and John Fitzgerald Kennedy.

Jonah — Hebrew: Dove
Jona, Jonas
Jonas Salk's 1954 polio vaccine was the medical breakthrough of the decade.

Jonathan/Jonathon — Hebrew: Gift of the Lord
Johnathan, Johnathon, Johnny, Jon, Jonnie, Jonny

Joram — Hebrew: The Lord is exalted
Jorie, Jory

Jordan — Hebrew: Descending
Jared, Jaret, Jerad, Jordie, Jordy, Jori, Joris, Jory, Jourdain, Jourdan

Jorge — See: George

Jory — See: Major

Jose — See: Joseph

Joseph — Hebrew: He shall add
Che, Guiseppe, Iosep, Ioseph, Joe, Joey, Jose, Josef, Josephe, Josephus, Joska, Josko, Jozef, Pepe, Pepito, Yoseph, Yussuf
Russian dictator Joseph Stalin was born Joseph Vissarionovich Djugashvili. He took the name Stalin, the Russian word for "steel," to signify his strength and grit.

Joshua — Hebrew: God of salvation
Josh, Joshuah

Josiah — Hebrew: May the Lord heal and protect

Judah — Hebrew: Praised one
Jud, Juda, Judas, Judd, Jude, Judson, Yehuda, Yehudah, Yehudi

Jules — See: Julius

Julian — See: Julius

Julius — Greek: Hairy-faced youthful one
Giuliano, Giulio, Giulius, Jule, Jules, Julian, Julie, Julien, Julio, Julion, Julot
Julius Winfield Erving II, now retired, was one of basketball's most beloved players. His nickname started in high school as "the Doctor," and when he went pro, the nickname was changed to Dr. J.

Junius — Latin: Born in June
Junias, Junior, Unot

Juri/Juris — Latvian: Farmer
Justin — Latin: Just, upright
Giustino, Giusto, Just, Justino, Justis, Justo, Justus, Justyn

K

Kadar/Kedar — Arabic: Powerful
Kadin — Arabic: Friend, companion
Kahlil — Arabic: Friend
Kalil, Khalil
Kaiser — See: Caesar
Kane — Hawaiian: God of men
Cane, Kain, Kaine, Kayne
Kaniel — Hebrew: Reed
Kareem — Arabic: Highborn, generous and powerful son of Allah
Born Lew Alcindor, this 7'3" basketball star changed his name to Kareem Abdul-Jabbar when he changed his religion from Catholic to the black orthodox Hanafi sect.
Karl — See: Charles
When Karl Malden became an actor, he changed his name from Mladen Sekulovich just so it would fit on theater marquees. Notice that his new last name is a variation of his original first name.
Keane — English: Sharp, bold
Kean, Keanan, Keen, Keenan, Keene
Keefe — Irish: Handsome, gentle, lovable
Keegan — Irish: Small and determined
Keenan — Irish: Very old and small
Keen, Keenen, Kienan, Kienen
Keir — Gaelic: Dark skinned
Actor Keir Dullea played the part of David Bowman in the film 2001: A Space Odyssey.
Keith — Welsh: From the forest
Kelley/Kelly — Irish: Warrior
Kelsey — Norse: Dweller by the water
Kelcey, Kelson, Kelton
Ken/Kenn/Kennie/Kenny — Nicknames for names starting with "Ken"

Kendall — English: From the bright valley
Kendal, Kendel, Kendell

Kendrick — English: Princely ruler
Kenric, Kenrick

Kenley — English: Dweller from the king's meadows

Kennard — English: Strong

Kennedy — English: Royal ruler

Kenneth — Gaelic: Handsome, fair
Ken, Kennet, Kenny

Kent — English: From the king's estate
Kenton

Kenward — English: Brave soldier
Conward, Kenway

Kenyon — Irish: White haired, blond

Kerem — Turkish: Nobility, kindness

Kermit — Gaelic: Free man
With the creation of Jim Henson's Muppets, the name Kermit has become synonymous with a frog.

Kern — Celtic: Mysterious
Kearne, Kearney, Kearny

Kerr — Celtic: Dark one
Keir, Keiran, Kerrie, Kerrin, Kerry, Kier, Kieran, Kiernan

Kerwin/Kerwyn — Irish: Little black one

Kevin — Irish: Gentle
Kevan, Keven, Kevon, Kevyn
This is a popular name for leading men in films and TV: Costner, Kline, and Dobson, to name just a few.

Kim — See: Joachim, Kimball

Kimball — English: Royal warrior
Kemble, Kim, Kimbell, Kimble, Kimmie, Kimmy
Fictional character Kimball O'Hara (he's no relation to Scarlett) is better known as Kim, in Rudyard Kipling's novel of the same name.

King — English: Ruling monarch

Kingsley — English: From the king's meadow
Kingsleigh, Kingston

Kinsey — English: Prince of victory

Kipp — English: From the pointed hill
Kip, Kippie, Kippy

Kirby/Kerby — Norse: From the church village

Kirk — Norse: Dweller by the church

Kirke, Kirkland, Kirkley, Kirwood
Born Issur Danielovitch, actor Kirk Douglas gave himself this not-too-common first name. When it came to naming his four sons, though, he kept it simple: Michael, Joel, Peter, and Eric.

Kit — See: Christopher
Kit Carson was an American frontiersman and guide in the West during the middle 1800s.

Kito — Swahili: Jewel

Kivi/Kiva — Hebrew: Protected

Knute — See: Canute
Knute Rockne, the famous Notre Dame football coach, was nicknamed by the press "the Great Man."

Konrad — See: Conrad

Konstantin — Latin: Steadfast, firm, constant
Constantin, Konstant, Konstanz, Kostas

Kornel — Latin: Hornlike

Kristian — Greek: Annointed Christian
Kris

Kristopher — Greek: Carrier of Christ
Kris, Kristofer, Kristoffer, Kristophor
Kris Kristofferson is probably the only Rhodes Scholar to use his Oxford education to become a country-music writer.

Kurt — See: Conrad

Kwamen — Akan, Ghana (African): Born on Saturday

Kyle — Celtic: Cattle-grazing hill

L

Lachlan — Gaelic: From the water, belligerent

Ladd — English: Boy, servant
Lad, Laddie, Laddy

Lael — Hebrew: He is God's

Lafayette — French: Faith

Laird — Scottish: Proprietor of land

Lal — Hindi: Beloved

Lalo — Latin: To sing a lullaby
This musical name belongs to one of television's most successful

composers, Lalo Schifrin. One of his memorable musical contributions is the pulsating, jazz-oriented theme for "Mission Impossible."

Lamar — Latin: From the sea; German: Land-famous

Lambert — German: Bright land
Lamberto, Landbert

Lamont — Norse: Lawyer; Spanish and French: The mountain
Lamond, Lammond

Lance — Latin: One who serves, light spear
Lancelot, Lancing, Lansing, Launce, Launcelot

Landers — French: From the grassy lawn
Landis, Landman, Landon, Landry, Langdon, Langston, Lannie, Lanny

Lane — English: Path
Laney, Lanie, Layne, Laynie

Langley — English: Long meadow

Langston — English: Tall man's town
Novelist, composer, playwright, and poet Langston Hughes was discovered by poet Vachel Lindsay. They met when Langston was working as a busboy in a Washington, D.C., hotel restaurant and left some poems by Vachel's plate.

Lanny — See: Landers

Larkin — See: Lawrence

Larry — See: Lawrence
This popular name belongs to an interviewer (Larry King), a basketball player (Larry Bird), a novelist (Larry McMurtry), a boxer (Larry Holmes), a TV star (Larry Hagman), and one of the Three Stooges.

Lars — See: Lawrence

Laszlo — Hungarian: Famous ruler

Latham — Norse: From the barn
Lathe, Lathrop

Latimer — English: Teacher, interpreter

Laughton/Lawton — English: Man of refinement

Lauren — See: Lawrence

Lavi — Hebrew: Lion

Lawford — English: From the ford at the hill

Lawler — Gaelic: Soft-spoken

Lawrence — Latin: Laurel crowned
Larkin, Larrie, Larry, Lars, Larson, Lauran, Lauren, Laurence, Laurens, Laurent, Laurentius, Laurie, Lauritz, Lawrance, Lawrie,

Lawron, Lawry, Lawson, Loran, Loren, Lorenz, Lorenzo, Lorin, Lorne, Lorrie, Lorry, Lowrance

T. E. (Thomas Edward) Lawrence, British adventurer, soldier, and scholar, was also known as Lawrence of Arabia.

Lazarus — Hebrew: God will help
Eleazar, Lazar, Lazare, Lazaro, Lazer, Lazlo

Leal — English: Loyal friend

Leander — Greek: Lionlike
Leandre, Leandro

Lear — German: Of the meadow

Lee — Nickname for names starting with or containing the sound of "Lee"

Lido Anthony Iacocca, called Lee for short, is the corporate superman responsible for turning Chrysler around.

Leif/Lief — Norse: Beloved

Leif Eriksson, Norwegian navigator, discovered Vinland, which is now thought to have been coastal North America. When he returned to Norway, he was honored with the name Leif the Lucky.

Leighton — English: From the meadow farm
Layton, Leigh

Leland — English: From the meadowland

Lemuel — Hebrew: Consecrated to the Lord
Lem, Lemmie, Lemmy

Lennon — Gaelic: Little cape

Lenny — See: Leonard

Leo — Latin: Lion

Leon — Latin: Lionlike
Leone, Lion, Lionel, Lionello, Lyonel

Leonard — French: Strong, brave as a lion
Len, Lenard, Lennard, Lennie, Lenny, Leonard, Leonardo, Leonardus, Leonerd, Lienard

Leopold — German: Patriotic, brave for the people
Leopoldo, Leupold

Leor — Hebrew: Light is mine

Leroi/Leroy — French: The king

Les — See: Leslie

Leslie — Gaelic: From the gray fortress
Les, Leslee, Lesley, Lezley

This name was thought of as an American girl's name and an English boy's name. Now, with the success of the "Naked Gun"

films, actor Leslie Nielsen has made the name more acceptable for boys in this country.

Lester — English: From the shining lamp; Latin: camp, protected area

Levi — Hebrew: Harmonious, uniting
Leavitt, Lev, Levic, Levy
Levi Strauss went west in 1849 in the California gold rush. A friend who was mining for gold complained that his pants weren't durable enough. Levi sewed together a more durable pair from tent canvas. They were the first "Levi's" — and the start of a major industry worth more than gold for Levi Strauss.

Lew/Lewis — See: Louis
The real name of Lewis Carroll, the creator of Alice in Wonderland, *is Charles Lutwidge Dodgson. It is said that he got his pen name by translating his given names into Latin (Carolus Ludovicus), then reversing them and translating them back into English-sounding names. It might have been easier just to keep his original name.*

Liam — See: William

Lincoln — English: Place by the pool
Linc, Link

Lindall — English: From the linden tree
Lin, Lind, Lindal, Lindberg, Lindbergh, Lindel, Lindell, Lindsay, Linsey, Lyndsay

Lindsay — See: Lindall

Linus — Greek: Flaxen haired

Lionel — See: Leon
Lionel (Leo) Hampton is king of the vibes (vibraphone). Because "the Hamp" (one of his nicknames) found a spiritual home in Israel, he earned another nickname, "the Great Rabbi of Jazz."

Llewellyn — Welsh: Lionlike
Lew, Llewellen, Llewelyn

Lloyd — Welsh: Gray haired, sacred
Floyd, Floydie, Lloydie

Locke — English: From the enclosed place

Lodge — French: Campground

Logan — Gaelic: From the little hollow

Lombard — Latin: Long bearded
Lombarda, Lombardi, Lombardo

Lon/Lonnie/Lonny — See: Alphonse

Lord — English: Guardian of the manor

Lorimer — Latin: Harness maker
  Lorimar, Lorrie, Lorrimer, Lorry
Lorin — See: Lawrence
Lorne — See: Lawrence
  "Saturday Night Live" fans know the name Lorne Michaels, the
  executive producer who helped formulate the show.
Lou — See: Louis
Louis — German: Famous warrior
  Aloysius, Lew, Lewes, Lewie, Lewis, Lou, Louey, Louie, Ludvig,
  Ludwig, Luigi, Luis
  Louis Armstrong, the great jazz trumpeter and singer, was called
  Satchelmouth by a London journalist. Eventually it was short-
  ened to Satchmo. When Armstrong was asked if he objected to
  that nickname, his answer was a widemouthed grin.
Lowell — French: Little wolf
  Lovel, Lovell, Lowe, Lowel
Loyal — French: Faithful, true
  Loy
Lucius — Latin: Bringer of light
  Luca, Lucas, Lucca, Luce, Lucian, Luciano, Lucias, Lucien, Lucio,
  Luck, Lucky, Lukas, Lukash, Luke
Ludlow — English: From the prince's hill
Ludwig — See: Louis
Luke — See: Lucius
  Luke Perry is a teenage heartthrob and a star of the hit TV series
  "Beverly Hills 90210."
Lundi/Lundy — French: Born on Monday
Luther — German: Renowned warrior
  Lotario, Lothar, Lothario, Lowther
  We have botanist Luther Burbank to thank for the Shasta daisy
  and the Burbank rose. It's no wonder he has been called "the
  Plant Inventor" and "an Architect of Nature."
Lyle — French: From the island
  Lisle, Lyall, Lyell, Lysle
  The very successful and somewhat controversial publisher Lyle
  Stuart has been affectionately referred to as "the Bad Boy of
  American Publishing."
Lyman — English: Man from the valley
Lyn/Lynn — English: From the waterfall
  Football player Lynn Swann said that with a name like Lynn, he
  had to become a football player!

Lyndon — English: Dweller at the linden-tree hill
Lindan, Linden, Lindon, Lindy, Lyndy
President Lyndon Baines Johnson was referred to as LBJ. His wife, Claudia Alta Taylor, was called Lady Bird, which gave her the same initials. The president liked the idea of that so much that he and his wife named their daughters Luci Baines and Lynda Bird, and one of their dogs Little Beagle.
Lysander — Greek: Liberator

M

Mac/Mack — Irish/Scotch/Gaelic: Son of (Also, nicknames for names starting with "Mac" and "Max")
Macdonald — Gaelic: Son of Donald
Macdonald Carey is one of America's most enduring actors. From the silver screen, he went to TV as part of the original cast of the soap opera "Days of Our Lives." That was over twenty-five years ago, and he has been there ever since.
Mace — Latin: Aromatic spice; English: Club
Macey, Macy
Mackenzie — Irish: Son of the leader
Macklin — Gaelic: Son of Flann
Maclean/McLean — Gaelic: Son of Leander
Madison — English: Good
Maddie, Maddison, Maddy, Madisson
Madoc — Welsh: Fortunate
Maddie, Maddoc, Maddock, Maddy, Maduc
Magnus/Manus — Latin: Great one
Mahir — Hebrew: Expert, industrious
Mahon — Celtic: Strong one
Mahoney
Maitland — English: From the meadowland
Major — Latin: Greater
Jorie, Jory, Maje, Majer, Mayer, Mayor
Malachai — Hebrew: My angel
Malachi, Malachy
Malcolm — Arabic: Dove

Malcolm X, whose birth name was Malcolm Little, was a black civil-rights leader and founder of the Organization of Afro-American Unity.

Malik — Islamic: Master

Malin — English: Little warrior
Mallin, Mallon, Malon

Mallory/Malory — German: Army counselor

Mandel/Mandell — German: Almond

Manfred — English: Man of peace
Manfredo, Manfrid, Manfried

Mannie/Manny — See: Emanuel/Emmanuel (Also, a nickname for names starting with "Man")

Manning — English: Son of the hero

Manuel — See: Emanuel/Emmanuel

Marcel — Latin: Little warrior
Marcellin, Marcellino, Marcello, Marcellus

Marcus — See: Mark
Marcus seems to be a name for healers of all types. There was the seven-year TV hit series "Marcus Welby, M.D.," and there was Roman philosopher Marcus Cicero, who recommended eating cabbage after drinking wine to prevent and/or cure a hangover.

Mario — See: Mark
Mario Lanza, considered one of the world's greatest operatic tenors, was born Alfred Arnold Cocozza.

Mark — Latin: Warlike
Marc, Marcel, March, Marco, Marcos, Marcus, Mario, Marion, Marius, Marjoe, Marko, Markos, Markus
Samuel Langhorne Clemens was a Mississippi steamboat pilot. When he began writing for a Nevada newspaper, he took the name Mark Twain, a nautical term that means "two fathoms deep."

Marlon — French: Little falcon
Marlen, Marlin

Marlowe — English: From the hill by the lake
Marlo, Marlow

Marshall — French: Keeper of the horses
Marsh, Marshal

Marston — English: From the place by the lake

Martin — Latin: Warlike
Mart, Martain, Marten, Martie, Martino, Marton, Marty, Mertin, Merton

Martin Luther King, Jr., the youngest person to win the Nobel Peace Prize, was baptized Michael Luther King, Jr. Six years later, his father, Rev. Michael Luther King, Sr., changed the Michael to Martin, for both himself and his son, in honor of the Reformation leader Martin Luther.

Marvel/Marvell — Latin: Miracle

Marvin — English: Famous friend
Marv, Marve, Marvyn, Marwin, Merv, Merven, Mervin, Mervyn, Morv, Morven
When award-winning composer Marvin Hamlisch was a young boy, his nickname was "Fingers" because he was always practicing the piano.

Mason — French: Stoneworker

Matt/Mattie/Matty — See: Matthew

Matthew — Hebrew: Gift of the Lord
Mata, Mateo, Mathia, Mathias, Mathieu, Mathius, Matias, Matio, Matt, Matteo, Matthaeus, Matthaus, Matthes, Mattheus, Matthias, Matthieu, Mattie, Matty

Matu — Native American: Brave

Maurice — Latin: Dark skinned
Maur, Mauricio, Maurie, Maurise, Mauruey, Maurite, Mauritis, Maurizio, Mauro, Maurus, Maury, Morice, Morie, Moritz, Moriz, Morrice, Morrie, Morris, Morritz, Morry, Mory
Artist Maurice Sendak is nicknamed "the Picasso of Children's Books."

Max — See: Maximillian, Maxwell

Maximillian — Latin: Greatest
Massimiliano, Massimo, Max, Maxie, Maxim, Maxime, Maximilliano, Maximilianus, Maximo, Maximus, Maxy

Maxwell — English: From the great well
Max, Maxey, Maxie, Maxy

Mayer/Myer — Latin: Great

Maynard — English: Mighty, brave
Mayne, Menard

Mayo — English: Kinsman

Mead/Meade — German: From the meadow

Medwin — English: Powerful friend

Meir/Meiri — Hebrew: One who shines

Melbourne — English: From the mill stream
Mel, Melborne, Melburn, Melden, Meldon, Mil, Milbourne, Milburn

Melville — English: Village near the mill
Mal, Malville, Mel

Melvin — Irish: Polished chief
Mal, Malvern, Malvin, Mel, Melvyn
Mel Brooks's name was Melvin Kaminsky. He said that he changed his name when he got a job as a drummer in the Catskills, because his real name wouldn't fit on the drums. So he used Mel, and Brooks came from his mother's maiden name, Brookman.

Menachem/Menahem — Hebrew: Comforter
Mendel, Mendeley, Mendie, Mendy

Mercer — Latin: Merchant; French: Dealer in textiles

Meredith — Celtic: Guardian from the sea
Meredeth, Merideth

Merle — French: Blackbird

Merlin — Welsh: Sea fort
Marlin, Merl

Merrick — English: Ruler of the sea

Merrill — French: Famous; English: Body of water
Merle, Merrel, Merrell, Merril, Meryl, Meryll

Merrit/Merritt — Latin: Valuable

Merton — English: From the town by the sea
Mertin, Merty

Merv/Mervin/Mervyn — See: Marvin
Merv (Mervyn) Griffin was the popular TV host who started "theme" talk shows.

Merwin/Merwyn — See: Marvin

Meyer — German: Head servant
Mayer, Myer

Michael — Hebrew: Like unto the Lord
Mica, Micah, Micha, Michael, Michal, Micheil, Michel, Michele, Michon, Mickel, Mickey, Mickie, Micky, Miguel, Miguelito, Mikael, Mike, Mikel, Mikey, Mikhael, Mikhail, Mikkie, Mikky, Mischa, Mishael, Mitch, Mitchel, Mitchell
For the past two decades this has been the most popular boy's name. Many celebrities with this name were born with it: Michael J. Fox, Michael Douglas, Michael Jackson, and Mikhail Baryshnikov.

Miles — Latin: Soldier; Greek: Merciful
Milan, Milo, Myles, Mylo
We all know that Miles Standish, one of the Mayflower settlers,

sent John Alden in his place to propose to Priscilla Mullins. But do you know that Miles was captain of the Pilgrims' military forces?

Millard — German: From the mill
Mill, Millais, Millay, Miller, Milman, Milne
Millard Fillmore, the thirteenth U.S. president, was born in a log cabin in New York State.

Milton — English: From the mill town
Milt, Miltie, Milty

Miner/Minor — Latin: Miner

Mitch/Mitchell — See: Michael

Mohammad/Mohammed — See: Muhammad

Mohan — Hindi: Delighted

Monroe — Irish: From the red marsh
Monro, Munro, Munroe

Montagu/Montague — French: From the pointed hill

Montgomery — French: From the rich man's hill castle
Monte, Monty
When Monty Hall, host of TV's "Let's Make a Deal," first started in show biz, he made a deal with his Toronto, Canada, radio-station manager to change his name from Monte Halparin.

Mordecai/Mordechai — Hebrew: Taught of God

Morgan — Celtic: One who lives near the sea

Morley — English: Meadow on the moor
Canadian-born Morley Safer is an investigative reporter on "60 Minutes."

Morris — See: Maurice

Morse — English: Son of the dark-complected one

Mortimer — French: From the quiet waters
Mort, Morty
Mortimer Benjamin Zuckerman is a self-made multimillionaire real-estate magnate and publisher.

Morton — English: Town near the sea
Mort, Morten, Mortin, Morty

Moses — Hebrew: A child saved from the water
Moe, Moise, Moises, Moishe, Mose, Mosheh, Moss, Moyes, Moys, Moyses, Mozes
Moses (Eugene) Malone, the first basketball player to sign a pro contract directly out of high school, became the youngest millionaire in sports history.

Mosi — Swahili: Firstborn

Muhammad — Arabic: Greatly praised
Mahmoud, Mahmud, Mohammad, Mohammed, Muhamet, Muhammed
Muhammad Ali, which is the Black Muslim name of one of the all-time greatest heavyweight prizefighters, was born Cassius Marcellus Clay, Jr. Ali's great-great-grandfather was a slave owned by Cassius Marcellus Clay, the American ambassador to Russia in the 1860s.

Mungo — Celtic: Lovable

Murdock — Gaelic: Wealthy sailor
Murdoch, Murtagh, Murtoch

Murphy — Irish: Sea warrior

Murray — Celtic: Sailor
Murrey, Murry
Murray Kaufman, better known as Murray the K, was the country's most popular disc jockey in the 1950s and 1960s.

Myron — Greek: Fragrant, sweet, perfumed

N

Nadim — Arabic: Friend

Namir — Hebrew: Swift as a leopard

Napoleon — Greek: New town
Napoleone, Nappie, Nappy

Nasser — Arabic: Victorious one

Nathan — Hebrew: God gave a gift
Nat, Nate, Nathon

Nathaniel — Hebrew: God has given
Nat, Natanael, Nataniel, Nate, Nathanael, Nathon, Natty, Nethanel
Singer Nathaniel Adams Coles had a group called the Nat Coles Trio. A manager renamed the group the King Cole Trio. Thereafter, the singer was known as Nat "King" Cole. He was the first black show host on national television.

Neal — Irish: Champion
Neale, Neall, Neel, Neil, Neill, Neils, Nels, Nial, Niall, Niel, Niels, Niles, Nils

Ned — See: Edgar, Edmond/Edmund

Nehemiah — Hebrew: Comforted by the Lord
Nahum, Nehamias, Nemiah, Nemian, Nemo

Neil — See: Neal
For men in show business, Neil seems to be the preferred spelling of the name — e.g., Neil Simon, Neil Diamond, Neil Sedaka.

Nelson — English: Son of Neal; son of a champion
Nealson, Nilson
South African activist Nelson Mandela has rekindled interest in this name, which nearly faded away since Nelson Eddy and Nelson Rockefeller were in the public eye.

Nero — Italian: Black one

Nestor — Greek: Wisdom of the aged

Neville — French: From the new town
Nevil, Nevile, Nevvy
History books taught us that Neville Chamberlain was England's prime minister, but did you know that he also invented the game of snooker?

Nevin — Latin: Of the snow; English: Middle; Gaelic: Holy
Nevins, Niven, Nivens

Newall/Newell — Latin: Kernel, fruit seed, something new

Newton — English: From the new town

Nicholas — Greek: Victory of the people
Niccolo, Nichol, Nick, Nickie, Nickolaus, Nicky, Nico, Nicol, Nicola, Nicolai, Nicolao, Nicolas, Nicolaus, Nicolo, Niki, Nikita, Nikki, Niklas, Nikolai, Nikolas, Nikolaus, Nikolos

Nick/Nickie/Nicky — See: Nicholas

Nicodemus — Greek: Victory over the people

Nigel — Latin: Dark one; Gaelic: Champion

Nissan — Hebrew: Banner, emblem

Nissim — Hebrew: Miracles, signs

Noah — Hebrew: Rest, comfort
Noach, Noak

Noble — Latin: Well known, famous

Noel/Noël — French: Born at Christmas
Natal, Natale, Nowell

Nolan — Irish: Noble, famous
Noland, Nolen, Nolend, Nolin, Nollan
In keeping with one of the meanings of the name, Nolan Miller is one of Hollywood's most famous fashion designers.

Norbert — Norse: Brilliant hero

Norman — French: From the north
Norm, Normand, Normen, Normie, Normy
The name Norman has never made it to the top ten, but many of its bearers have reached the top of their fields: TV producer/ director/writer Norman "All in the Family" Lear, film director Norman "Moonstruck" Jewison, actor Norman "Three's Company" Fell, novelist Norman Mailer, artist Norman Rockwell, clergyman Dr. Norman Vincent Peale, and military leader Norman Schwarzkopf.

Norris — French: Comes from the north
Norrie, Norry

Northrop — English: From the north farm
North, Northrup

Norton — English: From the northern town

Norville — French: From the north estate
Norval, Norvel, Norvell, Norvil, Norvill, Norvylle

Norvin — English: Friend from the north
Norvyn, Norwin

Norward — English: Northern guardian

Nova — Latin: New one

Noy — Hebrew: Beauty

Nugent — English: To shove

Nuncio — Italian: Messenger
Nuntius, Nunzio

Nuria — Hebrew: Fire of the Lord

Nye — English: Islander

O

Oakes — English: From the oak-tree grove
Oak, Oakie, Oakley, Oaky

Obadiah — Hebrew: God's servant
Oba, Obad, Obadias, Obed, Obediah, Obie, Oby

Oberon — French: Obedient
Oberon is king of the fairies and husband of Titania in Shakespeare's Midsummer Night's Dream.

Obert — German: Wealthy and bright one

Octavius — Latin: Eighth-born child
Octave, Octavian, Octavus, Ottavio

Odell — Norse: Rich man

Ogden/Ogdon — English: From the oak valley

Ola — Hebrew: Eternity

Olaf — Norse: Ancestor
Olaff, Olav, Olave, Olavi, Olen, Olin, Olof, Olov

Oliver — Latin: Olive tree (a symbol of peace)
Oliveiro, Olivero, Olivier, Oliviero, Olivio, Ollie, Olly, Olvan
The name Oliver attracted attention in the seventies, when Oliver Barrett IV, Jenny's husband in Love Story, *appeared in both book and film form. The name attracted even more attention in the eighties, when Colonel Oliver North made headlines during what has come to be known as Iranscam.*

Omar — Arabic: Highest
Omer, Omri
Omar Sharif is one of the few actors born with the name Michael who changed it. He went from Michael Shalhoub to Omar El Sharif in Egyptian films and Omar Sharif in English-language films.

Onan — Turkish: Prosperous

Oral — Latin: Speech
How appropriate that someone named Oral (Granville) Roberts is a preacher!

Oram — English: From the river-bank enclosure

Oran — Irish: Pale-complected one; Hebrew: Pine tree
Oren, Orin, Orren, Orrin

Orel — Latin: Listener
Every baseball fan knows about Orel Hershiser's records, titles, and awards.

Oren — See: Oran

Orestes — Greek: Mountaineer

Orien/Orion — Greek: Son of light

Orlan — English: From the pointed land
Orland, Orlando

Orman — English: Spearman

Orrick — English: Dweller at the old oak tree

Orson — Latin: Bearlike

Orville — French: From the golden city
Orval, Orvie, Orvy

Who says Orville is an unusual name? There are at least two of 'em: one of the two Wright brothers who flew the first motor-driven airplane; and the prince of popcorn himself, Orville Redenbacher.

Osbert — English: Divinely brilliant

Osborne — English: Divine warrior
Osborn, Osbourne, Oz, Ozzie, Ozzy

Oscar — Norse: Divine spearman
Oskar, Oskie, Osky, Ossie, Ossy
The Oscar is the film industry's most coveted award. Legend has it that it got its name when Margaret Herrick, the librarian at the Academy of Motion Picture Arts and Sciences, looked at the statuette and said that it looked like her uncle Oscar. Isn't that Wilde?

Osgood — English: Divine creator

Osmond — English: Divine protector
Osmont, Osmund, Osmunt

Oswald — English: Divinely powerful
Oswaldo, Oswell, Oswold, Oz, Ozzie, Ozzy

Otello/Othello — See: Otto
Othello, Shakespeare's protagonist, is a Moor in the military service of Venice and is married to Desdemona.

Otis — Greek: Keen of hearing

Otto — German: Rich
Odo, Otello, Othello, Otho

Ovid — Latin: Egg

Owen — See: Evan

Ozias — Hebrew: Strength of the Lord

Ozzie/Ozzy — See: Osborn/Osborne, Oswald
One of the perfect families during TV's Golden Age was the Nelsons, headed by Oswald "Ozzie" Nelson.

P

Pablo — See: Paul
Pablo Picasso's name at birth was Pablo Nepomuceno Cris-piniano de la Santissima Trinidad Ruiz y Picasso. He initially signed his paintings with his first initial, and then his mother's

and father's last names — P. Ruiz Picasso. He eventually dropped Ruiz, because it was a very common name, and stayed with his mother's more unusual name of Picasso.

Paco — Native American: Bold eagle

Paddy — See: Patrick

Paddy Chayefsky, the brilliant playwright and screenwriter, was originally named Sidney. When he was in the army and wanted to avoid K.P. duty one Sunday, he told his lieutenant that he had to go to mass. The lieutenant must have had a good sense of humor, for he nicknamed this Jewish soldier from the Bronx "Paddy," a classic Irish Catholic name. It stuck!

Page — French: Youthful attendant
Padge, Padget, Padgett, Paget, Paige

Palma/Palmer — English: Palm bearer

Paris — Place name: A city in France
This was the name of a prince of Troy who, according to Greek legend, abducted the beautiful Helen, thus causing the Trojan War.

Parker — English: Guardian of the park

Parnell — See: Peter

Parrish — English: From the churchyard
Parish, Parrie, Parrisch, Parry

Parvis — Latin: Of paradise

Pascal — Hebrew: Pertaining to Easter or Passover
Pace, Pasch, Paschal, Pascoli, Pasquale

Pat/Pattie/Patty — Nicknames for names starting with "Pat"

Patrick — Latin: Nobleman
Paddie, Paddy, Padraic, Padrick, Padruig, Pat, Patraic, Patric, Patricio, Patrize, Patrizio, Patrizius, Patsy, Patten, Pattie, Patty, Payton, Peyton
The popularity of actors Patrick Duffy and Patrick Swayze have done wonders for the popularity of this name.

Paul — Latin: Small
Pablo, Paley, Pall, Paoli, Paolino, Paolo, Paulie, Paulis, Paulot, Pauly, Paval, Pavel, Pavlo, Pavol, Pawl, Pawley, Poul
Here is a perfect example of how the meaning of a name didn't affect the person: Paul Bunyan. (Okay, so Paul Bunyan was a fictional character.) These real Pauls, no matter what their size, have all had big careers: Paul Anka, Paul Cezanne, Paul Gauguin, Paul Harvey, Paul McCartney, Paul Muni, Paul Newman, Paul Robeson, Paul Scofield, and Paul Williams.

Paxton — Latin: Town of peace
Pax, Paxon, Paxten, Paxtun, Payton
Penrod — German: Noted commander
Pen, Penn, Pennie, Penny
Pepin — German: One who seeks favors
Pepe, Pepi, Peppie, Peppy
Percival — French: Perceptive
Parsefal, Parsifal, Perce, Perceval, Percy
Percy — See: Percival
Percy Bysshe Shelley was one of the most radical of the English Romantic poets.
Perry — See: Peter
Perth — Celtic: Thornbush thicket
Peter — Greek: Stone
Panos, Parnell, Parry, Peadar, Pearce, Peder, Pedro, Peirce, Perkin, Pernel, Pero, Perrie, Perry, Petar, Pete, Petey, Petie, Petri, Petros, Petruscha, Pierce, Piero, Pierre, Pierrot, Piers, Piet, Pieter, Pietro
There are so many famous men with the name Peter, or a variation of the name, that it was hard for us to single out one. So here's a select list, to give you an idea of how popular the name was, is, and will continue to be: Saint Peter, Peter Stuyvesant, Peter Cooper, Peter Pan, Peter Falk, Peter O'Toole, Peter Jennings, Peter Bogdanovich, Peter Benchley, Peter Arno, Peter Max, Pete Rose, Pete Seeger, Pete Hamill (the list is starting to peter out), Perry Como, Perry King, Pierce Brosnan, Pierre Salinger, Pierre August Renoir, Piers Anthony, Piet Mondrian, and Pieter Brueghel.
Peverell — French: Whistler
Peverel, Peveril
Phillip — Greek: Lover of horses
Feeleep, Felipe, Filip, Filippo, Flip, Phil, Philip, Phillie, Phillipe, Phillipo, Philly
Phil Donahue was the first national TV talk-show host to make the audience an integral part of the show.
Philo — Greek: Loving
Phineas — Greek: Mouth of brass; Egyptian: Dark skinned
Fineas, Finnie, Finny, Pincas, Pinchas, Pincus
Pinchas Zukerman, world-renowned violinist, violist, and conductor, is called "Pinky" by friends.
Phoenix — Greek: Purple

Pierce — See: Peter

Pierpont — Latin: From the stone bridge
  Pier, Piers

Pierre — See: Peter

Pius — Latin: Devout, conscientious, kind

Placido — Spanish: Serene
  Opera singer Placido Domingo, one of the world's foremost tenors, made this name familiar to Americans.

Plato — Greek: Broad shouldered

Platt — French: From the flat land

Pomeroy — French: From the apple orchard

Pontius — Latin: Fifth one
  Ponce, Pontie, Ponty

Porter — Latin: Keeper of the gate

Prentice/Prentiss — English: Apprentice, learner

Prescott — English: From the priest's house
  Prescot, Prestcot, Prestcott

Presley — English: Priest's meadow
  Presleigh, Presly, Prestly
  Because of Elvis Presley's enormous popularity, it is now not unusual for Presley to be used as a first name.

Preston — English: From the priest's town

Price/Pryce — English: Value

Primo — Italian: First child (if a son)
  Primus

Prince — Latin: The first in rank
  Prince, born Prince Roger Nelson, is not just another pretty face. This talented musician writes and arranges the music on his albums and also plays more than twenty musical instruments.

Procter/Proctor — Latin: Leader, manager

Pryor — Latin: Head of a monastery

Pyne — English: Pine tree

Q

Quain — French: Clever one

Quennel — French: Dweller at the little oak tree
  Quenn, Quennell

Quentin — Latin: Fifth child (if a son)
Quent, Quenten, Quenton, Quint, Quintin, Quinton, Quintus
Quentin was the name of President Theodore Roosevelt's aviator
son, who was nicknamed "Quentin the Eagle." Quinton is the
name Burt Reynolds and Loni Anderson gave their son.

Quiller — English: Writer
Quill

Quimby/Quinby — Norse: From the woman's estate

Quincy — Latin: Fifth one; Place name: A town in Massachusetts
Quincy Jones, Jr., whose middle name is Delight, delights mil-
lions with his music.

Quinlan — Irish: Well shaped, athletic

Quinn — Celtic: Wise, intelligent

R

Radborne — English: Lives by the red brook
Rad, Radbourn, Radburn, Raddie, Raddy, Radley

Radcliffe — English: From the red cliff

Rafael — See: Raphael

Rafe/Rafer — See: Raphael

Raferty/Rafferty — Irish: Rich, prosperous

Rafi — Arabic: Exalting
Raffi, Raffy, Rafy

Raleigh — English: Dweller at the roe-deer meadow
Rawley, Rawly

Ralph — English: Fearless advisor
Raff, Ralf, Ralphie, Ralphy, Raoul, Rolf, Rolph
There are some names — and they're not always the most popu-
lar ones — that belong to many people from different walks of
life. Ralph is one of those names. To give you an idea of what we
mean, here are a bunch of Ralphs: Bunche, Nader, Abernathy,
Waldo Emerson, Lauren, Metcalfe, Macchio, and the famous but
fictional Ralph Kramden, whom Jackie Gleason played on "The
Honeymooners."

Ramon — See: Raymond

Ramsay/Ramsey — English: From the ram's island
Ram, Ramsy

Rance — French: A kind of Belgian marble

Randall — See: Randolph

Randolph — English: Shield-wolf (implying a protective cover)
Rand, Randal, Randall, Randell, Randie, Randle, Randolf, Randolfe, Randolphe, Randy

Randy — See: Randolph
This name seems to be catching on since country singer Randy Travis started winning all those Grammies.

Ranen/Ranon — Hebrew: To be joyous, to sing

Ranger — French: Guardian of the forest
Rainger, Range

Rankin — English: Little shield

Ransom — English: Son of a warrior

Raoul — See: Ralph

Raphael — Hebrew: God has healed
Rafael, Rafaelle, Rafaello, Rafe, Rafer, Raff, Rephael

Ravi — Hindi: Sun

Ravid — Hebrew: Jewelry, ornament

Raviv — Hebrew: Rain, dew

Ray — French: Kingly (Also, a nickname for names starting with "Ray")
Singer Ray Charles's last name is Robinson, but he chose not to use it because he didn't want to be confused with the boxer Sugar Ray Robinson.

Rayburn — English: From the roe-deer brook
Raybourn, Reyburn

Rayfield — English: Stream in the field

Rayford — English: Ford over the stream

Raymond — English: Wise protector
Raimond, Raimondo, Raimund, Raimundo, Ramon, Ray, Raymondo, Raymund, Raymundo
Long before he played Perry Mason, Raymond Burr worked for the Oregon Forest Service and spent five months on his own because he was snowed in. In this case, his last name was extremely appropriate: Burr!

Raynor — German: Wisdom, advice
Ragnor, Rainer, Rainier, Ranier, Raynar, Rayner, Regnier

Reade — English: With red hair
Read, Reed, Reid

Redford — English: From the red-river crossing

Reese — Welsh: Ardent one
Ree, Reece, Rees, Reiss, Rhett, Rhys, Rice

Reeve/Reeves — English: Steward
Regan — German: Wise
  Reagan, Reagen, Regen, Regin
Reginald — English: Powerful, mighty
  Reg, Reggie, Reginard, Reginauld
  *Reginald Martinez Jackson, known to baseball fans and candy
  lovers as Reggie Jackson, led the New York Yankees to a World
  Series victory in 1977 and tied Babe Ruth's record for World
  Series single-game homers by hitting three of them in the sixth
  game.*
Regis — Latin: Kingly, regal
  *Regis Philbin, living up to the meaning of his name, is one of the
  rulers of morning TV*
Remington — English: From the raven estate
  Remy
  *Remington Steele, played by Pierce Brosnan, was the handsome,
  cultured, and very charming detective on the TV series of the
  same name.*
Remus — Latin: Changeling
  Remi, Remo, Remy
Rene — See: Ronald
Renny — Gaelic: Small and powerful
Reuben — Hebrew: Behold a son
  Reubin, Reuven, Rouvin, Rube, Ruben, Rubie, Rubin, Ruby
Reuel/Ruel — Hebrew: Friend of God
Rex — Latin: King
Reynard — French: Fox
  Rainardo, Raynard, Raynardo, Regnard, Reinhard, Reinhart, Re-
  nard, Renart, Renaud, Rey
Reynold/Reynolds — See: Ronald
Rhett — See: Everet/Everett, Reece/Reese
Rhodes — Greek: Place of the roses
Richard — German: Wealthy and powerful
  Dick, Dickie, Dicky, Ric, Ricard, Ricardo, Riccardo, Ricci, Ric-
  ciardo, Ricco, Rich, Richart, Richie, Richy, Rick, Rickart, Rickert,
  Rickie, Ricky, Rico, Rikki, Ritchie, Ritchy
  *Because Richard and all its variations have been, and continue
  to be, quite popular, we could fill this chapter with Richard
  names. Here are just a few: Richard Chamberlain, Richard Bur-
  ton, Richard Nixon, Richard the Lionhearted, Richard Dreyfuss,
  Richard Pryor, Richard Avedon, Richard Dawson, Rick Blaine*

(Humphrey Bogart's character in Casablanca*), Ricky Nelson, Ricardo Montalban, Dick Cavett, and Dick Clark.*

Richmond/Richmund — German: Powerful protector

Rick — See: Richard (Also, a nickname for names starting or ending with "Ric" or "Rick")

Rider/Ryder — English: Horseman

Ridgley — English: By the meadow's edge
　　Riddley, Ridge, Ridley, Ridly
　　The hardly ever heard name Ridley can be seen on movie credits: Ridley Scott is the director of Alien, Aliens II, Blade Runner, Black Rain, Thelma & Louise, *and more.*

Rigby — English: Ruler's valley

Riley — Irish: Valiant
　　Reilly, Ryley

Rimmon/Rimon — Hebrew: Pomegranate

Ring/Ringo — English: Ring
　　Once upon a time in England, there was a group named Rory Storm and the Hurricanes. Each of the musicians decided to find American cowboy names for themselves. And so drummer Richard Starkey became Ringo Starr, keeping that name when he joined the Beatles.

Riordan — Irish: Royal poet
　　Reardon, Reorden

Ripley — English: From the shouter's meadow

Ritter — German: Mounted warrior, knight
　　Ritt

Roald — German: Famous ruler

Roarke — Irish: Mighty
　　Roark, Rorke, Rourke, Ruark

Rob/Robbie/Robby — See: Robert (Also, nicknames for names starting with "Rob")

Robert — English: Bright fame
　　Bert, Berty, Bob, Bobbie, Bobby, Rob, Robb, Robbie, Robbin, Robbinson, Robby, Roberto, Robertson, Robin, Robinson, Rupert, Ruperto, Ruprecht
　　As with the name Richard, Robert and all its variations have been and continue to be quite popular. It is said that Robert De Niro, when growing up in New York City's Little Italy, was nicknamed "Bobby Milk" because he was so pale and thin.

Robin — See: Robert

Robinson — English: Son of Robert

Rochester — English: Rocky fortress

Rockwell — English: From the rocky spring
Rocco, Rock, Rockne, Rocky

Rocky — Nickname for names starting with "Roc" and "Rock"
There were world boxing titleholders Rocky Graziano and Rocky Marciano, but the most famous boxing Rocky of all was Sylvester Stallone's fictional Rocky ("Yo, Adrian!") Balboa.

Rod — Nickname for names starting with "Rod"

Roderick — German: Renowned ruler
Roddie, Roddy, Roderic, Roderich, Roderigo, Rodrick, Rodrigo, Rodrique, Rory, Rurik, Rury

Rodman — English: One who clears the land, farmer

Rodney — English: From the island clearing

Roger — German: Famous noble warrior
Rodge, Rodger, Rogerio, Rogers, Rugero, Ruggiero, Rutger
While Roger has never been on the top-ten lists, it has been fairly popular through the years. There's Roger Moore, Roger Maris, Roger Williams, Roger Ebert, Roger Mudd, Roger Stevens, Roger Bannister, Roger Corman, Roger Vadim, Roger Rabbit, the Jolly Roger . . . and Roger, over and out!

Roland — German: From the well-known island
Roeland, Rolando, Roldan, Rollan, Rolland, Rollie, Rollin, Rollo, Rolly, Rowland
Roland, one of Charlemagne's most famous and accomplished knights, is the legendary prototype of the loyal, courageous, self-sacrificing hero of chivalry.

Famous psychologist and author Rollo May was named after the Little Rollo character in Jacob Abbott's series of books. As a kid, he hated his name until he found out that there was a Norman leader named Rollo the Conqueror.

Rolf — See: Ralph

Roman — Latin: Citizen of Rome
Romain, Rome, Romeo, Romer, Romualdo, Romulus

Romeo — See: Roman

Romney — Welsh: Curving river

Ronald — English: Powerful, mighty
Ranald, Raynold, Reinald, Reinaldo, Reinaldos, Reinhold, Reinwald, Renaldo, Renato, Renaud, Renault, Rene, Reynold, Reynolds, Rinaldo, Ron, Ronaldo, Ronnie, Ronny
This name enjoys the spotlight because of both a former U.S. president and a clown: Ronald Reagan and Ronald McDonald.

Ronan — Celtic: A pledge

Ronel — Hebrew: Joy of God

Roone — English: Counsel
ABC-TV sports and news fans know this unusual name because of Roone (Pinckney) Arledge, Jr.

Rooney — Irish: Red haired

Roosevelt — Dutch: Field of roses
Rosey, Rosie

Roper — English: Rope maker

Rory — See: Roderick

Roscoe — Norse: From the deer forest
Scoey
Roscoe Robinson brings honor to this name. In 1982, he was promoted to four-star general in the Army (becoming the first black to achieve that rank).

Rosey/Rosie — See: Roosevelt

Ross — Gaelic: From the island
Rossi, Rossy
Billionaire and 1992 presidential candidate Henry Ross Perot prefers being billed as H. Ross Perot and is generally referred to as Ross Perot.

Roswald — German: Mighty steed
Roswell

Roth — German: Red haired

Rowen — Gaelic: Red haired
Rowan, Rowe

Roy — French: King
Roi, Ruy

Royal — French: Royal one

Royce — English: Son of the king

Ruben/Rubin — See: Reuben

Ruby — See: Reuben/Reubin

Rudolph — German: Famous and glorious wolf
Dolf, Dolph, Rodolfo, Rodolfus, Rodolph, Rodolphe, Rudie, Rudolf, Rudolfe, Rudolfo, Rudulph, Rudy
Just one song ("Rudolph the Red-Nosed Reindeer"), and a name becomes associated with one of Santa's helpers; just one actor from Sweden (Dolph Lundgren), and a shortened version of that same name becomes associated with a muscle man.

Rudy — See: Rudolph

Rudyard — English: From the red enclosure

Rufus — Latin: Red-haired one
Rupert — See: Robert
Ruskin — French: Red-haired one
Russ — See: Russell
Russell — French: Redheaded
    Russ, Russel, Rustie, Rusty
Ryan/Ryen — Irish: Little king
> *Actor Ryan O'Neal was born Patrick Ryan O'Neal. He let go of Patrick so that people wouldn't confuse him with his third cousin, actor Patrick O'Neal.*

Rylan/Ryland — English: Dweller at the rye land

S

Sabian/Sabin — Latin: Of the Sabines (an ancient Italian tribe)
Saint — Latin: Holy
    Sanche, Sanchez, Sancho, Santo
Sakima — Native American: King
Salim — Arabic: Good
Salvador/Salvadore — Italian: Savior
    Sal, Sallie, Sally, Salvatore, Sauveur
Sam — Hebrew: To hear (Also, a nickname for names starting with "Sam")
> *For a time, this name belonged to the geriatric generation. Now, there are lots of young boys called Sam, and perhaps the resurgence of this name may be partially due to the popularity of the leading character on "Cheers." Actor Ted Danson as Sam Malone, the tall, attractive bachelor bartender with an eye for the ladies, has been charming TV audiences since 1982.*

Samir — Arabic: Entertainer
Samson — Hebrew: Like the sun
    Sam, Sammie, Sammy, Sampson, Sansao, Sansom, Sansome, Sansum, Shem, Shimson
Samuel — Hebrew: His name is God
    Sam, Samel, Sammie, Sammy, Samouel, Samuele, Shem, Shemuel
Sanborn — English: From the sandy brook
Sancho — See: Saint

Sancho Panza is the fictional peasant squire in Cervantes's Don Quixote.

Sanders — English: Son of Alexander
Sanderson, Sandor, Sandors, Saunders, Saunderson

Sandie/Sandy — Nickname for names starting with "San"

Sanford — English: From the sandy ford

Sargent — French: To serve
Sarge, Sergant, Serge, Sergeant, Sergei, Sergent, Sergi, Sergio

Saul — Hebrew: Borrowed
Winner of the Nobel Prize in literature, novelist Saul Bellow has also written plays. In keeping with the meaning of his name, Saul says his characters are borrowed from real people, including his relatives.

Savill/Saville — French: From the estate of willow trees

Sawyer — English: One who works with a saw

Saxon — English: Swordsman
Sax, Saxen, Saxin

Sayers — Welsh: Carpenter
Sayer, Sayre, Sayres

Scanlon — Irish: Charmer
Scanlan, Scanlen

Schuyler — Dutch: To hide, to shield
Shuylar, Skuyler, Sky, Skylar, Skyler

Scoey — See: Roscoe, Scoville

Scott — English: Scotsman
Scot, Scotti, Scottie, Scotty
Scott Joplin is called "the King of the Ragtime Composers." His musical composition "The Entertainer," which was the theme of the film The Sting, *won an Academy Award more than fifty years after he died.*

Scoville — French: From the Scotchman's estate
Scoe, Scoey

Scribe — Latin: Writer
Scribner, Scrivener

Scully — Irish: Town crier

Sean — See: John
Sean Connery's real first name is Thomas.

Searle — German: Armed one
Searl, Serle

Sebastian — Latin: Honored above others
Bastian, Bastien, Seb, Sebastiano, Sebastiao, Sebastien

Selby — English: From the farmstead

Selden/Seldon — English: Rare, strange, valley of willows

Selig — German: Blessed one, happy one

Selwin/Selwyn — English: Blessed friend

Seth — Hebrew: Appointed one

Seton — English: From the place by the sea
 Seaton, Seetin, Seeton

Seward — English: Victorious defender

Sewell — English: Wall near the sea
 Sewal, Sewald, Sewall

Sexton — English: Church official

Seymour — French: From the sea moors
 Seymore, Sy

Shafer — Aramaic: Good, beautiful

Shalom — See: Solomon
 Journalist and short-story writer Shalom Aleichem, born Sholem Rabinowitz, has been nicknamed "the Yiddish Mark Twain." Fiddler on the Roof is based on one of his stories.

Shamus — See: Jacob

Shanahan — Irish: Wise one

Shandy — English: Rambunctious

Shane — See: John
 Movie mavens agree that Shane is one of the greatest Westerns ever made. Alan Ladd portrayed the title character in this 1953 classic.

Shanley — Gaelic: Wise hero

Shannon/Shanon — Irish: Little wise one

Shaw — English: From the grove of trees

Shawn — See: John

Shea — Irish: Ingenious, majestic, courteous one

Sheehan — Irish: Little and peaceful

Sheffield — From the crooked field

Shelby — English: Sheltered town

Sheldon — English: Protected hill

Shelley/Shelly — English: Island of shells (Also, nicknames for names starting with "Shel")

Shephard/Shepherd — English: One who tends sheep
 Shep, Shepard, Sheperd, Sheppard, Shepperd, Sheppie, Sheppy

Sheridan — Irish: Wild one

Sheriff — English: Lawman

Sherlock/Sherlocke — English: Fair or white-haired one

Originally, Arthur Conan Doyle was going to name his fictional detective Sherrinford, but he thought the name was awkward-sounding, so he changed it to Sherlock. The name Holmes was inspired by author and physician Oliver Wendell Holmes.

Sherman — English: Sheep shearer

Sherwin/Sherwyn — English: Splendid friend

Sherwood — English: From the bright forest

Sidney — Phoenician: Enchanter
Sid, Sidon, Syd, Sydney
This seems to be a name for successful directors — Sidney Lumet, Sidney Poitier, and Sydney Pollack — who enchant moviegoers with their work.

Siegfried — German: Victorious peace
Siffre, Sigefredo, Sigfrid, Sigfroi, Sigvard

Sigmund — German: Victorious protector
Sig, Siggy, Sigimundo, Sigismond, Sigismund, Sigmond, Ziggy, Zigimond, Zigimund, Zigmon

Silas — See: Silvanus

Silvanus — Latin: Forest dweller
Silas, Silva, Silvain, Silvano, Sylvan

Simon — Hebrew: He who hears
Simeon, Simmie, Simmon, Simms, Simmy, Simone, Simpson, Symms, Symon, Ximenes

Sinclair — Latin: Clear sign
How many book reports were written on Nobel Prize–winner Sinclair Lewis's Babbit, Main Street, and Arrowsmith?

Skelly — Irish: Storyteller
Skelley, Skellie

Skipper — Dutch: Shipmaster
Skip, Skipp, Skippie, Skippy

Slade — English: From the valley

Sloan/Sloane — Irish: Warrior

Smith — English: Blacksmith
Smitty, Smyth

Sol — See: Solomon

Solomon — Hebrew: Peace
Salamon, Salman, Salmon, Salom, Salomo, Salomone, Shalom, Shelomoh, Shlomo, Sholom, Sol, Sollie, Solly, Solman, Zalman, Zalmen, Zalmon
If you look at a $10,000 bill, you'll see that Salmon P. Chase's name is on it. And rightfully so, considering that as secretary of

the treasury under President Lincoln he established a national banking system and issued a legal-tender currency.

Somerset — English: Summer settlement

Somerset Maugham was known as a novelist, playwright, and short-story writer. But did you know he was also a medical doctor? He first wrote about his experience as a physician in a London slum and then decided to continue writing, abandoning his medical career. Also, Somerset was his middle name; his real first name was William.

Sonny — Nickname for names starting or ending with "Son"

Sorrell — French: With reddish brown hair
Sorel, Sorell

Spalding — English: Divided field

Spangler — French: Glittering one

Spark — English: Flash of light
Sparky

Speed — English: Wealth, power, success
Speedy

Spencer — English: Administrator
Spence, Spense, Spenser

Spike — Latin: Ear of grain

Spike Lee, born Shelton Jackson Lee, is a moviemaker who attracts a lot of attention with his sometimes controversial work.

Spiro — Latin: To breathe

Squire — English: Attendant to nobility

Stacey — Latin: Firmly established
Stace, Stacy

Stan — Nickname for names starting with "Stan"

Baseball Hall of Famer Stan "the Man" Musial played for the St. Louis Cardinals (1941–63) and is one of the all-time great hitters.

Stancil — English: Upright bar, beam

Stanford — English: Stone river crossing

Stanhope — English: From the stony land

Stanislaus — Polish: Glorious position
Stanislao, Stanislas, Stanislav, Stanislaw, Stanislus

Stanley — English: Glory of the camp
Stanleigh, Stanly

Stanton — English: Town near the stony field
Stanten, Stantin

Stavros — Greek: Crowned

Steadman/Stedman — English: Occupant of farmstead
Stefan — See: Stephen
Stephen — Greek: Crown
    Estaban, Estevan, Etienne, Stefan, Stefano, Stephan, Stephanos,
    Stephanus, Stevan, Steve, Steven, Stevie, Stevin, Stevy, Tiennot
Sterling/Stirling — English: Genuine, valued
Sterne — English: Austere
    Stearn, Stearne, Stern
Steve/Steven — See: Stephen
Stewart — English: Steward of the manor
    Stew, Steward, Stewie, Stewy, Stu, Stuart
Stinson — English: Son of stone
Stockton — English: Town near the tree trunk
Stoddard — English: Keeper of the horses
Stoke — English: Village
Storm — English: Storm
    New York TV weatherman Frank Field named his son Storm.
    Now Storm Field is also a TV weatherman . . . how fitting!
Strom — Greek: Bed, mattress
Stuart — See: Stewart
Sullivan — Latin: Uplifter
    Sullavan, Sullie, Sully
Sultan — Swahili: Ruler
Sumner — English: One who summons or calls
Sutherland — Norse: From the southern land
Sutton — English: From the southern town
Sven — Norse: Youth
    Svend, Swain, Swen, Swend
Sweeney — Gaelic: Little hero
Sylvester — Latin: From the forest
    Silvester, Silvestre, Silvestro, Sly
    Bet Sylvester Stallone is the only actor in Hollywood who chose
    to use Sylvester (his middle name) instead of Michael (his real
    first name). And it works for him!

T

Tab — See: Tabor

Tabor — Persian: Drummer; Hungarian: Encampment; Gaelic: Well-spring
   Tab, Tabbie, Tabby, Taber

Tad — See: Thaddeus

Taffy — Welsh: Beloved one
   This beloved name is the Welsh version of David.

Taggart — Gaelic: Son of the church official
   Tag

Tait/Tate — Norse, Swedish: Cheerful one

Tal — Hebrew: Rain (Also, a nickname for names starting with "Tal")
   Tallie, Tally

Talbott — French: One given rewards from war gains
   Tal, Talbot, Tallie, Tally

Tallis — Persian: Learned, wise
   Tal, Tallie, Tally
   A tallis is a white fringed prayer shawl with blue or black bands and is worn by Jewish men during prayer.

Talmadge — English: Lake midway between two towns
   Tal, Tallie, Tally

Talman — Aramaic: Oppress, injure
   Tal, Tallie, Tally, Talmon

Tanner — English: Leatherworker
   Tan, Tann, Tannie, Tanny

Taro — Japanese: Firstborn male, big boy
   Taro is a tropical plant with an edible rootstock.

Tarrant — Welsh: Thunder
   Tarr, Tarrent, Tarrie, Tarry

Tauno — Finnish: World ruler

Tavish — Gaelic: Twin

Taylor — English: Tailor
   Tailer, Talor, Tayler

Teague — Irish: Poet
   Teige

Ted/Teddie/Teddy — Nicknames for names starting with "Ed" or "Ted"

Edward Moore Kennedy, the ninth and last child of Joseph and Rose Kennedy, is probably the most famous Ted/Teddy since Teddy Roosevelt. The current runner-up is "the King of Cable," Robert Edward Turner III, better known as Ted Turner and sometimes called "the Mouth from the South."

Telford — Latin: Shallow stream

Templeton — English: From the town of the temple
Temple

Terence — Latin: Tender, good, gracious
Terrel, Terrence, Terrie, Terrill, Terris, Terry, Terryal

Terry — See: Terence

Everyone knows Milt Caniff's famous comic strip "Terry and the Pirates." But do you know Terry's whole name? It's Terry Lee.

Teva — Hebrew: Nature
Tev, Tevie, Tevy, Tevya

Thaddeus — Greek: Gift of God; Hebrew: Praising God
Tad, Tadd, Taddeo, Thaddaus, Thaddeo, Thaddy, Thadeus

Thatcher — English: Roof mender
Thacher, Thatch, Thax, Thaxter

Theobald — German: Prince of the people
Ted, Teddy, Teobald, Thebaud, Thebault, Theo, Thibaud, Thibaut, Tibald, Tibalt, Tibold

Theodore — Greek: Gift of God
Feodor, Feodore, Ted, Teddie, Teddy, Tellie, Telly, Teodor, Teodoro, Theo, Theodor, Theodorus, Theodosios, Tudo
Theodore Roosevelt was the first president to ride in an automobile, fly in an airplane, and go in a submarine. Pulitzer Prize–winning author and illustrator Theodor Seuss Geisel was known to millions of children as Dr. Seuss.

Theodoric — German: Ruler of the people
Tedric, Teodorico, Theodric, Thierry

Thomas — Aramaic: Twin
Tam, Tamas, Tammeas, Tammen, Tammie, Tammy, Tavis, Tavish, Thom, Thoma, Thomaz, Thumas, Tom, Tomas, Tomaso, Tome, Tomkin, Tomlin, Tommie, Tommy
Now this name is popular! There's Thomas Jefferson, Thomas à Becket, Thomas Aquinas, Thomas Wolfe, Thomas Alva Edison, and former House Majority Leader Thomas Philip O'Neill, Jr. (better known as Tip O'Neill), to name just a few.

Thor — Norse: Thunder
Thorin, Thorley, Thorr, Tor, Tore, Torin
Norwegian explorer Thor Heyerdahl sailed a balsa-wood raft forty-three hundred miles from Peru to Polynesia and then wrote about his experience in the best-seller Kon-Tiki, *which was translated into sixty-four languages.*

Thormond — English: Thor's protection
Thormund, Thurmond, Thurmund

Thorndike — English: From the thorny meadow
Thorn, Thorndyke, Thornie, Thorny

Thorpe — English: From the village

Thurman/Thurmon — English: Servant of Thor

Thurstan/Thurston — Norse: Thor's stone
If you catch a rerun of the 1960's TV hit "Gilligan's Island," you'll see Thurston Howell III, the millionaire castaway played by Jim Backus.

Tim/Timmie/Timmy — Nicknames for names starting with "Tim"

Timon/Tymon — Greek: Reward

Timothy — Greek: Honoring God

Timur — Hebrew: Stately

Titus — Greek: Great size and power
Titan, Tito, Titos

Tobias — Hebrew: God is good
Tobe, Tobia, Tobiah, Tobie, Tobin, Tobit, Toby

Toby — See: Tobias

Todd — Latin: Fox
Tod, Toddie, Toddy

Toler — English: Tax collector
Toller, Tollie, Tolly

Tom/Tommy — See: Thomas
Have you ever thought about how many successful contemporary actors use the name Tom? Tom Selleck, Tom Cruise, Tom Hulce, Tom Berenger, Tom Hanks. Who did we leave out?

Tony — See: Anthony
This nickname is a popular show-biz name: Tony Danza, Tony Randall, Tony Curtis, Tony Bennett, and more.

Torrance/Torrence — Irish: From the place of little hills
Tor, Torrey, Torrie, Torry, Tory

Tracey/Tracy — Latin: Courageous
Tracy Tupman is the well-fed, well-groomed young man in Charles Dickens's Pickwick Papers.

Travis — Latin: From the crossroads
Traver, Travers

Trent — Latin: From the swift stream
Trenten, Trentin, Trenton

Trevor — Celtic: Prudent

Trini — Latin: Trinity, triad, three

Tristram — Latin: Sorrowful, mournful
Tris, Tristam, Tristan

Troy — Irish: Son of a foot soldier
Troy Donahue was a popular actor in the 1960s. In 1974, he played a character in The Godfather, Part II *named Merle Johnson, which, strangely enough, is Troy's real name.*

Truman — English: Faithful man
Writer Truman Capote was originally Truman Streckfus Persons. His mother divorced Truman's father and remarried Joseph Capote, who legally adopted the young boy.

Tucker — English: One who cleans and thickens cloth

Tully — Irish: To live with the peace of God

Turner — Latin: Lathe worker

Twain — English: Separated into two parts

Tyler — English: Tile and brick maker

Tynan — Gaelic: Dark haired, dark-complected

Tyrone — Greek: Sovereign
Tyrone Power was the oh-so-handsome romantic lead in films of the late 1930s and 1940s. Tyrone was also the name of Arte Johnson's strange little-old-man character on TV's "Laugh-In." Also, Tyrone Fletcher is the real name of Toonses, the driving cat on "Saturday Night Live."

Tyrus — Latin: One from Tyre (a port in Lebanon)

Tyson — French: Firebird

U

Udell — English: From the valley of the yew trees
Udale, Udall

Ulrick — German: Strong and powerful ruler; Danish: Wolf
Ulric, Ulrich, Ulu

Ulysses — Latin: Wrathful
   Ulises
   The eighteenth president of the United States was born Hiram
   Ulysses Grant. At West Point, his name was changed to Ulysses
   Simpson Grant so that his initials no longer spelled HUG. But he
   then had to put up with the new nickname of "Useless."

Umberto — Italian: Color of the earth
   The name Umberto Eco belongs to the novelist who wrote the
   best-seller The Name of the Rose.

Uno — Latin: The one

Upton — English: From the upper town
   American novelist Upton Sinclair was the voice of social protest
   during the first half of the twentieth century.

Uranus — Greek: Heavenly

Urban/Urbane — Latin: Courteous, from town
   Urbain, Urbano, Urbanus, Urvan

Uriah — Hebrew: God is my light
   Uri, Urie, Uriel

Ursel — Latin: Bear
   Ursa, Urshell

Uziel — Hebrew: My strength
   Uzi, Uzziah, Uzziel

V

Vachel — French: One who raises cows
   American poet Vachel Lindsay was called "the Tramp Poet"
   because of the time he had spent as a hobo trading poems for
   food.

Vada — Latin: Shallow place

Vail — English: From the valley
   Vale, Valle

Valdemar/Waldemar — German: Powerful, mighty

Valentine — Latin: Strong, powerful
   Val, Valentin, Valentino, Valerian, Valerio, Valerius, Valery, Vallie, Vally

Van — Dutch: From, of (usually used with another name)
   Vane, Vanne

Vance — English: Very high places

Vardon — French: Green knoll
  Varden, Verden, Verdon

Varian — Latin: Clever

Vasilis/Vassily — See: Basil

Vaughan/Vaughn — Celtic: Small

Vere — Latin: Faithful, true

Verlin — Latin: Flourishing
  Verion, Verle, Verlon

Vernon — Latin: Springlike
  Vern, Verne
  Popular and classical music composer Vladimir Dukelsky wrote songs such as "April in Paris" and "I Can't Get Started with You" under the name "Vernon Duke" and used his real name for the symphonies, concertos, sonatas, and ballet he composed.

Verrill — French: True one
  Verall, Verill, Verrall, Verrell, Verroll

Victor — Latin: Conqueror
  Vic, Vick, Vickers, Victoir, Victorien, Victorin, Viktor, Vitorio, Vittorio
  The great Danish pianist-comedian Victor Borge was born Borge Rosenbaum.
  Vic was the name of General George Armstrong Custer's horse.

Vidor — Hungarian: Cheerful

Vincent — Latin: Conquering
  Vin, Vince, Vincente, Vincenz, Vincenzio, Vincenzo, Vinicent, Vinicio, Vinnie, Vinny
  Vincent van Gogh lived in poverty, but exactly one hundred years after his death, his Portrait of Dr. Gachet *sold at auction for $82.5 million.*

Vinson — Latin: Son of Vincent

Virgil — Latin: Staff bearer
  Verge, Vergil, Vergit, Virge, Virgie, Virgilio
  In the film In the Heat of the Night, *Virgil Tibbs is played by Sidney Poitier.*

Vitas — Latin: Life
  Vida, Vidal, Vite, Vito
  "Asymmetric," "Five Point," "Eye-Eye," and "Greek Goddess" are some of the hairstyles that helped make Vidal Sassoon one of the world's wealthiest hairdressers.

Vito — See: Vitas

Vladimir — Slavic: Powerful prince
   Vladamir, Vladmir
   Vladimir Horowitz was one of classical music's greatest pianists.
Volley — Latin: To fly
   Vollon
Volney — German: Spirit of the people
Von — German: From, of (usually used with another name)

W

Wade — English: One who moves forward
Wadsworth — English: estate with a wading pool
Wagner — Dutch: Wagon driver
   Waggoner, Wagoner
Wainwright — English: Wagon maker
   Wain, Waine, Wayne
Walden — English: From the forest valley
Waldo — English: Ruler
   Waldron
   Where's Martin Handford? He's laughing all the way to the bank for creating those "Where's Waldo?" books.
Walker — English: One who thickens cloth
Wallace — English: Welshman
   Walach, Wallach, Wallie, Wally, Walman, Walsh, Welch, Welsh
Wallie/Wally — Nicknames for names starting with "Wal"
   Wally Cleaver, played by Tony Dow, was the Beaver's teenage brother in TV's "Leave It to Beaver" (1957–63).
Walt — See: Walter
   The great, innovative animator and producer Walt Disney was born Walter Elias Disney. He won a record seventeen Oscars from 1931 through 1969 (some of them awarded posthumously).
Walter — German: Powerful warrior
   Gauthier, Gualter, Gualterio, Gualtiero, Wallie, Wally, Walt, Walther
   Walter (Leland) Cronkite, Jr., has turned up on polls as the most trusted man in the country. His colleagues nicknamed him "Uncle Walter."

Walton — English: From the walled town

Ward — English: Guardian
  Warde, Warden, Worden

Warner — German: Protective warrior
  Werner, Wernher
  Warner LeRoy, the successful New York restaurateur (Tavern on the Green), is the son of film producer/director Mervyn LeRoy and Doris Warner, the daughter of one of film's famous Warner Brothers. This is a good example of a child being given the mother's maiden name as a first name.

Warren — German: Defender
  Ware, Waring, Waringer
  Warren Beatty! Need we say more?

Warwick — English: Village hero
  Warick, Warrick

Washington — English: From the washing place

Watson — English: Son of the warrior

Waverly — German: From the rippling water

Wayland — German: From the land by the highway
  Way, Waylan, Waylen, Waylin, Waylon
  Waylon (Arnold) Jennings, known for his special country-rock style, wrote the theme for the TV series "The Dukes of Hazzard."

Wayne — See: Wainwright
  As Nevada's highest-grossing entertainer to date, Wayne Newton is to Las Vegas what Mickey Mouse is to Disneyland.

Webster — English: Weaver
  Webb, Weber
  The TV sitcom "Webster" (1983–87) starred Emmanuel Lewis in the title role.

Welby — Scandinavian: From the farm by the spring

Weldon — English: Willow trees on the hill

Wells — English: From the spring

Wenceslaus — Slavic: Crown of glory
  Wenceslas, Wenzel

Wendel/Wendell — German: Wanderer

Werner — See: Warner

Wes — Nickname for names starting with "Wes"

Wesley — English: From the west meadow
  Wes, Westleigh, Westley

Westbrooke — English: From the west brook
  Wes, West, Westbrook

Westcott — English: From the west cottage
Weston — English: From the west town
Wheeler — English: Wheel maker
Whit — Nickname for names starting with "Whit"
Whitcomb/Whitcombe — English: Small valley
Whitelaw — English: From the small hill
Whitfield — English: Tiny field
Whitney — English: Small parcel of land near water
Whittaker — English: Small area of land
Wilbert/Wilburt — English: Bright willow
Wilbur — See: Gilbert
 Wilbur Wright and his brother Orville were American aviation pioneers who flew high in a heavier-than-air craft (1903) that they invented and constructed.
Wilder — English: Person from the wilderness
Wiley/Wylie — English: From the willow meadow
Wilfred — English: Hope for peace
 Wilfried, Willfrid
Will/Willie/Willy — Nicknames for names starting with "Wil"
Willard/Willerd — German: Courageous; English: Yard full of willows
William — German: Resolute protector
 Bill, Billie, Billy, Guglieimo, Guillaume, Guillermo, Uilleam, Uilliam, Wil, Wilek, Wilhelm, Wilkie, Will, Willan, Willem, Willet, Willie, Willis, Willy, Wilmar, Wilmer, Wilmot
 The name William is a solid name that, according to birth records, was in the top ten from the end of the nineteenth century through the 1960s. Here are just a few Williams and forms of William to give you an idea of the name's popularity throughout the years: William Shakespeare, William Butler Yeats, William Howard Taft, William Henry Harrison, William McKinley, William Penn, William Randolph Hearst, William Faulkner, William Devane, William Hurt, Willem Dafoe, Willie Mays, Willy Wonka, Willy Loman, Will Rogers, and Wil Shriner.
Wilson — German: Son of William
Wilton — English: Town near the well
 Wilt
 Born Wilton Norman Chamberlain, 7'1" "Wilt the Stilt" was responsible for rewriting a lot of pro basketball's records (he scored one hundred points in a single game), and supposedly made Casanova seem like a sissy.

Win/Winnie/Winny — Nicknames for names starting or ending with "Win"

And what about the name Winnie? Pooh!

Windell — English: Tree from which baskets are woven

Win, Windlan, Windy

Windsor — German: From the river bend

Winfield — English: Productive field

Winfred/Winfrid — English: Friend of peace

Wingate — English: Divine protector

Winslow/Winslowe — English: Victory hill

Winston — English: Town of victory

Sir Winston (Leonard Spencer) Churchill, prime minister of the United Kingdom, was born two months prematurely. That gave him two more months to smoke the more than 300,000 cigars that it is thought he smoked during his ninety-one years.

Winthrop — English: Victory at the crossroads

Wolf/Wolfe — English: Wolf

Wolff, Woolf, Woulfe

Wolfgang — German: Advancing wolf

Wolfgang Puck has made a name for himself as the owner and chef of Spago, the Los Angeles celebrity-hangout restaurant.

Wolfram — German: Wolf-raven

Woodley — English: From the woody meadow

Woodrow — English: From the hedge by the forest

Woody — Nickname for names starting or ending with "Wood"

The story goes that Woody Allen, whose real name was Allen Stewart Konigsberg, changed his first name to Woody because of his desire to be a great clarinetist like his musical idol, Woody Herman.

Worth — English: Valuable homestead

Wray — English: Accuser

Wren — Welsh: Chief or ruler

Wrennie, Wrenny

Wright — English: Artisan, worker

Wyatt — French: Guide

Wiatt, Wyatte

Wyatt (Berry Stapp) Earp was an American frontier law officer in Tombstone, Arizona.

Wycliff/Wycliffe — German: Village near the cliff

Wyche, Wyck

Wyman/Wayman — English: Warrior

Wynn — English: White, fair
Wynono — Native American: Firstborn son

X

Xavier — Arabic: Splendid, bright
Javier, Xever
As a young violinist, bandleader Xavier Cugat toured the country with opera great Enrico Caruso. They had something in common: They were both caricaturists.
Xenos — Greek: Stranger
Xeno, Zeno, Zenos
Xenophon — Greek: Strange voices
Xenophon was a Greek general and writer way back when. When? About 400 B.C.
Xerxes — Persian: Ruler; Greek: Pertaining to Caesar
Jerez, Xeres, Xerus
Xerxes was the king of Persia who invaded Greece in or about 400 B.C.
Ximens — See: Simon
Xylon — Greek: From the forest

Y

Yaakov — Hebrew: God is gracious
Yaacob, Yaacov, Yachov, Yacov, Yago, Yakob, Yakov
Comedian Yakov Smirnov is the Russian émigré who explains, "In America, you can always find a party. In Russia, the party always finds you."
Yagel/Yagil — Hebrew: To rejoice
Yale — German: One who pays or produces
Yancy — French: Englishman
Yan, Yance, Yank, Yankee, Yantsey

Yaphet — See: Japhet
Actor Yaphet Kotto is best known for his parts in Alien *and* Live
and Let Die.

Yardley — English: From the enclosed meadow

Yates — English: Keeper of the gates

Yavin — Hebrew: He will understand

Yehoram — Hebrew: God will exalt

Yehuda/Yehudah — See: Judah

Yehudi — See: Judah

Yigael — Hebrew: God will redeem
Yagel, Yigal

Yitzhak — Hebrew: Laughter
Itzak, Izaak, Yitzak
*Yitzhak is a popular name for Israeli leaders. There's Yitzhak
Shamir and Yitzhak Rabin.*

Yogi — Sanskrit: Person who practices yoga
*Baseball Hall of Famer Yogi Berra was born Lawrence Peter
Berra.*

Yona/Yonah — Native American: Bear; Hebrew: Dove

York — Celtic: From the farm of the yew trees
Yorick, Yorke

Yul/Yule — English: Jolly (as referring to the Christmas season)
*There are many stories about Yul Brynner's real name and
nationality. Most accounts say he was born Taidje Kahn, either
on the Siberian island of Sakhalin or in Outer Mongolia, and
that his mother was either a Russian or a Romany gypsy.*

Yuma — Native American: Son of a chief

Yvan — See: John

Yves — See: Ivar/Iver
*Yves Montand was born Ivo Montand Livi. He was an Italian
Jew. (And you thought he was French!) What about Yves Saint
Laurent? His real name is Henri Donat Mathieu, and he was
born in Oran, Algeria.*

Z

Zabdiel — Hebrew: God is my gift
  Zabdi, Zavdi, Zavdiel

Zachary — Hebrew: The Lord has remembered
  Zac, Zacarias, Zaccaria, Zach, Zachariah, Zacharias, Zacharie,
  Zack, Zak, Zakarias, Zechariah, Zecharias, Zeke
  *When the twelfth president of the U.S., Zachary Taylor, was a
  general in the Mexican War, he was nicknamed "Old Rough
  and Ready" because of his sloppy dress, tobacco chewing, and
  cussing.*

Zale/Zales — English: To sell

Zalman/Zalmen/Zalmon — See: Solomon

Zane — See: John
  *Pearl Zane Grey was called Pearl until he graduated from the
  University of Pennsylvania School of Dentistry and opened his
  practice. Then he was Dr. P. Zane Grey. When he gave up his
  practice, he dropped the "P" and went on to write fifty-four
  novels, including* Riders of the Purple Sage.

Zared — Hebrew: Ambush

Zebulon/Zebulun — Hebrew: To exalt, to honor
  Zeb, Zubin

Zedekiah — Hebrew: Justice of the Lord
  Zed

Zeeman — Dutch: Sailor, seaman

Zeke — See: Ezekiel, Zachary

Zelig — Yiddish: Blessed, holy

Zeus — Greek: Living
  *Zeus was the presiding god of the Greek pantheon, ruler of the
  heavens and father of other gods and mortal heroes.*

Zeviel — Hebrew: Gazelle of the Lord
  Zev, Zevi, Zevy, Zvi

Zion — Hebrew: A sign, excellent

Ziv — Hebrew: Full of life
  Ziven, Zivon

Zoltan — See: Sultan
  *Dr. Zoltan Ovary, a gynecologist, is listed in a local telephone
  book. We kid you not.*

Zubin — See: Zebulon/Zebulun

When Indian-born Zubin Mehta was appointed musical director of the Los Angeles Symphony, Californians started calling him Zubie Baby, and it stuck. Zubie Baby went on to become the conductor of the New York Philharmonic.

Zuriel — Hebrew: God is my foundation

Favorite Names of Girls

_____

_____

_____

_____

_____

_____

_____

_____

_____

_____

_____

_____

_____

_____

_____

_____

_____

_____

_____

Favorite Names of Boys

_____

_____

_____

_____

_____

_____

_____

_____

_____

_____

_____

_____

_____

_____

_____

_____

_____

Index

About the Authors

The Wilen sisters are quite experienced in the naming process. As TV and film scriptwriters, they've been responsible for naming dozens of fictitious characters. (And so far, not one of them has complained!)

To make a name for themselves, Joan and Lydia wrote the best-sellers *Name Me, I'm Yours!*; *Chicken Soup & Other Folk Remedies*; its sequel, *More Chicken Soup & Other Folk Remedies*; and *Live and Be Well*.